D0094441

SOUTHERN CIVIL RELIGIONS IN CONFLICT

SOUTHERN CIVIL RELIGIONS IN CONFLICT

Civil Rights and the Culture Wars

Andrew M. Manis

Mercer
University
Press
MMII

ISBN   0-86554-785-8 (cloth)
         0-86554-796-3 (paper)
MUP/H592//P224

© 2002 Mercer University Press
6316 Peake Road
Macon, Georgia 31210-3960
All rights reserved

∞The paper used in this publication meets the
minimum requirements of American National
Standard for Information Sciences—Permanence of
Paper for Printed Library Materials, ANSI Z39.48-
1992.

Library of Congress Cataloging-in-Publication Data

Manis, Andrew Michael.
Southern civil religions in conflict : civil rights and the
culture wars / Andrew M. Manis.
         p. cm.
Includes bibliographical references and index.
ISBN 0-86554-785-8 (alk. paper)—ISBN 0-86554-796-3 (pbk. :
alk. paper)
      1. African Americans—Civil rights—Southern States—History—20th
century. 2. Civil rights movements—Southern States—History—20th century.
3. Civil religion—Southern States—History—20th century. 4. Baptists—
Southern States—Political activity—History—20th century. 5. Southern
States—Race relations. I. Title.
   E185.61 .M29 2002
   323.1'196073075'088261—dc21

                                                            2002001094

For Linda

TABLE OF CONTENTS

PREFACE

No one who seriously studies American religious history or politics can avoid giving at least some attention to the interaction of religion and nationalism or the important concept of civil religion. By that abstract term historians, sociologists of religion, and political scientists generally refer to a blending of religion and patriotism with the nation as the focus of veneration, if not outright worship. Since 1967, when sociologist Robert Bellah brought the subject into vogue with a seminal article focusing on religion in presidential inaugural addresses, scholars and an occasional social commentator have produced an important body of literature on the topic.[1]

The first thinker to discuss the concept of civil religion was the French philosopher Jean-Jacques Rousseau in his reflections on the republican system of government called the *Social Contract,* written in 1762. He argued that a republic needs citizens who are convinced that their contract to live together in a society has ultimate validity. In effect, this meant that people in a society need to believe their society came from God and was not just a humanly-constructed social arrangement. In premodern societies such as medieval Europe with its religious monopoly, one dominating religion of society could provide the ultimacy necessary to legitimate the government and claim the allegiance of virtually all citizens. After the Reformation, however, the eventual proliferation of Christian denominations, organized religions, or *sects* as some called them, divided citizens' loyalties rather than gluing society together. In fact, Rousseau thought that by calling on its adherents to pledge allegiance to Jesus rather than Caesar, Christianity had a particular facility for dividing loyalties between God and country, and between the Kingdom of God and the social contract. Rousseau's solution was that the social order ought to be unified by a purely "civil (or civic) religion" that would symbolize the ultimate meaning of the society and earn the loyalty of the citizens.[2]

---

[1] Robert N. Bellah, "Civil Religion in America," *Daedalus* 96 (Winter 1967): 1-21.

[2] Jean-Jacques Rousseau, "The Social Contract," in *Rousseau: Political Writings,* translated and edited by Frederick Watkins (New York: Nelson and Sons, 1953) 148;

In the modern period, after the ratification of its Constitution, the United States more or less gave up on the idea of having a legal religious establishment or a state church. So instead of a legally established state church to unify citizens and make them more loyal and law-abiding, America developed a generalized civil religion that functions in modern times as a state church formerly functioned in premodern times. Thus, a civil religion differs from both the religious institutions and the political institutions of a society. The civil religion provides symbols that tell the citizens the ultimate or sacred meaning of their nation. Examples might be images of America as God's New Israel or America as a "city on a hill." The civil religion has sacred objects (for example, the Declaration of Independence, the Constitution, or the Liberty Bell). It has sacred shrines (The Lincoln or Jefferson Memorials, or the Gettysburg battlefield). It has sacred days with sacred rituals, such as the Fourth of July, Thanksgiving Day, or Memorial Day. The goose bumps one feels when hearing the "Star Spangled Banner," particularly if heard in church, are an expressions of civil religion. The anger many citizens feel when they think of someone burning an American flag is a reaction to the profaning of a civil religious object. The silence one hears upon entering the Lincoln Memorial is civil religious awe.

In this connection, one of the many ironies of southern history is that the region often considered America's most patriotic and most religious has in fact had an ambivalent relationship to the civil religion just described. While often heralded as the most American of regions, the South went through periods when it saw itself as distinct from mainstream America in the middle of both the nineteenth and the twentieth centuries. During the Civil War, the South literally thought of itself as a separate nation and spent four years of bloody war trying to become one. A century later, during the civil rights struggle (called by some historians the Second Reconstruction), many southerners once again viewed their region as different from the rest of the nation and as once again being punished for that difference. The result of this regional alienation was massive resistance to the federal government's efforts to end segregation. In both periods the process led the South's mythmakers to fashion a distinctive *southern* civil religion that conceived of America's historic calling

---

David Chidester, *Patterns of Power: Religion and Politics in American Culture* (Englewood Cliffs, NJ: Prentice-Hall) 81- 83, 88.

and destiny differently than did the traditional American civic faith. One of those differences has to do with race.

Many historians have thought of southern history as orbiting around the problem of race. Early in the twentieth century, Ulrich B. Phillips led this parade of historians by calling the commitment that the South should remain "white man's country" the "central theme of southern history." More recently Eli Evans amplified this point of view by observing: "Race permeates Southern politics like the twilight mist. . . . It is always just below the surface of every public utterance, a chorus of whispers in the clatter of elective politics."[3] For my own part, I would even go Phillips one better. Race is not only a central theme of southern history; to a great extent it is a central theme of American religious history, or arguably American history in general.

I hasten to add the disclaimer that this argument is not meant to imply that white southerners are more racist than other white Americans. The history of race relations in the United States before and since the civil rights movement has shown that wherever large numbers of African Americans settle, in the South or not, white Americans tend to react in similar ways. Now in the twenty-first century one could certainly argue that what used to be called the southern "Negro problem" has become (or always was) the American "race (or racism) problem." Simply because the South has been the region with the largest African American population, it may be understood as the focus of America's difficulty with race difference. Therefore, to address the intertwined themes of religion, American patriotism, and southern identity requires that race also be a significant part of the discussion.

This book is a continuing attempt to address these necessarily related issues. More specifically, it tries to show how two conflicting civil religions emerged in the South during the civil rights movement, each with its own understanding of America's calling and destiny, but both related to the question of race. Using black and white Baptists in the South as case studies, I interpret the civil rights movement as a civil

---

[3] Ulrich B. Phillips, "The Central Theme of Southern History," *American Historical Review* 34 (October 1928): 30-43; Eli Evans, quoted in John Shelton Reed and Dale Volberg Reed, eds., *1001 Things Everyone Should Know About the South* (New York: Doubleday, 1996) 101. With a slight change of emphasis the editors follow Phillips's lead, quoting Evans as an epigraph for a chapter entitled, "The Central Theme: Race and Politics."

religious conflict between southerners with opposing understandings of America. Central to their conflicting images of America, I submit, was race.

In the aftermath of World War II, citizens of every region drew together to affirm their common inheritance as a people and to celebrate the nation's military and moral victories. Such triumphs confirmed America as a beacon to the nations and a "city on a hill." When America and particularly the South turned inward to think about "the American dilemma" of racial segregation in a purported land of freedom and equality, the South became a battlefield of conflicting civil faiths. The growing civil rights movement, which called on the nation to "live out the true meaning of its creed," evoked within the South two separate civic creeds—one based on freedom by law and equality under God; the other finding in the Constitution a guarantee of states' rights and in the Bible a divine sanction of segregation. The civil rights movement thus introduced a forceful polarization among Americans: Some saw in desegregation the symbolic fulfillment of their view of America as a land of equality and inclusion. Opposing them and the civil rights struggle were those who feared desegregation as a threat to their image of America as a properly and predominantly white and Protestant nation.

Now the book re-appears in a revised, expanded form. The body and the thesis remain largely the same, but this volume expands the conversation in two new chapters. The overriding reason for the book's new edition is to broaden the argument by connecting the civil religious conflict I described in the civil rights movement to the culture wars of contemporary times. The expanded argument is important for at least four reasons.

First, the thesis reinterprets the civil rights movement as not only a fight for racial justice, but a cultural debate about the very meaning of America. In its first incarnation, the book was never intended to tell the whole story of the civil rights movement, or even the whole story of the churches' response to it. The intent was never to chronicle all the unfolding events of the movement or mine every churchly response to those events. Most of those stories were deliberately left out in order to focus on how the combatants during the civil rights struggle debated both Christianity's sacred scripture (the Old and New Testaments) and America's sacred documents (the Declaration of Independence and Constitution).

Moreover, this argument does not intend to suggest that civil religion is the only, best, or most important way to think about the civil rights movement. Nor did the original edition attempt to survey a sampling all southerners white and black and make generalizations accordingly. The intent was to test the thesis by examining two central and numerically dominant religious groups, white Southern Baptists and black National Baptists, as case studies. It is instructive to note, however, that according to more recent research the racial and civil religious views of white Southern Baptists were often shared among southern Methodists and Presbyterians.[4] Thus, while no one would claim or imply that black and white Baptists were the only important voices in the South, I remain willing to argue that their views were representative of most other southerners.

As in its initial appearance, this book seeks primarily to show how the civil rights movement was fundamentally a disagreement about whether or not America would symbolize to its own citizens and to the rest of the world a nation where racial diversity is ultimately accepted. Thus, my thesis views the civil rights movement and the debate it spawned as essentially, fundamentally, and primarily a conflict over America's acceptance of racial and other forms of cultural diversity.

This suggests a second reason for expanding the original argument. While this book reinterprets the civil rights movement, it also reinterprets more recent culture wars. One important way of understanding the culture wars is to recognize them as strong evidence for what John Egerton and other observers have called "the southernization of America." Religious historian Grant Wacker has made the point that after the 1960s the rest of America came to share many of the religious and cultural concerns of the South, observing that "this regional subculture has overflowed its sectional boundaries and permeated the mainstream."[5] In the process contemporary culture warriors fight out on the national

---

[4] See Andrew M. Manis, " 'City Mothers': Dorothy Tilly, Georgia Methodist Women, and Black Civil Rights," in Glenn Feldman and Kari Frederickson, eds., *Race, Rights, and Reaction in the American South, 1940-1956* (Fayetteville: University of Arkansas Press, forthcoming 2003); Joel L. Alvis Jr. *Religion and Race: Southern Presbyterians, 1946-1983* (Tuscaloosa: University of Alabama Press, 1994).

[5] Grant Wacker, "Uneasy in Zion: Evangelicals in Postmodern Society," in George Marsden, ed., *Evangelicalism and Modern America* (Grand Rapids: William B. Eerdmans Publishing Company, 1984) 28. See also John Egerton, *The Americanization of Dixie: The Southernization of America* (New York: Harper's Magazine Press, 1974).

stage conflicts that in earlier eras of American history were played out in a more regional setting.

Third, this edition of the book will attempt to show explicit chronological connections between the civil rights debates and the culture wars. Significantly more than previous commentators, I reinterpret the culture wars as having begun when Americans chose up sides over civil rights for African Americans. With its conflicting civil religious images of America, the civil rights era foreshadowed the culture wars. What began as a civil religious debate over civil rights was gradually transformed into the culture wars over a plethora of social issues. I wish to interpret the civil rights debates as a prelude to the culture wars—a chronological connection signaled by the new subtitle, "Civil Rights and the Culture Wars."[6]

This leads to a fourth and most important reason for expanding my original argument. Since the rise of the Religious Right and the culture wars of the 1980s and 1990s, having observed the polarized political discourse on social and religio-political issues, I maintain that the dual questions of race and diversity are the central issues of the culture wars. What in the culture wars has broadened into partisan conflict about matters such as prayer in schools, abortion, and family values, began as and largely remains at heart the question first raised by the civil rights debate: How diverse, racially and culturally, should America be? Thus, as W. E. B. Du Bois wrote that the color line would be the key problem of the twentieth century, this new, expanded argument agrees with Thomas C. Holt's recent title underscoring the continuing relevance of race in America: *The Problem of Race in the Twenty-first Century.*[7] Americans ought therefore not conceptualize any culture wars without seeing them, in more ways than meet the eye, as fundamentally about race and cultural difference.

Allow me then to acknowledge a number of persons who have influenced this work or given me professional and personal encouragement along the way. As this book re-presents what initially was my doctoral dissertation, I once again thank my advisor Bill Leonard, along with other

---

[6] The original title was *Southern Civil Religions in Conflict: Black and White Baptists and Civil Rights, 1947-1957* (Athens: University of Georgia Press, 1987).

[7] See DuBois's essay, "Of the Dawn of Freedom," in *Souls of Black Folks* (New York: Vintage Books, 1990 [orig. 1903]) 16; Thomas C. Holt, *The Problem of Race in the Twenty-first Century* (Cambridge: Harvard University Press, 2001).

committee members E. Glenn Hinson, Larry McSwain, Timothy George, and Glen Stassen. Other scholars who have encouraged this project, either in its first edition or in this one, are Samuel S. Hill, Wayne Flynt, Donald G. Mathews (who has on occasion used it as a course text), Sandy Dwayne Martin, and John Boles. In addition, I am especially grateful to Lewis V. Baldwin for his Foreword.

Special note is due to Jefferson P. Rogers, director of the Howard Thurman Center at Stetson University. Several years after the first edition had gone out of print, while reading one of my other writings, Rogers discovered my relatively little-known first book. Finding a used copy, he thought enough of its argument to invite me to his campus to deliver one of the University's 2000 Howard Thurman Lectures. Insisting that I deal with some of the issues in the civil religion book, he assigned me the task of addressing the topic of "Civil Religions and the Problem of Race in the New Millennium." A revised version of that lecture now appears as the concluding chapter of this volume. Rogers' interest in the topic and the audience's favorable response to those remarks eventually seduced me into re-presenting the book in an expanded form. Thus I thank Jeff Rogers, not only for the honor of being a Howard Thurman lecturer, but for giving me the opportunity to update my ideas for our contemporary situation and for pushing me to publish them.

This of course would not have been possible had not Marc Jolley, assistant publisher at Mercer University Press, been eager to bring the book out again. He has been both an encouraging and a demanding editor whose suggestions have improved the revision. Any glaring weaknesses and errors that remain, of course, are my own. In addition, my appreciation also goes to the rest of the staff at the press, with whom working on this project was a great pleasure: Cecil Staton, Edd Rowell, Amelia Barclay, Kevin Manus, Davina Rutland, James Golden, and Regina Toole.

I also wish to thank colleagues at Macon State College for their encouragement and friendship. Special among these are Harriet Jardine, Al McConnick, Ben Tate, Joe Lamb, Stephen Taylor, Robert Durand, Robert Burnahm, and Debra Slagle.

Finally, I thank my wife, Linda. She did not read the manuscript, correct my spelling, point out the weak spots in my arguments (at least not the ones in this book), or otherwise help me improve what readers may find herein. She did and does, however, improve my life in the ways that matter most—gracing it with love, affection, caring, humor, adventure, and beauty. Along with much else, including the dedication of this book, she has my deepest gratitude and devotion.

FOREWORD

Serious debate concerning the meaning and character of American civil religion began among a select group of scholars in the late 1960s. Inspired by the writings of the sociologist Robert N. Bellah, this debate surfaced at the height of the civil rights and anti-war movements, when questions about the relationship between religion and politics were widely discussed in both the academy and the public square. In more recent times, the debate has increased in intensity while drawing in scholars from many different backgrounds and disciplines.

This volume will undoubtedly advance the civil religion debate to another level. Initially published in 1987, twenty years after Bellah first directed scholarly attention to the shared religion of the American people, this book, which focuses largely on the 1950s, exists here in a revised and enlarged form, and it establishes Andrew M. Manis's importance as a key figure in the discussions concerning that religio-political phenomenon called American civil religion. Perhaps more than any other scholar up to this point, Manis extends the focus to a range of regional and racial considerations that often get lost in these discussions.

Manis challenges the notion that black and white southerners share a single, clearly-defined version of civil religion. While recognizing that blacks and whites in the South have long shared much in terms of spiritual and cultural values, Manis contends nevertheless that black and white Baptists represent two different traditions in civil religion, with each embracing its own perspectives on the meaning and significance of America's history and destiny. In other words, the black South's version of civil religion, which embraces universal rights, human equality, and interracial community under God, conflicts with that of the white South, which sanctions individual rights, white supremacy, and segregation on Biblical and theological grounds.

Manis's emphasis on the separate civic creeds of black and white Baptists provides one important angle for understanding the complexity of the South as a region, as an historical experience, and as a cultural entity. Employing what he terms "an interactive perspective" to explain both "the conflicts" and "the interplay of the South's two civil religions," Manis probes deeper into the complexity of the region by highlighting the historical factors, the social context, and the racial milieu that helped make the different "civil religious loyalties" of blacks and whites possible. This analysis is immensely important for both southern and American church historians, particularly in view of the continuing focus on the significance of regional trends in religious historiography.

Manis has added two very important and informative chapters to this new edition of his book. In one of these chapters, entitled, "Culture Wars: The Southern Theater," he discusses the relationship between religion and the South's role in national politics, placing his discussion in a broad historical context. Manis's reflections on the role of the Southern Baptist Convention in presidential politics over the last two or more decades are particularly important, and so are his comments regarding the Confederate flag issue during the 2000 elections. The Confederate flag disputes between black and white southerners are viewed not only as a more contemporary example of the different "civil religious loyalties" that existed in the 1950s, in the midst of the struggle for civil rights, but also as an indication of the continuing "culture war" over just how inclusive this nation will be in the twenty-first century.

The second new chapter skillfully builds on some of these concerns, with special attention to the larger and abiding question of race. Called "Civil Religions and the Problem of Race in the New Millennium," it concludes that "the culture war," which surfaced as civil faiths conflicted over racial and cultural inclusiveness during the civil rights years, will extend well into the twenty first century. Here Manis offers what some will label words of gloom, but no one can honestly deny the depth, power, and cogency of his discussion. Even as he envisions a future of "culture war" or civil religious conflict, Manis insists that "the door of inclusiveness" will remain open to new developments or possibilities in the areas of race, culture, politics, and religion.

Manis's book should be read alongside those of James D. Hunter, Robert Wuthnow, and numerous other scholars who are currently discussing and debating the nature and dimensions of the "culture war." By any standards, the book is a brilliant treatment of how public religion impacts political commitments, cultural values, and social outreach in this country.

Lewis V. Baldwin
Vanderbilt University
April, 2001

INTRODUCTION

From the inception of American life and history, sentiments of nationalism and religious fervor have often merged with religious fervor. Historians of American religion have produced an impressive and imposing body of literature analyzing this American phenomenon.[1] One of the most influential studies of the past thirty-five years was an article by sociologist Robert N. Bellah entitled "Civil Religion in America." This controversial article opened a new chapter in the historiography of American religion and created an important working concept by which historians and sociologists have interpreted the relation of religion and culture in America.[2]

The "civil religion debate" that has since raged among these scholars has most often focused on issues of definition and the theological and/or ethical desirability of this hybrid of religiosity and patriotism. More recent rounds of the discussion have centered on the varieties of civil religion, as expressed in the United States and in other nations as well.[3] Few scholars, however, have hinted at the various manifestations of civil religion *within* American society. Raising some of these issues in what has become a classic study is Charles R.

---

[1] The writings of these historians constitute some of the major works in American religious history. These include, among many others, Robert T. Handy, *A Christian America: Protestant Hopes and Historical Realities* (New York: Oxford university Press, 1971); Martin E. Marty, *Righteous Empire: The Protestant Experience in America* (new York: Harper & Row, 1970); Sydney E. Ahlstrom, *A Religious History of the American People* (New Haven: Yale University Press, 1972).

[2] Robert N. Bellah, "Civil Religion in America," in *Beyond Belief: Essays on Religion in a Post-Traditional World* (New York: Harper & Row, 1970). This article, which has been reprinted numerous times, actually gave new life and a new terminology to a scholarly discussion that was probably begun with the work of Sidney E. Mead. In many articles, most of which were compiled into his book *The Nation with the Soul of a Church* (New York: Harper and Row, 1975) Mead anticipated Bellah's concept with his own concept of "the Religion of the Republic."

[3] Robert N. Bellah and Phillip E. Hammond, *Varieties of Civil Religion* (New York: Harper & Row, 1980).

Wilson's *Baptized in Blood: The Religion of the Lost Cause, 1865-1920.*[4]

Wilson interprets the post-Civil War mythology of the Lost Cause as a distinctly southern expression of the American civil religion. He contends that in the aftermath of the Civil War, southern clergy developed a public theology that viewed the South as a peculiarly chosen region within the chosen land of America—the South as the purest of the pure, the chosen of the chosen. Wilson further suggests that this regional religious patriotism only slowly began to shift to a national focus as southern and American patriotisms were reunited by the fervor of World War I. From that point civil religious impulses in the South became increasingly "Americanized."[5]

Since the publication of Wilson's fine study, no scholarly work has attempted to follow the career of the southern civil religion into more recent history. A particularly appropriate period for such an investigation is that of the 1950s, the beginning of a period of southern history that has been called the "Second Reconstruction."[6] The obvious parallels between the 1950s and the period examined by Wilson justify an updated interpretation of civil religion in the South. Such an interpretation would provide a religious perspective on a critical period of southern history and clarify our understanding of both the American and southern versions of civil religion.

Despite an abundance of books and articles on the subject, studies with a southern regional approach to American civil religion are rare. Within such a perspective, the interaction of American and southern civil religious impulses must be taken seriously. Historically, that interaction has taken the form of conflicting patriotic loyalties to both America and the South. The interaction and the conflicting loyalties

---

[4]Charles Reagan Wilson, *Baptized in Blood: The Religion of the Lost Cause, 1865-1920* (Athens: University of Georgia Press, 1980). While Wilson's work is the first to give systematic exposition of the southern civil religion, Samuel S. Hill has long hinted at such an interpretation of southern religion. In his conclusion of John Lee Eighmy's *Churches in Cultural Captivity* (Knoxville: University of Tennessee Press, 1972) 200, Hill sees the South as unique among American regions in its penchant for investing its culture with divine sanction and creating its own peculiar mythology.

[5]Wilson, *Baptized in Blood,* 161-82; see especially 178ff.

[6]The term is standard among Southern historians. See C. Vann Woodward, *The Strange Career of Jim Crow,* rev. ed. (New York: Oxford University Press, 1966) 9-10, 139-41.

logically provide a key for interpreting the southern version(s) of the American public faith.

In this vein southern historian David Potter has reminded us that the South was not a completely separate culture even during the Civil War, when sectional conflict in the United States raged most intensely. Acknowledging the distinctiveness of the South, Potter nonetheless refused to equate distinctiveness with separateness. In this context he gave a cogent rationale for maintaining that sectional and national loyalties have always coexisted in the South: "Historians frequently write about national loyalty as if it were exclusive, and inconsistent with other loyalties, which are described as 'competing' or 'divided,' and are viewed as distracting from the primary loyalty to the nation. Yet it is self-evident that national loyalty flourishes not by challenging and overpowering all other loyalties, but by subsuming them all and keeping them in a reciprocally supportive relationship to one another."[7] Potter's insight suggests that any analysis of civil religion, if it is to accord with the historical experience of the South, must be sensitive to the interaction of these occasionally dual, though sometimes competing attachments.

The absence of this "interactive" perspective marks an important weakness in Wilson's analysis of the southern civil religion. He does not deal extensively with the *conflict* of civil religious impulses and gives scant attention to the pull of conflicting patriotic loyalties among southerners. Wilson also fails to note that many of the key values of the southern civil religion were derivatives of the larger American faith. As a result, he overlooks, or at least minimizes, the nuances of interaction and relationship between these two civil religions in the South. These are unfortunate omissions. For to apply the concept of civil religion to the South in a strictly regional manner, without analyzing the interplay of the southern and the American versions, is to ignore the relation of the part of the whole.

Another shortcoming, which Wilson shares with other writers on the subject of civil religion, is his exclusion of black perspectives from analysis. For a study of the 1950s, such an approach is problematic first of all because blacks' efforts in the civil rights movement marked

[7] David M. Potter, "The Historian's Use of Nationalism and Vice-Versa," *American Historical Review* 67 (July 1962): 932 and 943.

a noble expression of the American civic faith.[8] In such assessments, Martin Luther King Jr. often becomes the virtual personification of a prophetic manifestation of the American civil religion. The most significant evidence of King's rightful induction into the American civil religious pantheon is the recent designation of his birthday as a national holiday.

In a more general sense, however, to exclude black perspectives from these discussions is to ignore the profundity with which black Christians have sounded the themes of the American civil religion in their struggle for civil rights. Indeed, as Charles H. Long has noted, black Americans have not traditionally distinguished civil religion from church religion. This close connection has led James Melvin Washington to refer to black Baptists as "the church with the soul of a nation."[9] Excluding the views and attitudes of black southerners would serve to perpetuate an outmoded and provincial, if not also a benignly racist, historiographical approach.[10] But most important, in many ways race is at the heart of current debates about the meaning of America that make up so much of the current "culture wars."

These problems suggest that the interpreter of civil religion in the South must first employ an interactive perspective capable of explaining the conflicting religious patriotisms and their interrelationships. Such research must analyze both the American *and* southern civil religions. Set against this task is the necessity of an inclusive perspective that would survey both white and black perceptions. Indeed, a

---

[8] Bellah and Hammond, *Varieties of Civil Religion,* 171-72, 194-95. See also John. F. Wilson, *Public Religion in American Culture* (Philadelphia: Temple University Press, 1979) 36-37, and John Dixon Elder, "Martin Luther King and American Civil Religion," *Harvard Divinity School Bulletin 1* (Spring 1968): 17.

[9] Charles H. Long, "Civil Rights-Civil Religion: Visible People and Invisible Religion," in *American Civil Religion,* ed. Russell E. Richey and Donald G. Jones (New York: Harper & Row, 1974) 216; James Melvin Washington, *Frustrated Fellowship: The Black Baptist Quest for Social Power* (Macon GA: Mercer University Press, 1986) 135-57. Phillip E. Hammond has also criticized the tendency to ignore blacks and native Americans in discussions of civil religion. See "The Sociology of American Civil Religion: A Bibliographic Essay," *Sociological Analysis 37* (Spring 1976): 169-82.

[10] The consensus of Southern historians is perhaps best summed up by Donald G. Mathews, who rejects the "tacit assumption that white people and their experiences are the standard of judgment in our history." See his *Religion in the Old South* (Chicago: University of Chicago Press, 1977) xvi.

comparison of black and white attitudes sets in boldest relief and yields the clearest picture of the interplay of the south's two civil religions. Combining the interactive and the inclusive perspectives in therefore a central task of this book.

The era of the 1950s serves as an appropriate context for providing such a combination. This is because the central cultural issue of that period, the early rumblings of the black protest movement, addressed the key concerns of both civil religion and black-white relations. Obviously pertinent to the question of black-white relations, the nascent civil rights movement also addressed many important matters central to the concept of civil religion. The movement created a religious and political rhetoric that dealt with the identity, purpose, and values of American society. Further, the civil rights struggle sparked a concern for the cohesion of society amid an ongoing and threatening readjustment of the social order in the South.

All of these elements suggest more than the obvious truth that both race relations and civil religious concerns were crucial themes during the 1950s. They also point out that these themes were related because the goals of the civil rights movement raised serious questions directly relevant to civil religion. Moreover, the events of the decade stimulated impulses of both the civil religions. Early in the postwar period, crucial events in the nation and world gave impetus to a religious patriotism that focused on the nation. After the end of World War II, the nationalistic ardor of all regions, including the South, was sparked by the Korean War, the Cold War, McCarthyism antiCommunism, and the election of Dwight D. Eisenhower to the presidency. The events of the later 1950s, however, rekindled the southern sectional spirit. The 1954 Supreme Court decision on school desegregation, the Montgomery bus boycott of 1955-56, and the 1957 desegregation of schools in Little Rock, Arkansas, gave new strength to the southern civil religion.

These factors point to the 1950s as a context well suited for highlighting the interaction of the South's two civic faiths.[11] More spe-

---

[11]Samuel S. Hill has suggested that the South has historically participated in two cultural systems or frameworks of meaning, namely those of religiousness and southernness. See "The South's Two Cultures," in *Religion and the Solid South*, ed. Hill (Nashville: Abingdon Press, 1972) 46. Hill's dichotomy neglects the intermixing of Southernness and religion in the South. Southernness is more likely a constitutive part

cifically, this study centers on the years 1947 through 1957. In 1947 the Committee on Civil Rights, which was created a year earlier by President Harry S. Truman, published its study of the living conditions of American blacks and recommended measures for their improvement. The publication of *To Secure These Rights*, as the report was called, along with Truman's sending a bold civil rights bill to Congress, marked a major milestone in the growing movement for racial equality. Viewed in the Deep South as an assault on southern practices, Truman's civil rights policies were a significant beginning point in the resurgence of southern sectionalism and of the peculiarly Southern civil religion.[12] As to the latter date, the 1957 Little Rock school desegregation order became a crucial symbolic event revealing that the hardening of white response was well under way. This time frame allows one to interpret the patriotic fervor of the postwar era and continue through the Cold War years to the aftermath of the Little Rock crisis.

Inasmuch as the civil religion concept uses religious symbols to articulate the meaning of the nation, this study focuses on the early civil rights era as the period by which time the south's conflicting symbols of America had taken full form. The conflict of these two symbolic understandings of America precipitated increasingly dramatic events during the civil rights movement of the sixties. During the height of the civil rights struggle southerners appealed to conflicting symbolic images of America with increasing fervor. The shape and meaning of southerners' symbolic understandings, however, were largely determined by the 1950s and were not modified to any significant extent in the next decade.

This study examines the religio-patriotic themes that expressed southern religious attitudes on the meaning, purpose, and destiny of America. Editorials, articles, and sermons on and around the civil holidays are crucial, as are these southerners' specific responses to the important events of the period. An examination of these expressions from 1947 to 1957 serves as the means by which to monitor the shift-

---

of the South's religiosity than an addendum to it. I would differ with Hill by arguing that the division has more to do with the conflicting civil faiths in which the religion participates.

[12]Charles Roland, *The Improbably Era: The South Since World War II*, rev. ed. (Lexington: University of Kentucky Press, 1976) 31ff.

ing and conflicting civil religious impulses among black and white citizens of the South.

Thus a focus on the South of the 1950s and the inclusion of both black and white attitudes can facilitate what I have called the "interactive perspective." Perhaps more significant, however, is the suggestion of desegregation as the focal point—or better, the crystallization—of that interactive relationship. The civil rights movement and the increasing conflict of civil faiths after 1954 have a crucial common denominator in the concept of desegregation.

Analyzing desegregation as a religious symbol can illumine the relationship between these two civil religions. This is possible by examining the way desegregation symbolically functioned within the civil religions of certain southern blacks and whites in the 1950s. Where some have interpreted segregation as a religious symbol,[13] this study attempts to interpret its obverse, desegregation, as a civil religious symbol. My attempt is to analyze desegregation as a religious symbol and examine its effect on how Southerners' understand America religiously. The chief task is to discover comparisons between what these southerners saw as America's key values and the crucial developments they believed necessary for the actualization of these values in American society. More particularly, the analysis describes the ways desegregation was perceived to thwart (for some whites) or fulfill (for some blacks) the hope of actualizing their visions of the ideal America.

The chief question for analysis is, How did the specter or hope of desegregation relate to or modify the myth (i.e., image, idealization) of America among certain segments of the white and black populations of the South? In these southerners' civil religious understandings, desegregation functioned as a symbol that affected their respective images of America's religious meaning. For most blacks, desegregation symbolized the fulfillment or the actualizing of their images, while for many whites the concept embodied the threat of nonfulfillment.

Noting this divergent use of desegregation as a civil religious symbol suggests that the concept of civil religion need not be understood as national self-idolatry or mere jingoism. To interpret it in this

---

[13] See George D. Kelsey, *Racism and the Christian Understanding of Man* (New York: Charles Scribner's Sons, 1965) 96-116; James Sellers, *The South and Christian Ethics* (New York: Association Press, 1962) 115-27.

truncated manner is to minimize the moral ambiguity of any religion, civil or otherwise. Some have noted that while civil religion "may serve the high, universal ideals of a culture on the one hand, it may also be used for particularistic, self-serving ends."[14] Likewise, I assume that civil religion need not be intrinsically nonprophetic. The White Citizens Councilor and the civil rights activist of the 1950s were *both* preachers of an American civil religion, though of starkly different versions of it. The South in the 1950s was thus caught in the conflict between a prophetic and nonprophetic civil religion.

Two southern denominations, the Southern Baptist Convention among whites and the National Baptist Convention among blacks, serve as case studies for analyzing the conflict of these two civil religions. The Baptist denominations, both black and white, constituted a sizable portion of the religious population of the South. Baptists comprised roughly 50 percent of southern white population between 1950 and 1955.[15] The percentage of Baptists among southern blacks was even higher. Thus the statistical strength of these denominations in southern society lends itself to the emphasis on consensus necessary for any analysis of civil religion. Perhaps more important, however, is the degree to which Baptists, particularly Southern Baptists, have been the shapers of southern culture. As such, the use of these groups places any generalizations concerning the larger southern culture on somewhat more solid ground. The reader should understand the use of these groups as fairly representative case studies.

One should note, however, that the focus here is not primarily on the institutional interests of these denominations, but rather on the larger cultural issues. Thus I have not focused on these denominations in general, but rather on certain segments of them. Among white southerners my attention centers on the more reactionary elements of Southern Baptist life.[16] In this context "reactionary" refers to those

---

[14]John A. Christenson and Ronald C. Wimberley, "Who is Civil Religious?" *Sociological Analysis* 39 (Spring 1978): 82-83.

[15]John Shelton Reed, *The Enduring South: Subcultural Persistence in Mass Society* (Chapel Hill: University of North Carolina Press, 1972) 57-59.

[16]While emphasizing the reactionary response, I would not minimize the pluralism of racial attitudes that existed in the white South generally, nor in the Southern Baptist Convention in particular. As with any historical generalization, there are important exceptions to the views to which I point. Progressive Southern whites such as T. B. Maston, Henlee Barnette, Clarence Jordan, Will Campbell, and the Fellowship of

Southern Baptists most likely to have been influenced by the Citizens Council mentality. These persons sought to maintain the racial status quo, to enforce segregation, to justify racial arrangements in the Jim Crow South, and tended violently to berate "outside agitators."[17] Recently giving it the name "racial radicalism," Joel Williamson has argued that this mentality interpreted blacks in terms of natural savagery and bestiality and "insisted that there was no place for the Negro in the future American society." As such, Williamson deems this type of southerner the "most significant for race relations in the twentieth-century South."[18]

In investigating the attitudes of black Baptists, one should be aware that they exhibited greater solidarity in support of civil rights activism than did Southern Baptists in their opposition to it. Thus, what is said about the activist segment of the National Baptist Convention can, with some major qualifications, also be said concerning the denomination as a whole. Nevertheless, I give chief attention to those persons within the National Baptist Convention who most actively sought the attainment of blacks' civil rights. This focus necessitates the inclusion of certain elements of thought of Martin Luther King Jr. and other black preachers who participated in the activities of the Southern Christian Leadership Conference (SCLC). Consequently, while this study does not pretend to be another study of Martin Luther King, it does assume that his prominence as a spokesperson for southern blacks and as an enunciator of the American civil religion makes essential the inclusion of his perspectives.[19]

Southern Churchmen will not be the focus of this study. For these views see Robert F. Martin, "Critique of Southern Society and Vision of a New Order: The Fellowship of Southern Churchmen, 1934-1957," *Church History* 52 (March 1983): 66-80.

[17]This category of southern white response is borrowed from Davis C. Hill, "Southern Baptist Thought and Action in Race Relations, 1940-1950" (Th.D. diss, Southern Baptist Theological Seminary, 1952) 5-6. Hill posits two other categories of thought: the instructive, which simply presented factual information on racial matters, and the progressive, which showed serious concern for racial justice and for bettering the conditions of blacks.

[18]Joel Williamson, *The Crucible of Race: Black/White Relations in the American South Since Emanicipation* (New York: Oxford University Press, 1984) 6, 111-24.

[19]King obviously reflected the aspirations of blacks of all regions, not merely those of southern blacks. The American black community enjoyed great unity. Yet according to the 1940 census, 77 percent of American blacks still lived in the South. See Maxwell S. Stewart, *The Negro in America* (New York: Public Affairs Committee,

Comparing these more extreme portions of the two Baptist groups enables one more easily to highlight the conflict of public faiths in the South. Their images of America differed, to put it mildly. Their appropriations of the symbols of the American civil religion vigorously contradicted each other. To explore the extremes will highlight and clarify the conflicting loyalties and enables contemporary readers to feel more intensely the civil religious dilemma that forced so many in the middle into an immobilized silence concerning the issue of civil rights. One might argue, of course, that it is inappropriate to classify King and other activist ministers as extremists in the same sense as those of the Klan or Citizens Councils. From an overall perspective, one that includes those of northern, urban blacks like Malcolm X, King and the SCLC perspective were a more conservative option. For southern blacks, however, neither the black nationalist views of Malcolm and the Black Muslims (as they were then called), nor the more militant, more secular approach of Stokeley Carmichael, attracted much loyalty. For both the southern context and the chronological context of the 1950s, King was in this qualified sense. He and his followers were certainly viewed as such my most southern whites, even some of those who shared his integrationist hopes. Moreover, King himself accepted the designation of extremist in his 1963 *Letter From Birmingham Jail*.

Chapter 1 sets the stage for this story by defining the concepts of civil religion in both the American and southern versions—and by surveying the southern social context during the first half of the twentieth century. The heart of this study is the pivotal year 1954, when the United States Supreme Court's famous *Brown v. Board of Education* desegregation decision profoundly affected black and white images of America. Before 1954 the patriotic spirit of the era stimulated civil religious allegiances toward the nation as a whole. Chapter 2 therefore specifically analyzes the idealizations of America among

---

1944) 16. Moreover, even those blacks who lived in the North maintained Southern perspectives. J. Pius Barbour, prominent editor of the National Baptists' official organ, the *National Baptist Voice*, commented: "The day the Negro splits between North and South like the white folks we are sunk. No amount of chicanery has been able to drive a wedge between Northern and Southern Negroes. The real truth of the matter is: There are no Northern Negroes, just a lot of Southern Negroes up North." "Report on national Baptist Convention," *National Baptist Voice* 32 (October 1, 1947): 1-3, 5, 13. (*National Baptist voice* hereafter cited as *NBV*.)

whites and blacks, and delineates the mythic hopes black and white Baptists held for their nation's destiny during the early 1950s. Chapter 3 focuses on events after the *Brown* decision, which refocused white civil religious loyalties of the South while heightening blacks' appeal to the values of the American civil faith. In this process of refocusing, desegregation was interpreted as both the disappointed hope of many whites and the fulfillment of hope for most blacks. In chapter 4, the South of the civil rights era is analyzed more thematically than chronologically, emphasizing its conflict of civil faiths. There I suggest a socio-historical analysis of how these conflicting civil religions legitimated and consecrated the ways of life they symbolized. To see those values as consecrated, or rendered sacred, helps explain the era's extreme volatility by understanding the South of the civil rights era as a battleground for a civil religious holy war.

Chapter 5 represents the first of two new essays designed to show how the civil rights debates of the 1950s and 1960s are related to the late twentieth, early twenty-first century culture wars. Focusing on "Culture Wars: The Southern Theater," the chapter emphasizes the southern character of contemporary debates over social and religio-political issues. Since the heyday of the civil rights movement traditional southern concerns about unbridled pluralism have widened to other regions and become mainstream American worries. This argument attempts to show how such fears of cultural pluralism were related to race, particularly seen in the fundamentalist takeover of the Southern Baptist Convention, in the Religious Right's opposition to Bill Clinton, and in southerners' disagreements about the meanings and uses of the Confederate battle flag.

The book concludes with a reflection on "Civil Religions and the Problem of Race in the New Millennium," which takes issue with formulations of the current culture wars that give too little attention to the issue of race. This analysis shows how the culture wars began with the late 1960s "white backlash" against the civil rights movement. The opposition of white Americans to the gains of the civil rights movement, and to the federal government's efforts to institutionalize those gains, are currently embodied in the culture warriors' hostility towards affirmative action, political correctness, and other strategies for accepting racial and cultural differences. The debates of the civil rights era, in different form, thus remain in the present and for the foreseeable future a volatile part of American religious, social, and political discourse.

1

CIVIL RELIGION AND THE SOUTH:
THE SOCIAL CONTEXT

The America of the 1950s was a land of patriotism and piety. Internally America enjoyed a budding age of affluence, while ventures abroad stimulated a desire for another postwar return to normalcy. The result was a deep nostalgia for traditional American values and a rekindling of old-fashioned piety. This ambience reached its full expression, indeed its personification, in the presidency of America's warrior-priest, Dwight D. Eisenhower. Though differing in their interpretations of its nature and meaning, historians agree that some sort of "postwar revival" of religion occurred in America during that era of qualified peace and unprecedented prosperity. Some have understood the revival as a crest of popularity for religious practice; others have viewed it as the flourishing of an indiscriminate religion-in-general.[1]

It is, however, the Americanness of this revival more than its religiousness that makes it most noteworthy. Though patriotism has more than once in American history lived in flirtatious relationship with religiosity, the marriage never seemed to be on more solid ground than during the 1950s. While some may have asked, "What hath Jerusalem to do with Washington?" others, like sociologist Will Herberg, called it a renewal of the "American Way of Life."[2] Twelve years later, in his celebrated article, Robert N. Bellah gave that union of

---

[1]See Winthrop S. Hudson, *Religion in America*, 3d ed. (New York: Charles Scribner's Sons, 1981) 384; Martin E. Marty, *The New Shape of American Religion* (New York: Harper and Brothers, 1959.

[2]Will Herberg, *Protestant-Catholic-Jew* (Garden City, N. Y.: Doubleday & Co., 1955).

patriotism and piety a new name–"civil religion"–and discussions of the topic by historians and sociologists of religion continue unabated.

Discussing civil religion in the American South, however, requires uniting two themes that are ordinarily unrelated in the history of religion in America. Scholars in the field of American civil religion most often fail to note the South's distinctive way of participating in the American public faith. On the other hand, interpreters of southern or African-American religion rarely discuss the issue of civil religion. This study seeks to effect a successful marriage between these themes.

As far as the period of the 1950s is concerned, such a marriage depends upon the more than chance meeting of civil religious loyalties and common attitudes toward the race issue among southerners black and white. The southern social context, of course, provided the necessary common ground. That context simultaneously developed these loyalties and attitudes until, by the 1950s, they found a nexus in the symbol of desegregation. The story of that development takes us to the post-World War II period. On the way one can survey white and black Baptists' religio-patriotic attachments to America, as well as their views on the matter of race. These developments set the stage for the opening volleys in the South's holy war of civil religions. Before describing that warfare, however, some definitional clearing of ground may be warranted.

Definitions of the Central Terms

Providing operative definitions for the highly theoretical and oft-times controversial concept of civil religion is no simple matter. Among historians of American religion, the "civil religion debate" has been one of the most significant discussions in the last thirty-five years, and most of the controversy has dealt with the complex problems of definition.[3] Consequently, rather than highlighting all of the

---

[3] The bibliography of civil religion is quite large. Two bibliographical articles include Boardman Kathan and Nancy Fuchs-Kreimer, "Bibliography on Civil Religion," *Religious Education* 70 (September-October 1975): 541-50, and Hammond, "Sociology of American Civil Religion," 169-82. The most important works on civil religion are those of Robert N. Bellah, which will be cited in the discussion of his views. Other significant studies include *American Civil Religion*, ed. Russell E. Richey and Donald G. Jones (New York: Harper & Row, 1974) and Mead, *Nation with the*

important discussions of civil religion, I will lay a minimum of theoretical groundwork before suggesting a composite model of civil religion.

Most Americans are completely oblivious to the intellectual construct of civil religion. The mention of the term to the average religious person, or even to an average member of the clergy, will usually be greeted by a blank stare. Even among many academic interpreters of American religion the "popular" understanding of civil religion is that of a syncretistic, nonprophetic, American religion-in-general.[4]

Perhaps the clearest general definition of civil religion is that of Catherine Albanese, for whom the concept refers to "a religious system that has existed alongside the churches, with a theology or mythology (creed), an ethic (code), and a set of symbols and rituals (cultus) related to the political state. As a shorthand, we might say that civil religion has meant religious nationalism."[5] Albanese thus understands civil religion as a system of religious symbols by which people interpret "the meaning of their existence as a political community."[6] Many scholars have noted the religionlike components of nationalism. In a classic study, historian Carlton J. H. Hayes has characterized nationalism as a religion.[7] Given this similarity with nationalism, it is no wonder that civil religion is often understood merely as a kind of baptized patriotism. Civil religion can legitimately be viewed in this way. It can, however, be more fruitfully studied within the framework of the sociology of religion.

Soul of a Church. A rather offbeat, but insightful, study of civil religion, which will be important in the conclusion of this book, is John Murray Cuddihy, *No Offense: Civil Religion and Protestant Taste* (New York: Seabury Press, 1978).

[4] Martin E. Marty, who obviously knows and has written better in subsequent writings on American civil religion, originally described "civil religion" as religion-in-general in *The New Shape of American Religion*, 31-44. See also *A Nation of Behavers* (Chicago: University of Chicago Press, 1976) and "Two Kinds of Two Kinds of Civil Religion in America," in *American Civil Religion*, ed. Richey and Jones, 139-57. To his credit, Marty acknowledges that civil religion can be prophetic or priestly or both.

[5] Catherine L. Albanese, *America: Religions and Religion* (Belmont, Calif.: Wadsworth Publishing Co., 1981) 284.

[6] Ibid., 302.

[7] Carlton J. H. Hayes, *Nationalism: A Religion* (New York: Macmillan Co., 1960).

Emphasizing the Durkheimian tradition of societal integration, sociologist Robert N. Bellah has defined civil religion in general as "that religious dimension, found... in the life of every people, through which it interprets its historical experience in the light of transcendent reality." More specifically, he defines it as "a set of religious beliefs, symbols, and rituals growing out of the American historical experience interpreted in the dimension of transcendence."[8] This religious dimension, with all of its components—beliefs, symbols, and rituals—functions to outline the meaning of the nation.

Beneath these definitions, however, Bellah has laid a theoretical foundation that views civil religion as both essential to for a society's integration and as capable of bringing a prophetic word to that society. For Bellah, societies rest on a common set of religious understandings that "provide a picture of the universe in terms of which [its] moral understandings make sense." These religious understandings both legitimate and provide a "standard of judgment" for bringing prophetic criticism to bear on a society.[9] This dual role of legitimation and criticism of society allows this common set of religious understandings to be used for either the maintenance of the status quo or for social change.

Bellah touches on these concerns by describing the ways a society's religious and political realms may relate to each other. As one ascends the scale of societal and religious evolution, religious symbol systems become progressively more complex. Concurrently, the religious and political systems become more differentiated from one another.[10]

In primitive or less evolved societies, says Bellah, the religious and political systems are coterminous; one system performs both functions.[11] The religious systems of archaic societies are grounded in a

---

[8] Robert N. Bellah, *The Broken Covenant: American Civil Religion in Time of Trial* (New York: Seabury Press, 1975) 3, and "Response [to a symposium on the civil religion thesis]," in *The Religious Situation: 1968*, ed. Donald R. Cutler (Boston: Beacon Press, 1968) 389. The celebrated thesis of Robert Bellah's original essay asserted that "there actually exists alongside of and rather clearly differentiated from the churches an elaborate and well-institutionalized civil religion in America" ("Civil Religion in America," in Bellah's *Beyond Belief*, 168.

[9] *Broken Covenant*, x. See also Bellah and Hammond, *Varieties of Civil Religion*, vii-viii.

[10] "Religious Evolution," in *Beyond Belief*, 24.

[11] Ibid., 25-29; Bellah and Hammond, *Varieties of Civil Religion*, viii.

divinely instituted order and are partially independent from the political system. Established state structures and a hierarchy of religious specialists emerge. Yet submission to the divine king is equated with entry into the cosmic order; to oppose him is to be allied with demonic forces. The rudimentary civil religion that emerges at this stage tends to divide the world into such opposing groups.[12]

In more complex modern societies these two systems become differentiated from each other, usually taking the form of separation of church and state. These societies, however, still need religious legitimacy as much as their primitive counterparts. Thus, modern societies relate the religious and political realms by a kind of religious *tertium quid* that is completely identified with neither the state nor the church and can be considered civil religion proper.[13] In fifth-stage, or modern, societies civil religion must be specific enough to symbolize ultimate reality effectively, yet general enough to include all who live in a pluralistic society.[14]

From this evolutionary perspective Bellah deals with instances when a civil religion becomes idolatrous by divinizing the nation and demonizing outsiders. In this context he underscores the ethical ambiguity of the concept of civil religion, which "like all things human, is sometimes good and sometimes bad, but which in any case is apt to be with us for a very long time."[15] Negative forms of civil religion manifest themselves when modern civil religion reverts to archaic forms. Archaic religion, as noted earlier, tends to divide the world into "good guys" and "bad guys."

Archaic civil religion is capable of reasserting itself in more advanced stages of societal development. The American penchant for dualistically dividing the world into the free and Communist realms provides a salient example. Similarly, Americans' tendency to assert a

---

[12] Bellah, "Religious Evolution," 29-32; Bellah and Hammond, *Varieties of Civil Religion,* viii-ix. Bellah's evolutionary scale includes primitive, archaic, historic, early modern and modern religions. See Bellah, "Religious Evolution," 20-50.

[13] Bellah and Hammond, *Varieties of Civil Religion,* xi.

[14] "Rejoinder to [Joan] Lockwood: 'Bellah and his Critics,'" *Anglican Theological review 57* (October 1975): 420-421.

[15] "American Civil Religion in the 1970s," in *American Civil Religion,* ed. Richey and Jones, 257.

jingoistic chosenness—for example, that America's power is identical to morality and God's will—is an example of archaic regression.[16]

Bellah views these impulses not only as regressive, but also as perversions of the basic intent of the American civil religion. They are aberrations that he believes are judged by the transcendent values of the public faith. Admitting the possibility of perversion, he asserts, "Without question our civil religion has been a cloak for petty interests and ugly passions, but it does provide us with a standard and with an obligation to use the political process to gain a transcendent goal—establishing equality and justice."[17]

The implicit universalism of this goal suggests that in order to accord more fully with the pluralism of modern society, the American civil religion must be faithful to its present task of helping attain a "viable and coherent world order."[18] It must become the basis for a "world civil religion." Such a universal responsibility is not only within the purview of America's civic faith; it is the logical outworking of its quintessential value. "Indeed," Bellah argues, "to deny such an outcome would be to deny the meaning of America itself."[19] Hence, as part of a *modern* society the American civil religion must disavow the pull toward archaic regression and, in a sense, lose itself for the sake of a true global community. If successful, its values will thus cause America to lead the other nations of the world in the adoption of a truly global consciousness.

Bellah's theoretical distinctions between prophetic and nonprophetic varieties of civil religion are particularly important in a study such as this, which argues that during the 1950s southern Americans were torn between two differing yet related versions of their national faith. His perspective cannot be used, however, without certain important modifications.

Long a perceptive interpreter of religion in American culture, historian John F. Wilson has registered cogent disagreements with Bellah from the outset of the civil religion debate. He has argued that

---

[16] Bellah and Hammond, *Varieties of Civil Religion,* xi-xiii.

[17] Robert N. Bellah, "Civil Religion: The Sacred and the Political in American Life," *Psychology Today,* January 1976, 58.

[18] Robert N. Bellah, "Commentary and Proposed Agenda: The Normative Framework for Pluralism in America," *Soundings 61* (Fall 1978): 371.

[19] Robert N. Bellah, "Civil Religion in America," in *Beyond Belief,* 185-86.

in differentiated societies two forms of religion coexist. One is a nonspecific religion identified with "a residual realm of values"; the other constitutes an institutionalized pattern of belief and behavior clearly distinguishable from social, political, or economic activities.[20] Insofar as civil religion exists in America, it is religion in the first form. The second form of religion may be seen in the more sectarian belief-systems of the denominations.

In Wilson's view the nation has no fully coherent meaning system. One finds only a "cluster of interpretations of American society."[21] Wilson thus disagrees that the American civil religion is, in Bellah's words, "clearly differentiated" from the political system or from the specific, formal religions in the society. There *are* what Wilson calls "mythic elements" in the culture that have embodied for Americans the meaning of their nation. Moreover, these elements are expressed in symbols and images that celebrate a God-given national purpose.[22]

My "mytho-cultural" model of civil religion borrows heavily from the perspectives of Robert Bellah and John Wilson. Bellah's scale of religious evolution is accepted, as is his view that civil religions appear in all societies. Wilson's stress on mythic, cultural materials provides the best theoretical description of civil religion.[23] This model agrees with Bellah that in primitive societies, in which the institutions of the social system are less differentiated, one system provides both political and religious functions of the society. In less differentiated societies, such as, for example, Medieval Christian Europe, traditional religion provides social integration and relates the religious and political systems to one another. Modern societies, however, are too differentiated and pluralistic for any one system of meaning to provide an ideological basis for the whole society.[24] On the other hand,

---

[20] John F. Wilson, "The Status of 'Civil Religion' in America," in *The Religion of the Republic*, ed. Elwyn A. Smith (Philadelphia: Fortress press, 1971) 11.

[21] Wilson, *Public Religion in American Culture*, 95.

[22] Ibid., 20.

[23] See Bellah, "Religious Evolution," 20-50; Bellah and Hammond, *Varieties of Civil religion*, v-xi; Wilson, "Status of 'Civil Religion' in America," 11; Wilson, *Public Religion in American Culture*, 25-27.

[24] This understanding of modern societies is elaborated in the work of sociologist Richard K. Fenn. See especially his *Toward a Theory of Secularization* (Storrs: University of Connecticut Press, 1978). Fenn argues that American society,

modern societies do continue to have "mytho-cultural" understandings, created out of the society's common history. Because they arise
from the common history and culture of the people, these understandings can help provide integrative or binding elements for the
society. Insofar as they also interpret for citizens the meaning of their
collectivity, they may be viewed as religious in nature. Because these
understandings function, in George B. Tindall's words, as "mental
pictures that portray the pattern of what a people think they are (or
ought to be)," they may be characterized as "mythic."[25] They are
cultural in that they do not constitute a formal or differentiated religious tradition within the nation, but rather are diffused throughout
American culture.

This model focuses on "mytho-cultural" meanings because the
religious symbols of the denominational traditions in America are too
specifically sectarian to bind the pluralistic culture together. The
religio-patriotic symbols of the nation, however, can provide meaning
for the collectivity, even if they cannot perfectly integrate the society.
The national symbols, or the mytho-cultural meanings, do function as
shorthand images that refer to what Americans view as normative,
"taken-for-granted reality" about their nation. As Clifford Geertz has
suggested in another context, these meanings connect America, or
citizens' idealization of it, ultimate value.[26]

Civil religion, then, is the symbolic component of a modern
society that can serve to integrate the society by providing a common
understanding of its place and role in history. Such an understanding

---

for example, institutionalizes pluralistic systems of meaning, which are in turn
internalized by individuals. The competition between these meaning systems carries
the potential for ideological conflict. This possibility may be seen as a likely
description of what took place in the South of the 1950s.

[25] See Tindall's "Mythology: A New Frontier in Southern History," in *The Idea
of the South: Pursuit of a Central Theme,* ed. Frank E. Vandiver (Chicago: University
of Chicago Press, 1964) 1-2, and Melville J. Herskovits and Frances S. Herskovits,
Dahomean Narrative: A Cross-Cultural Approach (Evanston, Ill.: Northwestern
University Press, 1958) 81-82. See also Mircea Eliade, *Myth and Reality* (New York:
Harper & Row, 1963); Alan W. Watts, *Myth and Ritual in Christianity* (Boston:
Beacon Press, 1953); and Phillip Wheelwright, "The Semantic Approach to Myth," in
Myth: A Symposium, ed. Thomas A. Sebeok (Bloomington: Indiana University Press,
1958).

[26] See "Ethos, World View, and the Analysis of Sacred Symbols," in *The Interpretation of Cultures* (New York: Basic Books, 1973) 127.

is embodied in mytho-cultural symbols and usually set within some framework of ultimacy. This concept can be more specifically defined for the American context: Civil religion is that cluster of mytho-cultural meanings (or symbols) by which Americans represent and communicate the significance and purpose of their national experience. In addition to enabling Americans to interpret their experience, these meanings, as John Wilson suggests, "provide frameworks for self-understanding for individual and collective behavior."[27]

For my purposes the term civil religion refers to southerners' beliefs about the meaning and purpose of America, and to a lesser degree about the South's role in the national purpose, as expressed in traditional religious language. This narrow focus on civil religious beliefs may seem somewhat arbitrary. One might cogently argue that such a discussion must include some mention of the ritual dimension of civil religion. Many interpreters—Bellah for a significant example—include this aspect in their most basic definitions of civil religion. Yet even Bellah, who began his study of civil religion by examining a ritual event—American presidential inaugurals—has tended to look through the rituals to explain the beliefs and values of the American public faith.

Three aspects of this mytho-cultural model argue for its appropriateness in understanding civil religion. One is that it does not describe a civil religion differentiated from either the religious or the political systems of the society. These mytho-cultural meanings are diffused over various institutions. This is to say that our political and religious institutions, as well as American voluntary associations, appeal to these meanings. Civil religion is "housed" exclusively in neither the religious nor the political systems. Rather, both appeal to it to help give meaning and integration to the society. Thus, against Bellah one might argue that civil religion is culturally diffused rather than structurally or institutionally differentiated.

A second strength of this approach is its harmony with the privatization of religious belief in modern society. The plurality of available frameworks of meaning in modern life forces the individual to construct his or her own symbol system out of various selections.[28]

---

[27] Wilson, *Public Religion in American Culture*, 94 and 115.

[28] For a discussion of this aspect of modern society, see Peter L. Berger, *The Sacred Canopy: Elements of a Sociological Theory of Religion* (Garden City, N.Y.:

This in part suggests why civil religion cannot integrate or provide meaning for the entire society. To the degree that modern society allows a privatization of religion, it also allows members of the society to choose not to include civil religious meanings in their personal symbol systems. Not everyone in the society will want to give specific religious interpretations to the nation, those who view civil religion as national self-idolatry being the most significant examples. Thus the civil religion cannot bind together the collectivity in ways Bellah hopes it might.[29]

This suggests a third and related advantage of the mytho-cultural perspective. It allows for divergent subcultural manifestations of the civil religion. Interpreting the American civil religion as a cluster of meanings with reference to the nation, John Wilson argues that "this kind of approach to the religious understanding of American culture makes it possible to deal with the empirical observation that there are sub-cultures, or particular combinations of the meanings. A subset has intense reality for a particular segment of the society, while other subsets have significance for other groups."[30] Insofar as it emphasizes meaning rather than social integration, the mytho-cultural approach allows a significant pluralism of civil religion in America.

Pluralism is a central characteristic of religion in America, even its civil religion. Highlighting this pluralism, Dick Anthony and Thomas Robbins have noted that diverse ideological groupings put forward different variations that embody "different visions of America's destiny and its relationship to social ideals." Meredith

---

Doubleday & Co., 1969); Thomas Luckmann, *The Invisible Religion: The Problem of Religion in Modern Society* (New York: Macmillan Co., 1967); Berger and Luckmann, *The Social Construction of Reality: A Treatise in the Sociology of Knowledge* (Garden City, N. Y.: Doubleday & Co., 1966).

[29] For Bellah the (American) Revolutionary faith serves as the normative content—the "heart and soul"—of the American civil religion. That faith thus includes an implicit universalism and sanctifies pluralism and can become the basis for a "world civil religion." This is one reason why Bellah does not equate civil religion with national self-idolatry. See "Civil Religion in America," in *Beyond Belief*; "The Revolution and the Civil Religion," in *Religion and the American Revolution*, ed. Jerald C. Brauer (Philadelphia: Fortress Press, 1976) 55-56, 62; "Commentary and Proposed Agenda," 371; and "Civil Religion and the Use of Power" (Address to the National Seminar of the Southern Baptist Christian Life Commission, Dallas Texas, march 23, 1981, Transcript) 2-3.

[30] Wilson, 117.

McGuire holds a similar view: "What emerges from sociological descriptions of American civil religion is a picture of diverse—even conflicting—values associated with what is central to the American people."[31]

Such an understanding thus fits the intention of this study. In order to analyze the conflict of civil religious loyalties in the American South, one must proceed from a definition of civil religion that such a perspective provides the theoretical foundation necessary for contrasting the American civil religion with the southern versions of it.

What I am calling the southern civil religion is one of the subcultural, or regional, manifestations of the American civil religion. It is an American faith, but one with its peculiar distinctions. It is, above all, a system of mixed symbols. The images of this public faith resemble a mythic Rorschach. At one glance they embody and communicate the faith of an American's American; another peek, and they gather before the undulating Stars and Bars and intone, "Forget, Hell!"

Samuel S. Hill rightly understands the South as, in Geertz's terms, a "cultural system," in which southern mores are given divine sanction. Southerners, Hill contends, have usually regarded theirs as "the most moral type of arrangement for human living, and [believed] that the southern churches are the purest in Christendom. In a word, many southern whites have regarded their society as God's most favored. To a greater extent than any others, theirs approximates the ideals the Almighty has in mind for mankind everywhere."[32] In this vein Charles R. Wilson writes of a full-fledged southern civil religion during the post-Civil War and twentieth-century South. He describes a set of values that could be designated the "southern way of life," and that differed from the American civil religion—"less optimistic, less

---

[31] Dick Anthony and Thomas Robbins, "Spiritual Innovation and the Crisis of American Civil Religion," in *Religion and America: Spirituality in a Secular Age,* ed. Mary Douglas and Steven Tipton (Boston: Beacon press, 1982) 230; Meredith McGuire, *Religion: The Social Context* (Belmont, Calif.: Wadsworth Publishing Co., 1981) 153.

[32] Hill, "The South's Two Cultures," in *Religion and the Solid South,* 36 and 45.

liberal, less democratic, less tolerant, and more homogeneously Protestant."[33]

The undeniably southern distinctions in the civil religion,
however, ought not lead one to minimize the historic Americanness of
the South. The southern civil religion mixes its symbols in accord with
the historical experience of the American South. The southern civil
religion is thus a southernized version of the American public faith,
with the necessary changes. It is distinctively southern not because it
gives sole allegiance to the South, but because it mixes the symbols of
allegiance to both America and the South. Moreover, it very often
interprets loyalty to the southern way of life as the epitome of
allegiance to America: One best fulfills his or her loyalty to America
by being loyal to the southern way.

Southern whites in the 1950s thus believed in what Swedish
scholar Gunnar Myrdal called the "American creed" of equality, freedom, and justice. Yet many also believed in the "creed of segregation."
The opposing pulls of these creeds underscored the pathos of the
"American dilemma."[34] That dilemma also revealed the essentially
mixed character of the southern civil religion.

The horns of the "American dilemma" came sharply to bear on
the loyalties of these southern whites as the entire nation began to
come to grips with the challenge of racial desegregation. My use of the
term desegregation in this context highlights its symbolic meaning and
is used synonymously with the term integration. In the 1950s and
1960s most whites unquestionably understood segregation as an important, if not the all-important, southern value. Prominent journalist James McBride Dabbs illustrated this by quoting an elderly southern farmer's confession of faith: "You can take my property.... But
take away the customs of my fathers, and I have nothing to live for."[35]

---

[33] Wilson, *Baptized in Blood*, 12-13.

[34] Gunnar Myrdal, *An American Dilemma: The Negro Problem and Modern
Democracy*, vol. 2 (New York: Harper & Brothers, 1944) 3; Ernest Q. Campbell and
Thomas F. Pettigrew, *Christians in Racial Crisis: A Study of Little Rock's Ministry*
(Washington, D. C.: Public Affairs Press, 1959) 59-60.

[35] James McBride Dabbs, *Haunted by God: The Cultural and Religious Experience of the South* (Richmond, Va.: John Knox Press, 1972) 9. For his full discussion
of Southern white valuations of segregation, including the social and economic, see
114-15.

In analyzing a value system that placed such import on the maintenance of the status quo, coldly cognitive definitions may miss the symbolic power of segregation. They miss the fact that most white southerners in the 1950s could only understand desegregation and integration as synonymous. Further, even though black activists in the civil rights era and afterward tended to distinguish between the terms, in striving for their ideal of integration they of necessity had to focus their activities on the practical first step of desegregation.[36]

Midcentury Racial Milieu

National and Southern Baptist attitudes concerning the "Negro problem" form the framework for understanding desegregation as a symbol in the civil religions of the South. Black-white relations constituted the central social question of the period, indeed one could say for all of southern history and caused southerners of both races to relate their views to their images of America.

Martin Luther King Jr. is most accurately viewed as the leading voice of black hopes in the 1950s. His phenomenally rapid rise to the leadership of the nascent black movement and the degree to which his perspectives were shared by much lesser-known Baptist preachers suggest that King's work expressed an ongoing ferment in the black church and community. More particularly, this receptivity to King's leadership among blacks, Baptists and non-Baptists alike, was one of the most significant manifestations of a stirring of attitudes on the race issue. These stirrings among National Baptists, of course, grew out of the general tendencies in the twentieth-century black church.

Most contemporary interpreters agree on the definitive character of black Christianity. That character, born of the experience of oppression in America, has been described by historian Gayraud Wilmore as a thrust for liberation. "Black religion," he argues, "always

---

[36] George D. Kelsey has described the important distinction in his book *Racism and the Christian Understanding of Man*, 114-15. Among black leaders, integration constituted a "realized condition of community, involving mutuality, reciprocity, and respect among persons." Desegregation, on the other hand, was merely the legal effort to end discriminatory public policy. Thus, to have a desegregated society was not necessarily to have an integrated on. See also Faustine C. Jones, "Ironies of School Desegregation," *Journal of Negro Education* 47 (Winter 1978): 2.

concerned itself with...the yearning of a despised an subjugated people for freedom."[37]

Wilmore holds, however, that the impulse toward liberation has been occasionally clouded over by an otherworldliness that failed to challenge the oppression of white society. One such occasion was during the 1920s and 1930s, when black churches largely retreated into "enclaves of moralistic, revivalistic Christianity" centrally concerned with institutional maintenance. This tradition within the black church, argues Wilmore, led many black religionists to withhold support from Martin Luther King Jr. viewing him as too radical.[38]

While Wilmore and others have rightly called attention to the otherworldly, conservative strain in black Christianity, most interpreters have also noted the "worldly otherworldliness" of black religion. Students of the black spirituals characteristically read between the otherworldly lines to highlight a black faith that always concerned itself with liberation. Lawrence W. Levine and James H. Cone have both called attention to the power of the spirituals to speak in otherworldly terms to the pain of blacks' very earthly oppression.[39]

In addition, the black preacher, depending on his training and intelligence, historically has given an otherworldly dimension to his "civil rights emphasis." Such "heavenly" images might be expected, for the preachers were often describing the nature of the kingdom of

---

[37] Gayraud S. Wilmore, *Black Religion and Black Radicalism*, 2d ed. (Maryknoll, N. Y.: Orbis Books, 1983) x. Other scholars have agreed that liberation has always been a central emphasis of black Christianity in America. See, for example, Eugene D. Genovese, *Roll, Jordan, Roll: The World the Slaves Made* (New York: Pantheon Books, 1974); Donald G. Mathews, *Religion in the Old South* (Chicago: University of Chicago Press, 1977); and Albert J. Raboteau, Jr., *Slave Religion: The Invisible Institution" in the Antebellum South* (New York: Oxford University Press, 1978).

[38] Wilmore, *Black Religion and Black Radicalism*, 161 and 180.

[39] The most recent treatment of this conservative tradition in black Christianity is James Melvin Washington, *Frustrated Fellowship: The Black Baptist Quest for Social Power* (Macon, Ga.: Mercer University Press, 1986). Lawrence W. Levine, *Black Culture and Black Consciousness* (New York: Oxford University Press, 1977) 30-54; James H. Cone, *The Spirituals and the Blues* (New York: Seabury Press, 1972) 1-33. See also Miles Mark Fisher, *Negro Slave Songs in the United States* (New York: citadel Press, 1953) 1-67 and Benjamin E. Mays's early study, *The Negro's God* (New York: Atheneum Press, 1968) which interprets the black spirituals in a more otherworldly vein.

heaven. Nevertheless, as William Washington asserted, "at the same time he [the black preacher] was talking about the here and now. And these kind of messages, even though they were sublimated, got through to the people.... It was almost like Jesus with his parables: you couldn't put your finger on what he was talking about, but everybody knew what he was talking about."[40]

Beyond this code language of the slave spirituals and black preaching lay efforts of southern black preachers increasingly to address the social conditions of their people throughout the century. Martin Luther King's father and maternal grandfather provided significant examples. Commenting on lessons learned from his father-in-law, the elder King wrote of the minister's larger responsibility to his community: "In the act of faith, every minister became an advocate for justice. In the South, this meant an active involvement in changing the social order all around us."[41]

Thus, two generations before Martin Luther King Jr. came to maturity as a minister, black pastors in the South were moving away from exclusively otherworldly understanding of their ministerial roles. While these ministers were perhaps atypical among black pastors in the South, the younger King's meteoric rise to prominence at least suggests an increasingly fertile ground for a "this-worldly" ministry. Black views of segregation indicate that this was true.

The traditional bromide of most southern whites in the 1950s and sixties held that blacks preferred segregation as a social arrangement. An examination of black leaders' comments regarding Jim Crow quickly disabuses the historian of that suggestion. King testified to an early sense of antipathy toward segregation. As a boy he refused to patronize a particular theater that forced blacks to enter through a rear door and sit in a separate gallery. At fourteen, returning from an oratorical contest where he had spoken on "The Negro and the Constitution," Martin and his teacher were ordered to give up their bus seats to whites. Cursed for not moving quickly enough, they were forced to stand for the entire ninety-mile trip to Atlanta. King

[40] William Washington, director of public relations for the National Baptist Convention, interview with author, Nashville, Tenn., April 14-15, 1984.
[41] Martin Luther King, Sr., *Daddy King: An Autobiography* (New York: Harper & Row, 1980) 82.

recalled: "That night will never leave my memory. It was the angriest I have ever been in my life."[42]

Personal experiences of humiliation under Jim Crow were determinative for most black ministers who by the 1950s were ready to fight for their rights. In Lynchburg, Virginia, young pastor W. J. Hodge began to refer to himself by his initials rather than allow whites to address him by his first name.[43] Fred Shuttlesworth, who in 1963 summoned King and the SCLC to Birmingham, Alabama, for a direct action campaign, also felt a growing resentment over racially moti- vated discrepancies in the country's system of justice. "Blacks [were] abused," he recalled, "taken advantage of, closing their property, [would] go to courts and have absolutely no standing before the law. I think all of these things built up in me residually, on top of each other."[44] Segregation often generated among blacks a poignant bitterness toward the South. J. Pius Barbour wrote of the incom- parable feeling of being forced into a Jim Crow car on a railroad trip into the South: "When one takes a trip South, he is filled with bitter- ness when he gets to his destination and is in no condition to ap- preciate the better South.... I think this one thing fills the Negroes with bitterness about the South more than anything else. One always re- turns home with a degree of bitterness."[45]

Why were these feeling of distress so rarely noted by southern whites? At least one explanation was the southern black's tendency not fully to speak his or her mind in the presence of whites. Barbour

[42] Cited in John J. Ansbro, *Martin Luther King, Jr.: The Making of a Mind* (Maryknoll, N. Y.: Orbis Books, 1983) 76-77. These statements originally appeared in King, *Stride Toward Freedom: The Montgomery Story* (New York: Harper & Row, 1958) 18-20, and *Playboy Interviews* (Chicago: Playboy Press, 1967) 349.

[43] `W. J. Hodge, interview with author, Louisville, Kentucky, April 2, 1984. Hodge was a prominent pastor of the Fifth Street Baptist Church in Louisville. An important advocate of civil rights on the local scene, Hodge was interviewed as a representative of the "average" black minister. By "average" I mean ministers who addressed the issue of civil rights in their preaching, but who could not be considered "activists" in ways similar to ministers like Martin Luther King Jr. or Ralph David Abernathy. Having begun his ministry during this period, Hodge also represents the perspectives of younger black ministers.

[44] Fred Shuttlesworth, interview with author, Cincinnati, Ohio, March 10, 1984.

[45] "Editor Barbour Spends a Week in Mississippi," *NBV 31* (November 1, 1946): 3.

regarded blacks' characteristic reserve around whites as an effect of living in America. He sensed such reserve even among non-American whites. Commenting on a bus trip in Italy, he wrote poignantly that "after living in America all your life I do not think it is possible to completely throw off the feeling of Race. Somehow it grips you and a Negro surrounded by whites is a study in reserved behavior."[46] One should probably interpret this, however, as a studied reserve. An important tradition in blacks' relations with whites, dating from the slave experience was the practice of masking. James H. Cone notes that surviving in an oppressive society required making the oppressors think the victims were what they themselves *knew* they were not. A slave song put it thus: "Got one mind for the boss to see / Got another for what I know is me."[47]

Blacks began to move away from that tradition in the postwar period, however. At times, black preachers spoke "white" in the presence of whites. Addressing the white Baptist Convention of Alabama in 1955, the president of the black Alabama Baptist Convention, U. J. Robinson, sounded themes close to the Southern Baptist heart. He appealed for financial help for Selma University in order to help "stand the storm of Communism, Atheism, and other idolatries. That is our number one need today."[48] Privately, however, his words were more "black." Asked his opinion of the Supreme Court's desegregation decision, Robinson's parabolic reply was, "It must be all right, nine white men did it."[49]

Not only was there encouragement from the actions of the federal government, in both the Supreme Court's *Brown* ruling and in President Truman's desegregation of the armed forces, there were also improvements in race relations. In 1946, for example, the black and white Baptist conventions of Georgia met together in a fellowship meeting. One black spokesman, Roland Smith, believed the meeting marked an important epoch. He further exhorted, "If ever we are not to make a mockery of Christianity this kind of spirit must manifest

---

[46] "A Bus Trip in Europe, Article 5," *NBV 32* (December 15, 1947): 5.

[47] Cone, *Spirituals and the Blues*, 27.

[48] U. J. Robinson, "Selma University's Place In Colored State Baptist Convention," *Alabama Baptist 120* (December 1, 1955): 5. (*Alabama Baptist* hereafter cited at AB.)

[49] Washington, interview with author, March 14-15, 1984.

itself more and more."[50] Developments such as this, coupled with the
Federal government's efforts toward establishing civil rights, added to
black hopefulness and led many blacks to think the time was ripe for
pressing their demands. Thus King could affirm that "we stand on the
threshold of the most constructive period of our nation's history. This
is an exciting age, filled with hope."[51] President Joseph H. Jackson of
the National Baptist Convention, who disagreed with King on other
matters, also felt a similar hopefulness among blacks in recalling that
period: "Nineteenth Hundred and Fifty-three was a time when
prospects of freedom presented a dream and the hope of multitudes,
not the dream of a chosen few. It was believed that the possibility of
realizing the dream was no longer a faint vision, it was a goal in
sight.... No one could be in step with the times and not behold this
revelation of freedom and feel the urgency and power of its thrust. To
be on the side of the movement for freedom was no question; it was a
certainty in the minds of all. The only question was one of
methodology."[52]

Jackson's assessment suggests not only the sentiment of
hopefulness among blacks in general, but also the more specific policies
of the National Baptist Convention.

Gayraud Wilmore interpreted the black church in its national
institutional form as more "a sympathetic spectator than a responsible participant" in the struggle for blacks' civil rights. This, he
believed, was evidenced by hesitant support for Martin Luther King
Jr. He further argued that the National Baptist Convention "simply
refused to be identified with him."[53] The relation of the National
Baptist Convention to King's work was not quite as simple or as
monolithic as Wilmore suggests. Many individual congregations
helped raise money for the SCLC, as Wilmore admits, and numerous
ministers joined King's marches. Beyond this, one can argue that King
enjoyed fairly strong institutional support from the National Baptist

---

[50] Statement by Roland Smith, editor of the black Baptist newspaper in Georgia,
cited by Gainer E. Bryan, Jr., in "Georgia Baptists of White and Negro Conventions
Join in Fellowship Meeting at Savannah," *Christian Index* 126 (November 28, 1946):
5-6. (*Christian Index* hereafter cited as *CI*.)

[51] "A View of the Dawn," *Interracial Review* 30 (May 1957): 82.

[52] Joseph H. Jackson, *A Story of Christian Activism: The History of the National
Baptist Convention, U. S. A.* (Nashville: Townsend Press, 1980) 231.

[53] Wilmore, *Black Religion and Black Radicalism*, 179.

Convention despite the strong criticism he sometimes received from its president.

As an ecclesiastical body the Convention had a long tradition of calling for the civil rights of its constituency. Its presidents almost always participated in the struggle for first-class citizenship and better race relations. D. V. Jemison of Selma, Alabama, president from 1940 to 1953, illustrated such leadership in his 1943 address to the Convention. Commenting on the failure of white ministers to address the race problem, he instructed his listeners as follows:

"The difference between the white and Negro preacher is this: the Negro preacher makes the sentiment for his people, but with a white preacher the people make the sentiment for him. This is true because the white minister dare not preach against traditions and customs handed down by his people; if he does he will lose his position. They preach Christ but are sadly lacking in applying Christ in all of their doings as it relates to the Negro group.

"Another underlying cause of this deplorable condition is wanting and urging the people and especially the Negro to accept that which is called peace but in the meantime there is no peace.... He who at all today warns against false prophets in the visible church is looked upon as narrow-minded and an arrogant bigot and a disturber of the peace of the church."[54]

To be sure, as some scholars have argued, older black ministers were less militant than the younger generation.[55] D. V. Jemison's influence, however, was not lost on his minister son, Theodore. In 1953 the younger Jemison, then secretary of the National Baptist Convention and pastor of the Mount Zion First Baptist Church of Baton Rouge, Louisiana, led blacks in the South's first bus boycott. Martin Luther King copied elements of this boycott two years later in the Montgomery boycott.[56] Thus, emboldened by developments in the

---

[54] Quoted in Jackson, *Christian Activism*, 181. See also Jackson, *Unholy Shadows and Freedom's Holy Light* (Nashville: Townsend Press, 1967) 73-75.

[55] See David L. Lewis, *King: A Critical Biography* (New York: Praeger Publishers, 1970) 158; C. Eric Lincoln, *The Black Church Since Frazier* (New York: Schocken Books, 1974) 119. Lincoln's work was published as part of a single volume that includes E. Franklin Frazier's *The Negro Church in America;* Frazier's book was originally published in 1963 by the University of Liverpool.

[56] The influence of the Baton Rouge boycott on the similar effort in Montgomery, Alabama, is noted in King, *Stride Toward Freedom*, 75. The best source

World War II and postwar years, the new militancy of the younger black ministers grew naturally out of the traditions of leadership in the National Baptist Convention.

The Convention had long and strongly supported the work of the NAACP, support that carried over into the formation of the SCLC. While the latter organization was not officially connected with the Convention, many of its original leaders were active members of it.[57] Joseph Jackson wrote an optimistic appraisal of this support: "Many of us felt that in this particular move [the founding of the SCLC] we, of the National Baptist Convention, would have within our reach a group dedicated not only to civil rights but to America and to the Christian point of view. We believed that now the Convention... has brought into existence a group of young men who understand the visions of the founders of their convention and who were willing to make a sacrifice...to make the Christian ideals of brotherhood a practical reality in the United states of America."[58]

The support of the National Baptist Convention, one must admit, would have been stronger had there not developed a bitter rift between president Joseph H. Jackson and Martin Luther King. Though Jackson early supported the work of King and the SCLC, Jackson eventually came to view King as an "upstart, a provocateur, and ultimately a menace to the best interests of the Black people and the clerical profession."[59]

---

on the Baton Rouge boycott itself is Judy Barton's oral history interview with Theodore J. Jemison and Johnnie Jones, April 12, 1972, transcript, Oral History Collection, Martin Luther King Jr. Center for Nonviolent Social Change, Atlanta, Ga. One should perhaps note that Jemison later served as the president of the National Baptist Convention. Jemison recently set a precedent for the president of the convention by endorsing the Reverend Jesse Jackson" 1984 candidacy for president of the United States. Such a politically partisan action represents a significant change from the policies of former president Joseph H. Jackson. It also testifies to the continuing strength of the King tradition within the National Baptist Convention.

[57] In addition to King and Abernathy, National Baptist participants in the founding of the SCLC included Rev. A. L. Davis of New Orleans, Rev. Theodore J. Jemison of Baton Rouge, Rev. W. T. Crutcher and Rev. R. E. James of Knoxville, Tennessee, and many others. See Jackson, *Unholy Shadows*, 77; on the convention support with the NAACP, see also 42-43.

[58] Jackson, *Unholy Shadows*, 77.

[59] Lincoln, *The Black Church Since Frazier*, 119.

On the philosophical level, their differences centered on Jackson's rejection of King's acceptance of civil disobedience. Jackson believed in a limited methodology for protest. Only methods sanctioned by the "supreme law of the land" were justifiable. For Jackson protest had its place in the Bill of Rights and the Constitution, as evidenced by the right to assemble to petition the government for redress of grievances. Citizen groups, however, were not to go beyond petition to redress their own grievances. By doing so, the protesters would be punishing persons innocent of the evils they wish to remove. The accused would be denied the right to appear in their own defense. Such an eventuality would constitute redress without due process of law.[60]

Jackson feared that "unknown conspirators in pseudo-patriotic cloak" might join the protest movement in order to overthrow the government rather than to correct injustice. Persons advocating civil disobedience, Jackson believed, were "enemies to the American way of life and are liabilities to her body politic."[61] Such leaders unnecessarily created tensions and stirred up animosities in the vain hope that these tensions might generate constructive solutions to contemporary problems. Jackson considered this approach a type of "confusionism" holding that "lawlessness can be substituted for law and thereby bring to pass an ordered society."[62]

Criticism so pointed could only have had King in mind, though Jackson was careful not to repudiate King by name. Interestingly enough, Jackson's book-length apologia for his approach to civil rights specifically mentions Martin Luther King only once, and then favorably.[63] At the very least, this suggests that Jackson was loath to condemn King directly, presumably because of his popularity, thus indicating a significant personal dimension to the Jackson-King rift. King's meteoric rise to prominence within the National Baptist Convention, and in the black community in general, surely created some ministerial jealousy in the older black leader.

Nevertheless, black Baptist approval of King remained hearty despite the hesitancy of Joseph H. Jackson. W. J. Hodge recalled that at the popular level most National Baptists, by far, identified with the

---

[60] Jackson, *Christian Activism*, 233-35.
[61] Jackson, *Unholy Shadows*, 107; Jackson, *Christian Activism*, 234.
[62] Jackson, *Unholy Shadows*, 170.
[63] Ibid., 76.

efforts of Martin Luther King: "There were always enough to galvanize a sufficient number of people in the black community to participate and be supportive."[64] The interest of many local black pastors helps explain the strength of the movement within the black churches. Behind this pastoral interest, however, was a certain psychological morale that came from the National Baptist Convention's civil rights tradition and its blanket approval of the growing black movement.[65] Later, in the student-led protest movement of the sixties, poor, rural, uneducated southern blacks protected the young workers, gave shelter, and attended mass meetings in innumerable churches across the South.[66] The movement of the 1950s and sixties did not arise *de novo*, however. In many ways, specific actions by black Baptists in the South prepared the way for King's movement.

The mid-forties saw black Baptists in the Deep South become increasingly restive. In 1946 several whites attended the convention of black Baptists held in Montgomery, Alabama. J. Pius Barbour noted that "they heard a plenty as those preachers made out they were talking to God but were shooting at those white folks." Barbour also pointed out that "the Negroes were politically conscious and were all stirred up about that new amendment that Alabama had adopted to keep them from the polls. They intended to fight it out in the courts."[67] Two years later black pastors in Birmingham made a public statement repudiating segregation. They acknowledged that segregation would continue to be practiced but declared that the time had now come for Christian people to take the lead in abolishing the practice.[68]

Many prominent National Baptist pastors in the Deep South began to raise the consciousness of their parishioners during this early postwar period. In Montgomery, King's predecessor at the Dexter Avenue Baptist Church, the Reverend Vernon Johns, prepared the way for King's movement by instilling a sense of pride in his church members. King's ministry was acceptable to the people of Dexter

---

[64] W. J. Hodge, interview with author, April 2, 1984.

[65] Washington, interview with author, March 14, 1984.

[66] Barbara L. Carter, "Making a Difference," in *Protest, Politics, and Prosperity: Black Americans and White Institutions, 1940-1975*, ed. Dorothy K. Newman (New York: Pantheon Books, 1978) 19.

[67] "Editor Barbour Spends a Week in Alabama," *NBV 31* (December 15, 1946): 3 and 14.

[68] J. Pius Barbour, "Among the Brethren," *NBV 32* (January 15, 1948): 8.

Avenue, one observer believed, "largely because Vernon Johns had already passed that way."[69] A firebrand who instilled a sense of pride in his congregation, Johns encouraged the parishioners to demand respect and their rights from the white power structure. One of his clerical colleagues described Johns as "one of the men who helped to keep what we would ordinarily call 'the pot boiling' because he stood out and preached against the cruelties and injustices of the community....He put [such] outstanding subjects out there on the bulletin board that the police would question him concerning race relations, while he was preaching here."[70]

Black Baptist leaders in neighboring states followed suit. President Harrison H. Humes of the black Baptist Convention of Mississippi declared at the 1948 annual session, "We don't want the white leadership in Mississippi to misrepresent the Negroes' request. The Negro is requesting free participation in a government that he has given his blood to defend from the Revolutionary War to the Recent World War II."[71] The president of the Georgia Baptist Missionary and Educational Convention, William Holmes Borders, admonished his fellow preachers to get in the forefront of the struggle for their people's rights. "The Negro preacher," he argued, "must take the lead in fighting for the civic rights of the southern Negro and he must not flinch before the Klu Klux Klan [sic] or any other race hating group. We must serve notice...that we will not be intimidated."[72] Curious as to whether rural southern blacks were as concerned about civil rights as were blacks in the cities, J. Pius Barbour personally reported on that meeting in Pelham, Georgia. He learned that "not only was there no compromise but rather an intensifying of the demands that Negroes

[69]Charles E. Boddie, God's "Bad Boys" (Valley Forge, Pa.: Judson Press, 1972) 70.

[70]S. S. Seay, interview by Judy Barton, January 25, 1972, transcript, 3-4, Oral History Collection, Martin Luther King Jr. Center for Nonviolent Social Change, Atlanta GA. See also Barton's January 24, 1972, interview with R. D. Nesbitt (a member of Dexter Avenue Baptist Church) transcript, 17-18, Oral History Collection, King Center.

[71]Coleman W. Kerry, "Mississippi Baptists Hold Great Meeting," NBV 32 (August 15, 1948): 3.

[72]Quoted in J. Pius Barbour, "Borders Re-elected President of Georgia Baptist Missionary and Educational Convention," NBV 32 (December 1 1948): 3.

would take no back ground in their fight for their rights. Things are stirring in the South and don't you forget it."[73]

Encouraged by these early admonitions and, of course, by the support of the federal government, black Baptists increased their civil rights activities throughout the 1950s and into the sixties. The racial milieu within the black community in general encouraged this burgeoning activity among black Baptists. The stirrings among National Baptists set the stage for the work of Martin Luther King, the Montgomery Improvement Association, and later the SCLC.

Beyond the work of the para-church organizations associated with King, National Baptists made their own distinct but related efforts. Thus, for example, the black Baptist Convention of Virginia conducted a voter registration drive in 1958. At their May meeting the Convention created a civil rights commission and sent a letter to every black Baptist church in the state, calling on pastors to encourage their members to pay the poll tax and register to vote.[74]

Thus, rather than revealing a black community satisfied with the status quo, the racial milieu indicated that black Baptists were increasingly dissatisfied, militant, and insistent that America become what it claimed to be. The remarkable solidarity of black Baptists' attitudes contrasts quite clearly with the divided mind of Southern Baptists.

Although rank-and-file Southern Baptists tended to maintain a hard line against the incursions of the growing black movement, the Southern Baptist Convention in this period was unusually divided in its racial attitudes. While the segregationist impulse found very strong support at the local level, Convention leadership tried, albeit timidly, to provide a more progressive direction.[75] This bifurcated mind

---

[73] Ibid.

[74] Letters from the reverend Dr. L. C. Johnson, chairman of the Civil Rights Commission of the Virginia Baptist State Convention, July 5 and October 9, 1958, Correspondence, File, SCLC Collection, King Center, Atlanta, Ga. Letters were mass-mailed to all black Baptist churches and/or ministers in Virginia.

[75] This division within Southern Baptist views of civil rights and the race issue continued through the sixties. The division also became more crystallized and thus more noticeable after the death of Martin Luther King. See Andrew M. Manis, "Silence or Shockwaves: Southern Baptist Responses to the Assassination of Martin Luther King Jr." *Baptist History and Heritage* 15 (October 1980): 19-27, 35.

among Southern Baptists must, of course, be interpreted within the general response of the white South to the events of the era.

The 1948 Dixiecrat revolt against Truman's civil rights policies, prefigured the South's more general and more volatile reaction to the Supreme Court's desegregation decision. Because of similarities with southern sentiments toward the federal government after the Civil War, southern historians have often called the period after 1954 "the Second Reconstruction." The Southern Baptist racial milieu of the 1950s was set within such a cultural context.

The mood of the South in the mid-1950s closely approximated that of 1948. As Numan Bartley has noted, however, the climate grew even more intense in response to the direct threat of forced integration—embodied in the symbol of the Supreme Court—and the growing militancy of southern blacks.[76] The heightened sense of paranoia created a southern challenge to federal authority stronger than at any time since the Civil War. The South's demand for conformity of thought and its intolerance of dissent were reminiscent of its antebellum reaction to the abolitionist movement.[77] The radical white South hoped to form a united front in the face of the threat. Not surprisingly, prominent southern journalist Hodding Carter could suggest, "As far as many white southerners were concerned, the [Civil] war had begun again, and the blanket salvos of the 'outsiders' were reason enough for togetherness."[78]

Besides the reinvigorated activities of the Klan the most extreme response of the white South was the rise and growth of the Citizens Councils. Founded in the summer of 1954 in Yazoo City, Mississippi, the Councils expanded into an area wide apparatus claiming three hundred thousand members. It propagated its message through a newspaper, regional television and radio shows, and large numbers of speakers.[79] By the end of 1955, at least 568 segregationist organizations

---

[76] Numan V. Bartley, *The Rise of Massive Resistance: Race and Politic in the South in the 1950s* (Baton Rouge: Louisiana State University Press, 1969) 82.

[77] Hodding Carter, *The South Strikes Back* (New York: Doubleday & Co., 1959) 17.

[78] Ibid., 18.

[79] Ibid.

had arisen throughout the South, with high membership figures in each of the Deep South states.[80]

The Citizens Councils contributed greatly to the South's growing alienation from the rest of the nation. Benjamin Muse has noted that many southerners came to refer to "the government in Washington" as they would have spoken of a foreign power. Perhaps the best indication of this was a 1959 series of articles in the periodical the *Citizens' Council*, identifying the enemies of the South. It named seventy-four national organizations in the November issue and an additional thirty-three in the August issue. "The list as a whole," Muse wrote, "was a startling revelation of how largely the Citizens' Councils had assumed an attitude of belligerence toward the government and people of the United States."[81] Many African Americans viewed the Citizens Council as the Klan without the sheets.

The institutional church in the South found itself caught within such a context. The leadership generally criticized the vitriol of the Councils and the violence of the Klan. Their voices were muted, however, because their parishioners, if they were not outright members of the councils, quite often shared their views. As Bartley suggests, the churches did not shape events. They generally reacted only when the society, and thus when their vested institutional interests, were threatened. His conclusion—that "their failure to exert a more positive stabilizing influence was an integral element in the rise of massive resistance"—is difficult to refute.[82] To find an affirmation of segregation among Southern Baptists is thus hardly a surprise.

Southern Baptist historian Leon McBeth has correctly argued that his coreligionists held "a Reconstruction posture" on the race issue until the eve of World War II, with significant change since then.[83] That posture was expressed in 1950 by then-president of the Southern

---

[80] John Bartlow Martin, *The Deep South Says "Never"* (New York: Ballantine Books, 1957) 37. Martin cites membership totals for the following states: South Carolina, forty thousand; Mississippi, seventy-five thousand; Georgia, sixty thousand; Louisiana, twenty thousand. He also notes that councils were organized in the states of Alabama, Texas, Oklahoma, Missouri, and Arkansas.

[81] Muse, *Ten Years of Prelude: The Story of Integration Since the Supreme Court's Decision* (New York: Viking Press, 1964) 176-77.

[82] Bartley, *Rise of Massive Resistance*, 294.

[83] Leon McBeth, "Southern Baptists and Race Since 1947," *Baptist History and Heritage* 7 (July 1972): 155.

Baptist Convention, R. G. Lee. Interviewed by the black newspaper the *Pittsburgh Courier*, Lee said he did not favor sermons that addressed issues like civil rights.[84]

Southern Baptist actions matched their attitudes against integration. In 1956 two Baptist colleges, by a decision of the trustees and through a student referendum, banned blacks from admission.[85] Influence from extreme segregationist thought often made itself felt within the churches. On one occasion fifty hooded and robed, but unmasked, Klansmen visited a church near Mobile, Alabama. Greeted warmly by the pastor, the visitors solemnly marched into the sanctuary as the pianist played "Onward Christian Soldiers."[86]

Typical southern justifications for these attitudes and actions found expression among Southern Baptists. Their spokespersons were most often quiet segregationists who held that however laudable the goal of integration might be, too rapid strides toward that goal would disturb the peace. Thus, Leon Macon, editor of the *Alabama Baptist*, argued the segregationist case: "It is not unChristian to endorse measures which lead to peace, harmony, and order. It is not matter of prejudice but a matter of wisdom and common sense. We heartily wish all men well but we cannot believe that any of our parents, of any race, want their children to live in a hostile environment caused by unwise idealism."[87] Not surprisingly, many Southern Baptists believed with David Gardner, the editor of the [Texas] *Baptist Standard*, that the vast majority of blacks in the South preferred segregated schools even as they preferred separate churches.[88] That these were the majority views among Southern Baptists can hardly be doubted. This was particularly true of laypersons and many ministers at the local level of denominational life. The national leadership of the Convention, however, harbored some significantly different perspectives.

---

[84] Cited in Hill, "Southern Baptist Thought and Action," 299-300.

[85] "Anti-integration Action at Two Baptist Schools," *American Baptist 121* (January 12, 1956): 4. (*American Baptist* hereafter cited as *AmB.*)

[86] "Klansmen Visit Baptist Church," *Baptist Record*, 80 (November 1, 1956): 1. (*Baptist Record* hereafter cited as *BR.*)

[87] Leon Macon, "Using Churches for Schools," *AB 123* (February 20, 1958): 3.

[88] David Gardner, "The Segregation Problem," *Baptist Standard 66* (October 14, 1954) 2. (*Baptist Standard* hereafter cited as *BS.*)

Social ethicist George B. Kelsey detected a shift of Southern
Baptist racial attitudes during the period after World War II. He
attributed the change to new cultural forces that had been developing
for a long while but were loosed by the war. He acknowledged, however, a significant division in Southern Baptist thinking: "While the
old ideas continue to persist alongside the new after World War II,
there is an increase in the prophetic criticism of racist attitudes and
practices."[89] These new attitudes toward race were mostly located in
the leadership of the Southern Baptist Convention, particularly the
heads of the denomination's national agencies. The agency most
devoted to raising the consciousness of Southern Baptists on this
matter was the Christian Life Commission. The Commission supported the Supreme Court's desegregation decision in 1954 and gave most
of the space in its publication, *Light*, to the question of race relations.
In 1956 the commission engaged ethicist T. B. Maston to write what
became a controversial pamphlet generally in support of integration.[90] The Christian Life Commission would thus become the lightning rod for criticism from the more reactionary elements of the
Southern Baptist Convention.

Negative reaction did not have the stage to itself, however.
Progressive views on integration were at times expressed by Southern
Baptist pastors. In the wake of the Little Rock debacle, pastor Dale
Cowling of that city's Second Baptist Church defended the Supreme
Court's desegregation ruling, stating: "One seriously wonders if the
high court could have interpretated [sic] otherwise. We must remember that the *very heart* of America is *freedom*. Her strength has
been her rebellion against caste systems and her insistence upon the
worth of every individual. The design of our Constitution was to
provide freedom for all."[91]

---

[89] George B. Kelsey, *Social Ethics among Southern Baptists, 1917-1969* (Madison
N J: Scarecrow Press, 1973) 206.

[90] Thomas Buford Maston, *Integration* (Nashville: Christian Life Commission
of the Southern Baptist Convention, 1956.)

[91] Dale Cowling, "A Christian Looks at Integration in Little Rock" (Sermon
preached at Second Baptist Church, Little Rock, Arkansas, September 1, 1957) tran-
script, Boyce Centennial Library of the Southern Baptist Theological Seminary,
Louisville, Ky. Cowling's sermon is also included in DeWitte Holland, *Sermons in
American History: Selected Issues in the American Pulpit, 1630-1967* (Nashville:
Abingdon Press, 1971).

Agency leaders, though generally more quiet on the issue, occasionally expressed similar views. In April 1956, a group of such leaders published a statement calling for a "Christian spirit in race relations." They based their admonition of six principles, among them humankind's creation in God's image and God's impartiality.[92] This leadership elite constituted a progressive vanguard within the Southern Baptist Convention. Its members controlled the levers of power, as well as some of the Convention's sources of communication (namely, the state newspapers), but not the attitudes of the "average" Southern Baptist. In reality, however, even their control of the denominational machinery was tenuous. Their tentative influence on the views of the laity stemmed from the decentralization of Southern Baptist polity and the usual chasm between the leadership and laity of any large denomination. Because of this gulf and the Convention's political decentralization, these leaders always had difficulty convincing the rank and file and usually moderated their pronouncements in the interest of denominational unity. The division was real and was integrally related to the conflict of civil religions in the South.

In describing the racial milieu, however, it is sufficient merely to note the diversity of opinion within the Southern Baptist Convention. Most Southern Baptists clearly opted for the segregationist perspective, although the most reactionary attitudes are, surprisingly, somewhat difficult to document from the Baptist newspapers and convention minutes. The explanation for this is that the papers and convention machinery were in the hands of more moderate or progressive denominationalists who above all worked to hold the convention together. Most of the attitudes surveyed in the remainder of this book come from the dominant reactionary perspective. To be fair to Southern Baptists as a whole, however, one must also note the growing dissent from the racial orthodoxy of the majority.

---

[92] "Christian Spirit in Race Relations," *CI 135* (April 12, 1956): 3. Among the leaders signing this statement were Alma Hunt, executive secretary of the Women's Missionary Union; Duke K. McCall, president of Southern Baptist Theological Seminary; Baker James Cauthen, executive secretary of the Foreign Mission Board; Courts Redford, executive secretary of the Home Mission Board; Porter Routh executive secretary of the Southern Baptist Convention; and Sydnor L. Stealey, president of Southeastern Baptist Theological Seminary. Certain prominent pastors also signed the document.

Development of Civil Religions Loyalties

Surveying the southern milieu regarding white and black attitudes reveals that the race question struck close to the matter of American identity. Alongside the development of southern racial attitudes was a developing set of images of America. These images suggest a developing conflict of civil religious loyalties. That these conflicting loyalties should be noticeable in the years before 1947 should thus be no surprise. The South has always attempted to be both American and southern—indeed, its inhabitants have argued proudly that to be a good southerner was to be a good American. Yet within these dual loyalties, there were also certain subtle shifts of civil loyalty. Thus, the years between 1917 and 1947 may be understood as a period of ambivalence.

The ambivalence of the white South is understandable. The twentieth-century experience of southerners has included competing, alternating loyalties to American and their native region. On the one hand, as regards patriotic loyalty to America, the twentieth-century South largely moved back into the national mainstream. On the other hand, as historian Fletcher M. Green correctly observed, the South retained a powerful but dormant sectionalism that with sufficient and periodic provocation reawakened to challenge southerners' loyalty to the nation.[93]

Among southern blacks, however, the ambivalence was of a different sort. Blacks experienced little vacillation between civil loyalties to America and to the South. Their public faith always focused on the entire nation. The ambivalence was in their remaining true to themselves while staying faithful to the nation that had not yet truly come to terms with their otherness. During these years of prelude American blacks served patriotically in their country's wars, despite the continuance of Jim Crow in America. In response to this indignity, blacks in the United States developed much of the assertiveness that later burst through the barriers of segregation during the civil rights movement. The power of that movement is very largely traceable to the confluence of two dynamic impulses at work in the African-American community: an increasingly fervent black con-

---

[93] Fletcher M. Green, "Resurgent Southern Sectionalism, 1933-1955," *North Carolina Historical Review* 33 (April 1956): 223-25.

sciousness and a heightened appeal to the American civil religion. The development of civil religious loyalties among both white and black southerners between the years of 1917 and 1947 thus included a component of ambivalence. Southern whites being torn between Americans and being southerners, while southern blacks experienced what W. E. B. Du Bois called a "double-consciousness" of being simultaneously black and American.

"The Americanization of Dixie" has been an important theme in the South's post World War II development, as well as in recent southern historiography. Scholarly discussion has centered on the degree to which the South has disappeared as a regional entity as it has become more like the rest of the nation.[94] Most interpreters have noted the reassimilation of the South into the national mainstream during and after the period of Reconstruction.[95] Those who describe the reconciliation of the South and North in dramatic, almost miraculous, terms have tended to overestimate the degree of division between them.[96] That understanding rests on the dubious assumption that the South had developed a completely separate nationalism by 1865. Southern civil religious loyalties, however, remained quite mixed even during the Civil War. David Potter rightly reminds us of the swift readiness with which the South reaffirmed its loyalty to the United States. Despite its clinging to the Lost Cause, southerners by and large once again became fervent American patriots by the time of the Spanish-American War in 1898. Such a rapid return to the American fold defies explanation unless southern loyalty to America was never

[94] For an introduction to some of these issues, see John Egerton, *The Americanization of Dixie: The Southernization of America* (New York: Harper's Magazine Press, 1974); Reed, *The Enduring South,* and *One South: An Ethnic Approach to Regional Culture* (Baton Rouge: Louisiana State University Press, 1982); and Roland, *Improbable Era,* who noted the reassimilation of the South into the national mainstream; and "The Ever-Vanishing South," *Journal of Southern History* 48 (February 1981).

[95] See chapter 7 of Wilson, *Baptized in Blood*; Paul H. Buck, *The Road to Reunion, 1865-1900* (Boston: Little, Brown & Company, 1937); and Paul M. Gaston, *The New South Creed: A Study in Southern Mythmaking* (Baton Rouge: Louisiana State University Press, 1970).

[96] Arthur Schlesinger once called the reunion of the North and South within thirty-five years (1865-1900) "one of the unnoticed miracles of modern times." Quoted by Frank L. Owsley, review of *Road to Reunion,* by Paul H. Buck, *Yale Review* 27 (September 1937): 171. Buck's study interprets the reconciliation similarly.

completely obliterated by the Civil War. Rather, a white southern loyalty to the United States was eclipsed by other loyalties that temporarily came into conflict with it.[97]

A residual patriotism toward the nation enabled the South to move quickly back into the mainstream. As a result, through the course of the twentieth century the South saw a waning of its distinctiveness and its sectionalism. Kenneth K. Bailey has argued for a decreasing sectionalism in southern religion, suggestion that "the South and the southern churches are being brought into closer association with the rest of the nation as the nation moves into closer association with the rest of the world."[98] With respect to attitudes toward international affairs the South has increasingly come to resemble the nation as a whole. One scholar has even argued that after 1935 Southern Baptists, for example, were a microcosm of the larger society.[99] Though probably a glaring overstatement, this evaluation rightly underscores the reawakening of the South's dormant nationalism and the solidarity of the North-South reconciliation.

In this period America's wars contributed greatly to the reunion. The "splendid little war" with Spain gave southern boys an opportunity to prove their (American) patriotism. The martial ardor of the South burned still warmer in the global wars of the twentieth century.[100] Politicians from the South led the way. "Traditionally quick on the military draw, they were the political vanguard of American participation in both world wars," notes Charles Roland.[101] Returning into the American fold, southerners brought with them a certain sense of regional destiny that meshed with that of the nation. Even before World War I Southern Baptists adopted a providential interpretation of the rise of Woodrow Wilson, a son of the South, to the presidency. In 1917, Southern Baptist Convention president W. J.

[97] Potter, "Historian's Use of Nationalism," 947-48.

[98] Kenneth K. Bailey, *Southern White Protestantism in the Twentieth Century* (New York: Harper & Row, 1964; Gloucester, Mass.: Peter Smith, 1968) 166.

[99] Robert Benjamin Ferguson, "The Southern Baptist Response to International Affairs and Threats to Peace, 1931-1941" (Ph.D. diss., Carnegie-Mellon University, 1981) 264.

[100] Frank E. Vandiver, "The Southerner as Extremist," in *The South: A Central Theme?*, ed. Monroe L. Billington (Huntington, N. Y.: Robert E Krieger Publishing Co., 1976) 74.

[101] Roland, *Improbable Era*, 5.

McGlothlin predicted proudly that "it is Woodrow Wilson, a southern man, who will be the principal factor in using this nation for the emancipation of other nations."[102] Later, Southern Baptist biblical scholar A. T. Robertson saw Wilson's call to "make the world safe for democracy" as a virtual extension of Southern Baptist efforts to "universalize religious democracy."[103] Once America entered the war, Southern Baptist rhetoric took on apocalyptic overtones. Germany was identified with the Antichrist, while America was the nation chosen by God as the repository of freedom. God had sheltered America in isolation from international politics that democracy might grow unhindered. Beyond this, as Southern Baptist theology professor W. O. Carver believed, "God had commanded America to destroy German autocracy and to carry civil and religious democracy to the world."[104]

Southern Baptist support went far beyond mere rhetoric, however. James J. Thompson has described Southern Baptist financial contributions to the war effort and the fervor with which they sent their sons to Europe to fight.[105] In this they were little different from other Southerners, of whom nearly a million entered the army during the Great War. Such support for America's war effort suggests a significant diminution of the sectional spirit. Doubtless a great surprise to dyed-in-the-wool Yankee haters, at times this cooling of southern allegiance came through deliberate effort. Note, for example, Virginia congressman Carter Glass's admonition: "There should be intermingling of troops from all the States. We should submerge provincialism and party spirit in one powerful flood of nationalism, which would carry us on to victory."[106]

The era of the First World War thus saw a bona fide "Americanization" of the South. Yet paradoxically it was a southernized America on which these southerners focused. George Tindall describes an

---

[102] W. J. McGlothlin, "Christianize the South, *BS 29* (June 14, 1917): 22.

[103] A. T. Robertson, *The New Citizenship: The Christian Facing a New World Order* (New York: Fleming H. Revell, 1919) 166-67.

[104] W. O. Carver, "Some Aspects of Education in the Light of the War's Revelations," *Review and Expositor 17* (January 1920): 78-79.

[105] James J. Thompson, Jr., *Tried As by Fire: Southern Baptists and the Religious Controversies of the 1920s* (Macon, Ga.: Mercer University Press, 1982) 3.

[106] George B. Tindall, *The Emergence of the New South, 1913-1945* (Baton Rouge: Louisiana State University Press, 1967) 53-54.

Americanization that sublimated sectional loyalty, at least temporarily, for the sake of unity. "Indeed," he argues, "the idea of a
peculiarly pure Americanism in the South, with overtones of Anglo-
Saxon racism and anti-radicalism, became an established article of
the regional faith."[107] Baptists and other white southerners carried this
regional faith with them as they moved into the post-World War I era.
Along with other Americans, Southern Baptists entered the "tribal
twenties" with a fearful idealism. Fearing that foreign influence
would subvert American life, they idealistically anticipated a prominent role for America in the creation of a better world. The South, of
course, would lead the way.

Such leadership, however, demanded that Southern Baptists
beware of the dangers lurking in America's vicinity. The influence of
immigrants demanded significant limitation. Beyond this, Southern
Baptists admonished themselves to propagate their regional faith for
the sake of the nation and the world. To Southern Baptist xenophobes
the new immigrants of the early twentieth-century constituted a
serious peril to the nation, threatening to subvert the minds of the
masses. They believed that these peoples had brought with them
"national strains inimical to those of America and...religious and
political ideals...inferior to the standards of America."[108] Not surprisingly, Southern Baptists solidly supported the passage of the
Johnson-Reed Act, which placed strict quotas on the new and, in the
view of these Southerners, un-American immigrants.[109]

Intense Southern Baptist opposition to the presidential candidacy
of New York's Catholic governor, Al Smith, arose naturally from such
attitudes. Arch-fundamentalist J. Frank Norris reflected the consensus, declaring that Smith's election "would be the beginning of the
end of our civilization."[110] Growing out of their solicitude concerning
foreign influence was an unambiguous call to propagate a 100-

---

[107] Ibid., 63-64.

[108] Victor I. Masters, "Who Shall Inherit the United States?" *Western Recorder*
98 (February 14, 1924): 12-13; Charles T. Alexander, "World's Call for Historic
Christianity," *Western Recorder* 98 (June 5, 1924): 4. (*Western Recorder* hereafter
cited as *WR*.)

[109] See the official statement of the Southern Baptist Social Service Commission
in support of the Johnson-Reed Act, *Annual of the Southern Baptist Convention*,
1924, 114-15.

[110] Quoted in Thompson, *Tried As by Fire*, 188.

percent American faith, which had its deepest roots in southern soil. A widely published article interpreted the region as a bastion against foreign subversion and called for southerners to help shape the destiny of the world through evangelism.[111] These southerners thus understood the South as the hope of America's complete conversion. Southern Baptists were called to convert the South, which in turn would convert America. Editor Victor I. Masters articulated this faith, suggesting that "as goes America, so goes the world. Largely as goes the South, so goes America. And in the South is the Baptist center of gravity of the world."[112]

During this era one senses an implicit and at times explicit sectionalism hiding within Southern Baptists' civil religious loyalty to America. Southerners alternated between their desire to be true blue Americans and the need to maintain the distinctiveness of their region. Thus amid the "Americanizing" process was a recurring sectionalism. Part of this sectionalism stemmed from the bad publicity bequeathed to the South by the fundamentalist crusade and the Scopes trial. In the abusive editorials of pejorative journalists like H. L. Mencken the region during the twenties discovered its image as "the benighted South."[113] The policies of Franklin D. Roosevelt also affected this sectional reawakening. Early in his first term in the White House, having noted the findings of an economic survey, Roosevelt called the South the nation's "economic problem number one." Given the South's historic sensitivity to criticism from other regions, such a comment could not but cause southerners to rally around the rebel flag. In addition, the president's wife's interest in the advancement of blacks gave rise to a growing sectional perspective.[114]

This sectionalism could be temporarily suspended, however. The threat of Nazi Germany and the trauma of Pearl Harbor gave new impetus to the national perspective, and persuaded southerners to hold

---

[111] Richard H. Edmonds, "The South a Great Mission Field," *BS* 36 (May 1, 1924): 7. During the same month, this article was reprinted in at least three other state Baptist papers: the *Alabama Baptist,* the *Religious Herald* (Virginia) and the *Christian Index* (Georgia).

[112] "Baptists and the Christianizing of America in the New Order," *Review and Expositor* 17 (July 1920): 297.

[113] Tindall, *Emergence of the New South,* 208-9.

[114] Green, "Resurgent Southern Sectionalism," 225-26; see also Roland, *Improbable Era,* 4.

their regional fealty in abeyance. As Paul M. Gaston notes, "The war thus worked to affirm the national myth of a powerful Republic devoted to preserving liberty and justice and, simultaneously, to strengthen the image of the South as a fully integrated part of the Republic and its calling."[115] Having thus reidentified with the national purpose, and again appealing to its "military-patriotic" tradition, the South threw itself into an American war once more. And it did so fervently, judging from contemporary public opinion. According to a 1941 Gallup poll, 88 percent of southerners believed the defeat of Germany to be more important than America's neutrality. That figure compared with a range of 63 to 70 percent in other regions.[116] Prominent southern historian C. Vann Woodward, noting the South's eager response to patriotic slogans, is probably accurate in interpreting this ardor as "the zeal of recent converts."[117] Recently converted or not, southerners definitely transcended their regional loyalty during the war. Indeed, as Robert Benjamin Ferguson argues, "The militant views...expressed by Southern Baptists and much of the South in the early years after 1935 were to become indistinguishable from those of the majority of Americans."[118] Hence, southern support for the war effort was solidly American and usually (civil) religious in nature.

Not surprisingly, Southern Baptists led the way in religious interpretations of the war. One writer suggests that the ease with which they participated in the war "attests to the power of civil religion in their lives." Beyond this, their call to missions blended with a sense of messianic nationalism to help them decipher the meaning of the war.[119] Southern Baptists understood the conflict not only as the struggle for the survival of democracy, but also of the belief in the

---

[115] Gaston, *New South Creed*, 233.

[116] Tindall, *Emergence of the New South*, 687-88.

[117] *The Burden of Southern History*, rev. ed. (Baton Rouge: Louisiana State University Press, 1977) 194.

[118] Ferguson, "Southern Baptist Response to International Affairs," 261.

[119] Joseph L. Price, "Attitudes of Kentucky Baptists toward World War II," *Foundations* (April-June, 1978): 135.

individual and of Christianity itself—for if democracy failed, so would Christianity.[120]

So close was the identification of Christianity with American democracy that some went beyond the usual Southern Baptist rejection of pacifism; some equated it with atheism. To at least one Southern Baptist in Kentucky these views were allies. In an unusual twist of logic, H. H. Hargrove argued that "extreme pacifism renders all to God and leaves Caesar out and is to that extent atheistic for Caesar is ordained of God."[121] This uniting of the purposes of Christian faith and American patriotism is best summed up in a paragraph from one local church's monthly servicemen's bulletin: "What does it mean to you to fight under two flags, the Christian flag and Old Glory? For as surely as you defend your country's banner and keep aggressors from maintaining strongholds on our soil, so surely do you keep the banner of Christ waving full and free."[122]

The attitudes of southern whites, particularly Baptists, revealed civil religious ambivalence. True to their historic yet often stormy relations with the rest of the nation, southerners alternated the focus of their civic piety between their nation and their region. The inherent paradox of southern whites' civil religious allegiances proved fertile ground for the South's soon-to-be-sprouting conflict of civil religions.

Ambivalence also characterized the lives and loyalties of the "other" southerners, the blacks. Despite increased migration out of the South during the 1920s, blacks remained heavily southern in orientation and affection. Their civil allegiances, however, tended to transcend the boundaries of Mason-Dixon and to focus on the nation.[123] The paradox was that they could remain loyal Americans

---

[120] Ferguson, "Southern Baptist Response to International Affairs," 106, n. 121. He also argues that they desired to protect the idea of the brotherhood of man. This is doubtful; Southern Baptists have long questioned that doctrine.

[121] "Atheism, a Cause of War," *WR 117* (February 4, 1943): 10.

[122] Marjorie Green, "Under Two Flags," *A Salute to You Who Are Serving God and Coutnry* 1 (February 1944): 2.

[123] My discussion of black perspectives is not reserved to black Baptists. Black Baptists, however, generally reflected the perspectives of the larger black community and their views can be highlighted indirectly by examining more general black sources. In addition, this approach can more readily show the context out of which black Baptists spoke.

despite their country's reluctance to come to terms with their blackness. As Gunnar Myrdal suggested, blacks knew that the nation was not living up to the American creed. Yet they remained under its spell, at least to some degree believing that the creed actually ruled America.[124]

Blacks' tenacious belief in their country was no new departure. Mid-twentieth-century manifestations simply varied a theme sounded throughout the previous century. More accurately, as Leonard I. Sweet notes, blacks had combined two important themes throughout the nineteenth century: "They asserted both their identity as blacks and their identity as Americans. At the same time that blacks were nationalistic in their pride of color, pride of black capabilities,...they were nationalistic about the superiority of American ideals, their stature as Americans, and their rights as citizens of the American nation. Blacks were bifocal in their identification and affections."[125] Thus believing in the ideals of America, blacks committed themselves to equality, a cause they expected to purge the nation and redeem its destiny as a beacon to the oppressed.[126]

Edward Wheeler agrees that blacks managed to keep their faith in America. In a study of southern black ministers at the turn of the century, he notes that even the harshest clerical critics conceded the superiority of American institutions. These ministers wanted to be considered loyal Americans. "They called for the inclusion of black people into the mainstream of American life," Wheeler writes, "and they believed it would happen."[127] Yet there was an incipient impulse toward protest among black leaders, and the twentieth century would see the gradual change toward more aggressive efforts of achieving equality.

Both their loyalty and the strengthening protest were visible in African-Americans' response to America's wars. Blacks had long believed what turned out to be an illusion—that by fighting for and thus proving their love for their country they might win their full rights.

---

[124] Myrdal, *An American Dilemma*, 4.

[125] Leonard I. Sweet, *Black Images of America, 1784-1870* (New York: W. W. Norton Co., 1976) 175.

[126] Ibid., 5.

[127] Edward Lorenzo Wheeler, "Uplifting the Race: The Black Minister in the New South, 1865-1902" (Ph.D. diss. Emory University, 1982) 73-74.

Thus, during World War I, leaders such as W. E. B. Du Bois called for black support: "Let us not hesitate. Let us, while this war lasts, forget our special grievances and close our ranks shoulder to shoulder with our white citizens and the allied nations that are fighting for democracy."[128] Others spoke in more pointed terms. The Reverend C. W. Walker of Aiken, South Carolina, argued that "no man has the right to claim the protection of the American flag who is not willing to fight for it."[129]

As a result blacks strongly supported the war. At the beginning of America's participation, black soldiers composed only 20,000 of 750,000 American troops. On the first registration day after the passage of the Selective Service Act of 1917, over 700,000 blacks enlisted. Moreover, blacks sought few exemptions from service and gave generous financial support. In South Carolina, counties with high black populations had the highest per capita contributions in the Liberty Loan and war saving stamp drives.[130] Like other Americans blacks imbibed Wilsonian rhetoric about the meaning of war. They interpreted it as a contest between good and evil, between freedom and oppression.[131] This struggle for democracy in Europe, however, was not matched by a similar concern at home. During the war era the frequency of lynchings rose, precipitating a number of race riots. Forty blacks were killed in a riot in East St. Louis, Illinois, in 1917. Some months later, responding to the brutality of the riot, blacks staged a major march in New York. Protesting the plight of blacks in America, one of the banners offered this challenge: "Mr. President, why not make *America* safe for democracy."[132] The "Red Summer" of 1919 preceded the "Red Scare," as numerous race riots sprung up across the nation when black veterans sought to compete with whites for available employment.

---

[128] From Du Bois's editorial "Close Ranks" in the black journal *Crisis*, July 1918. Quoted in John Hope Franklin, *From Slavery to Freedom: A History of Negro Americans*, 3d ed. (New York: Alfred A. Knopf, 1967) 476.

[129] Theodore Hemmingway, "Prelude to Change: Black Carolinians in the War Years, 1914-1920," *Journal of Negro History* 65 (Summer 1980): 214-15.

[130] Black participation in the war effort is discussed in Franklin, *From Slavery to Freedom*, 455-56, and Hemmingway, "Prelude to Change," 216-18.

[131] Franklin, *From Slavery to Freedom*, 484-85; Hemmingway, "Prelude to Change," 214.

[132] Franklin, *From Slavery to Freedom*, 474-75.

After the war blacks discovered that their situation had not improved despite their contributions to America's victory. As a contemporary interpreter suggested, "It would be difficult to prove, despite the fluent words about democracy which emanated from the public press and from the propaganda platform, that the Negro received a single additional right of citizenship above that which he enjoyed prior to 1917."[133] In his autobiography, prominent black educator Benjamin Mays noted the nation's recrudescent racial tension in the immediate postwar years. Black servicemen, he recalled, were often told, "Take off those uniforms and act like a nigger should."[134]

Thus a poignant sense of disillusionment settled over black Americans. Returning soldiers, experiencing economic discrimination in the North, learned that American racism was not limited to the South. The black vision of America's pristine ideas that had been so much a part of black rhetoric in the previous century was lost. The hope of America living up to its principles flickered. Suspicions were growing "that Americans were in fact living up to their principles, for their principles were racist."[135] Yet the disappointment stimulated a rapid development of blacks' incipient protest impulses. Martin Luther King Sr. captured black sentiment: "The terms of the struggle during that period were harsh and coldly efficient. To change what needed to be changed required a solid effort across the country, not just in the South."[136] Blacks increasingly called for improvement of their lot. Organizations like the National Equal Rights League and the National Race Congress, as well as the NAACP, redoubled their efforts toward first-class citizenship.[137] Also, in October 1919, the National Baptist Convention publicly called for more complete integration of blacks into American life. Local activities by Baptists became more bold, if not more widespread. Led by two Baptist clergymen and the local president of the NAACP, blacks in Richland County, South

---

[133]Guion Griffis Johnson, "The Impact of the War upon the Negro," *Journal of Negro Education* 10 (July 1941): 607.

[134] Benjamin E. Mays, *Born to Rebel* (New York: Charles Scribner's Sons, 1971) 68.

[135] Sweet, *Black Images of America*, 178-79.

[136] Martin Luther King, Sr., *Daddy King: An Autobiography* (New York: Harper and Row, 1980) 104.

[137] Franklin, *From Slavery to Freedom*, 486-92.

Carolina, protested the 1915 showing of *The Birth of a Nation*, a popular film expressing the views of the Ku Klux Klan.[138]

Perhaps surprisingly, the postwar disillusionment did not create a widespread attraction to any "Back to Africa" movement, at least not among religiously oriented blacks in the South. While the black nationalist efforts of Marcus Garvey became what was then the largest mass movement of blacks in American history, its appeal was predominantly Northern and urban.[139] Black Baptists in the South were never so fully disillusioned with America as to be enamored of a Garveyite sentiment. William Washington, a longtime observer of black Baptists has suggested that black ministers never "felt that [in] America with all its imperfection, that a 'Back to Africa' movement... would have solved the problem. They have always felt that the problems could be worked out."[140]

Civil rights activist Ralph David Abernathy agreed, noting the attachments that southern blacks maintained for their country: "They loved America and [felt] that this was our home. And that we were not going to give up on our country,...not going back to Africa. Nobody in my family accepted the teachings of Marcus Garvey....We have made too great an investment in this country to forsake [it]. But they just believed that one day a better day would come."[141] As most southern blacks viewed America, apparently, be it ever so racist, there was "no place like home."

This sense of being at home in America expressed one side of black Americans' dilemma of double-consciousness, as described by W. E. B. Du Bois in *The Souls of Black Folk*: "One ever feels his two-ness—an America, a Negro; two souls, two thoughts, two unreconciled strivings; two warring ideals in one dark body....The history of the

---

[138] Franklin, *From Slavery to Freedom*, 486-92; Hemmingway, "Prelude to Change," 219-20.

[139] See Ahlstrom, *A Religious History of the American People*, 1066-67, and Wilmore, *Black Religion and Black Radicalism*, 145-52.

[140] Washington, interview with author, March 14-15, 1984.

[141] Ralph David Abernathy, interview with author, Atlanta, Ga., March 21, 1984. Abernathy probably underappraises the extent of black response to Garveyism in America, though he is probably more accurate in assessing the response of Southern blacks. The best treatment of the appeal of Garveyism is Randall K. Burkett, *Garveyism as a Religious Movement: The Institutionalization of a Black Civil Religion* (Metuchen, N. J.: Scarecrow Press, 1978).

American Negro is the history of this strife."[142] This American part of their souls once again led blacks to defend their country in another world war. Yet the other horn of their classic dilemma was never far away, as American propaganda described the Nazi doctrine of Aryan superiority that sounded uncomfortably like the doctrines of American white supremacy.

In response blacks expressed a wide range of emotions. At the beginning of the war some blacks evidenced a sense of alienation from America's fight. Quipped one black youth to a white acquaintance, "By the way, Captain, I hear the Japs done declared war on you white folks." Others vented their feelings with irony, as did a black service- man who, offended by segregated blood banks, suggested, "Just carve on my tombstone, 'Here lies a black man killed fighting a yellow man for the protection of a white man.'"[143] Of course, there was also the unmitigated anger of the soldier who felt the sting of discrimination in the army: "Every day since I've been in the Army some white person has reminded me through some word or act that, although I wear the uniform of an officer of the United States Army, I'm still nothing but a 'nigger....'" What the hell do we want to fight the Japs for anyhow? They couldn't possibly treat us any worse than these 'crackers' right here at home."[144] The paradox was that southern blacks did maintain their civil religious loyalties in the face of such pain. They kept their faith in the ideals of America. Admittedly, they knew that they might have to push harder and dig deeper into the soul of America to get the nation to actualize those ideals. But ideals— viable ideals—they remained.

Thus southern blacks entered the post-World War II era ready to appeal for their civil rights based on the civil religious values of the nation. Justifiably tempted to repudiate that nation and its racism,

---

[142] On the double-consciousness of American blacks, see W. E. B. Du Bois, *The Souls of Black Folk,* in *Three Negro Classics* (New York: Avon Books, 1965) 214-15; William B. Gravely, "The Dialectic of Double-Consciousness in Black American Free- dom Celebrations, 1808-1863," *Journal of Negro History* 67 (1982): 302-17; Peter J. Paris, *The Social Teaching of the Black Churches* (Philadelphia: Fortress Press, 1985) 27-56.

[143] Horace R. Cayton, "Fighting for White Folks?" *Nation,* September 26, 1942, 267-69.

[144] Earl Brown, "American Negroes and the War," *Harper's Magazine,* April 1942, 547.

southern blacks yet clung to its deepest values. Benjamin Mays, mentor of young Martin Luther King Jr. explained why blacks might still pledge their civil religious allegiance:

> I know that the Declaration of Independence was not meant for me; that its chief architect, Thomas Jefferson, was a slave owner; that the Thirteenth, Fourteenth, and Fifteenth Amendments have not been fully implemented; and that the "land of the free" and "sweet land of liberty" are not equally applicable to black and white. But these are ideals to which the nation clings and the goals toward which it strives when it is at its best and thinks nobly. It is not always easy for a black man to swear allegiance to the flag, but the American dream is embodied in that allegiance, and until it is repudiated one can still hope for and work toward the day when it becomes a reality.[145]

As they greeted the postwar era, armed with the values of the American civil religion and led by Mays's protege, southern blacks stood at the beginning of the beginning.

---

[145] Mays, *Born to Rebel*, 275.

2

IMAGES OF AMERICA BEFORE THE STORM

Most historians and sociologists acknowledge that the South's regional distinctiveness has diminished to some degree through the course of the twentieth century and particularly since World War II. The South, however, has refused to be completely assimilated by the nation. In its relations to the nation as a whole, southern culture has always been marked by ambiguity and ambivalence. As such the region maintains features that relate it to the nation while keeping its distinctive identity.[1] By the mid-twentieth century, however, the ambiguity and ambivalence had become more prominent and profound.

Particularly is this true regarding southerners' civic piety during the 1950s. That decade set this ambivalence in bold relief because its important events helped stimulate loyalties both to America and to the South. At least among most southern whites, the significant events after 1954 gave impetus to the southern civil religion. On the other hand, events in the years before the Supreme Court's desegregation ruling stimulated civil religious impulses more focused on the nation as a whole.

Reacting to these events, southern and National Baptists in the early postwar period reflected the patriotic spirit of the era, and that ardor created a revitalization of the American civil religion. Out of this revitalization, Southern and National Baptists used religio-patriotic images in referring to their nation, though they developed these images in different directions. Whites, as represented by Southern Baptists, held a version of the civil religion that matched the ambiguity of the South's relationship to the nation during those years.

---

[1]William C. Harvard, "The South: A Shifting Perspective," in *The Changing Politics of the South* (Baton Rouge: Louisiana State University Press, 1972) 36.

It was a simultaneously "Americanized," yet distinctively southern, civil religion. During the same period, black Baptists strengthened their appeal to the values and images of the American public faith. The differences between these southerners' images of America would prove significant enough to provide the basis for civil religious conflict later in the decade.

The Patriotic Context, 1947-1954

American religion in the postwar era developed a widespread tendency to associate religiosity with patriotic commitment. This form of "patriotic piety," suggests Sydney E. Ahlstrom, saw religion as an indispensable component of patriotism and united religion and Ameri-canism to perhaps an unprecedented degree.[2] The postwar years stimulated the euphoria of a holy cause vindicated and thankfulness for an enemy vanquished. In such an atmosphere a surge in piety might naturally accompany a rise in patriotic fervor. The result was what historians of American religion have called "the postwar revival."

Interest in religion during the 1950s soared to unprecedented levels. No doubt the war effort itself contributed to this resurgence, as did the postwar situation in the nation and world. Amid the multiplying international crises of the era, religion provided Americans with much-needed reassurance. The need for peace, whether personal or political, deepened as the tensions of the Cold War surfaced. Commentators, particularly clerical ones, often interpreted the ideological combat between the United States and the Soviet Union in dualistic, apocalyptic terms. The uncertainty of this ideological struggle, coupled with the growing fear of annihilation in the nuclear age, created a desire for the unearthly comforts that, according to many, only religious faith could provide.

These conditions made possible the religious boom of the period. Consequently, church membership and attendance rose sharply, with edifice construction following suit.[3] The boom affected American

---

[2] Ahlstrom, *A Religious History of the American People*, 954.

[3] Ibid., 952-53. Ahlstrom notes that church membership rose to a century-high level of 69 percent by 1960, an increase of one point per year throughout the previous

culture as well as church life. Led by presidential high priest Dwight D. Eisenhower, "piety on the Potomac" came into vogue. Before the end of the decade this civic religiosity would insert the phrase "under God" into the Pledge of Allegiance and emblazon the inscription "In God We Trust" on the nation's coins.

The revival was not without its critics, however. Martin E. Marty notes that a number of Protestant social activists, such as Reinhold Niebuhr and the editors of *Christianity and Crisis,* viewed the upsurge as superficial.[4] Such detractors found few, if any, counterparts in the South. While Southern Baptist commentators admitted that spiritually America was far from the ideal, they generally delighted in the booming interest in religion, both in the churches and in the culture. Rather than finding fault with the revival, they were much more inclined to criticize the critics.

Baptists applauded almost every official effort to advance the cause of religion in American life. Leon Macon, editor of the *Alabama Baptist,* for example, commended the Pentagon's efforts to meet the spiritual needs of American servicemen. Later in the decade, Southern Baptists strongly supported the American Legion's "Back to God" movement.[5] Southern Baptists avidly commended President Eisenhower for his leadership in bringing the nation back to God. The Baptist papers frequently printed articles highlighting religious sentiments in his speeches. Georgia's *Christian Index* carried, for example, excerpts from the president's 1954 State of the Union Address and a speech to the national conference of the Methodist Student Movement.[6] The President's practice of beginning all cabinet meetings with

---

twenty years. Money spent annually on church construction rose $990 million from 1945 to 1960.

[4]Cited in *Righteous Empire,* 257. Others criticized the revival in a similar vein, as a vacuous, watered down religion-in-general. See Marty, *New Shape of American Religion,* 67-89; A. Roy Eckardt, *The Surge in Piety in America: An Appraisal* (New York: Association Press, 1958) 42-67; and Winthrop S. Hudson, "Are the Churches Really Booming?" *Christian Century 72* (December 21, 1955): 1494-96.

[5]Macon, "Religion in the Armed Forces," *AB 116* (February 14, 1952): 3. A great deal of publicity was given to the "Back to God" movement in the Baptist papers. See for example "President Opens Legion's Back to God Movement," *Baptist Message 72* (March 3, 1955): 1 and 4. (*Baptist Message,* published in Louisiana, hereafter cited as *BM.*)

[6]See "President Sounds Religious Theme," *CI 133* (January 28, 1955): 4.

silent prayer, received high praise from an editor who advised that "every Christian in the land should thank God every day that the man in the White House is devotedly dedicated to leading his nation in public and private paths of peace and righteousness."[7]

Such wholehearted support for the religious reawakening reflected a cultural milieu that effortlessly idealized the nation in religio-patriotic images. Given their conservative political and religious traditions, Southern Baptists, and probably white southerners in general, felt little hesitation about articulating their understandings of America's meaning in religious language. An investigation of the images by which they communicated those meanings, however, requires an appraisal of the social conditions in the postwar South.

The South's traditionally ambivalent relationship with the rest of the nation persisted throughout the 1950s. On the one hand, postwar social change made the South more like the nation than ever before. On the other hand, by the mid-1950s the South began to retreat to traditional southern patterns. George B. Tindall notes, for example, the Americanness of the South regarding international issues. Domestic affairs, however, led southerners to "retreat back within the parapets of the embattled South" in their efforts to withstand the massive social change of the era. The critical issue for the postwar South, Tindall maintains, was whether the broader vision or the defensiveness would prevail.[8]

Perhaps the greatest result of this social change was the beginning of the end of southern homogeneity. Though a constant in American history, pluralism was slow in coming to the South. Samuel S. Hill has pointed to World War II as a watershed whose cultural impact disturbed the homogeneity of the South.[9] In effect, however, the social changes began even before the war.

If the wars of the late nineteenth and twentieth centuries served to Americanize the South, the same might be said of the economic equivalent of America's wars, the Great Depression. That experience

---

[7]E. S. James, "Christianity at the White House," *BS 67* (January 28, 1955): 4. This editorial was also printed in *AB 120* (February 10, 1955): 4.

[8]Tindall, *Emergence of the New South*, 731.

[9]Samuel S. Hill, "The Strange Career of Religious Pluralism in the South," *Bulletin of the Center for the Study of Southern Culture and Religion* 4 (July 1980): 22.

had a significant unifying effect on the nation as Americans of all regions suffered from the same poverty stricken conditions. Beyond this, as historian Dewey W. Grantham Jr., suggests, the encouragement of the New Deal sparked a real stirring of the South's "proletariat"—the sharecropper, textile worker, and the black domestic worker. The New Deal accomplished this by popularizing standards that increasingly undermined the doctrine of states' rights.[10]

After the war economic changes increasingly brought the South more closely into line with the rest of the country. The region experienced higher levels of prosperity than at any other time in its history. Northern industry moved South and brought significant changes in southern society through increased immigration. While comparatively still a "poorer cousin" to other regions, Dixie was catching up rapidly. This industrialization, with its concomitant urbanization, tended to subvert older sectional attitudes.[11]

The South moved back into the American mainstream politically as well as economically. As a result of the nationally solidifying events during and after the war, the South was as American as it had ever been. Charles P. Roland points to southern strength in Congress at this time. By 1960 southerners headed 60 percent of the committees in both houses. Never to be outdone in military-patriotic issues, southern legislators also led Congress in supporting the Cold War and American participation in the Korean War.[12]

Potent as it was, the Americanizing process could not shield the South from the assault of social and cultural change or abort a renascent sectional spirit. Not surprisingly, the attitudes slowest to change were those related to race. As Numan Bartley writes, "Most white southerners... continued to approve of segregation even though the region was undergoing economic and demographic changes that demanded social adjustments. The North, moreover, had resumed its role as protector of the nation's black minority. Outside intervention

---

[10]Dewey W. Grantham Jr. *The Democratic South* (Athens: University of Georgia Press, 1963) 70.

[11]See Roland, *Improbable Era*, 11-29; Dewey W. Grantham Jr., "An American Politics for the South," in *The Southerner as American*, ed. Charles Grier Sellers Jr. (Chapel Hill: University of North Carolina Press, 1960) 176-77.

[12]Roland, *Improbable Era*, 71.

and environmental transition too swift for the southern social system to assimilate set the stage for political reaction."[13]

The outside intervention came quickly on the heels of the war; the reaction, at least among religionists took somewhat longer. Harry S. Truman's civil rights policies marked the beginning. The president appointed a Committee on Civil Rights to study the problem in 1946. A year later the committee's report was published and became one of the most important statements on civil rights in American history. The recommendations of the committee included the establishment of a permanent commission and joint congressional committee as well as the creation of the Civil Rights Division of the Department of Justice. It strengthened existing civil rights laws and established the Fair Employment Practices Committee.[14]

Truman's civil rights efforts raised the ire of many southern politicians. A number of southern governors warned against any national legislation to abolish segregation or the poll tax. The reaction became particularly acute when Truman announced his intention to campaign openly on the civil rights issue in the 1948 election. As a well-known result, southern Democrats bolted their party to form the Dixiecrat ticket headed by Governor Strom Thurmond of South Carolina.

For southern whites, therefore, this ambivalent milieu created images that celebrated the civil religious meaning of the nation without extensively commenting on the issue of race. That their federal government was beginning to call the southern way of life into question did not lead them immediately to adjust or repudiate their images of America. Such would come later. Among black southerners, increasing efforts by the federal government in behalf of their civil rights precipitated a heightened appeal to *their* images of America. As one might expect, given the relative degree to which the federal government had aided the struggle for black equality, African Americans' images were more national and less regional than those of their white counterparts.

[13]Bartley, *Rise of Massive Resistance*, 17.

[14]United States President's Commitee on Civil Rights, *To Secure These Rights* (New York: Simon and Schuster, 1947) 151-73.

Southern Versions of the American Civil Religion

The differences between these sets of images would not break into a full-scale conflict of civil religions until after 1954. While both versions of the civil religion were in a sense Americanized, they included obvious differences of focus. They also differed in terms of their hopes for America. Such differences were largely shaped by these southern groups' traditional sentiments toward non-southern America.

As southern culture by midcentury had become increasingly Americanized, so had its version of the American civil religion. Its themes, images, and values mirrored those of the larger American culture. Yet it also included important undercurrents of distinctiveness. Like almost all of the country, the South perceived an imminent danger during the Cold War era. Amid apocalyptic rhetorical strains, American culture in general divided the world between the virtuous "us" and the evil "them."

Certain southerners, however, did not view the world precisely in such terms. For them the world was not a vast dualistic struggle, but a perilous "triangle of threat."[15] Three great powers, rather than two, grappled for supremacy in the world. America faced *two* mortal enemies and sensed a double paranoia. The righteous nation struggled to withstand the onslaughts of Roman Catholicism as well as "international Communism." This triangular socioreligious world view constituted the distinguishing mark of the Southern Baptist version of the American civil religion. Conforming to the South's historically ambiguous relationship with the nation, this version of the American civil religion bore both American and distinctively southern characteristics.

The ambiguity of this version of the American civil religion raises the general question of southern distinctiveness. What is uniquely southern about this phenomenon? In this regard, of first importance is the matter of uniqueness itself. Scholars of southern history and culture have often desired to note the *unique* distinctiveness in southern ways of being. Particularly in the area of

---

[15.]This term is borrowed from Professor W. O. Carver of the Southern Baptist Theological Seminary, who articulated the implicit world view of his fellow Baptists in his article "America in a Triangle of Threat to the World," *WR 121* (July 31, 1947): 8.

southern religion, this has been a laudable and often fruitful effort. Occasionally, however, this quest has mistaken distinctiveness for what might redundantly be called "absolute uniqueness." The ambiguity of regional expressions of national traits rarely if ever allows one to find in the South traits that exist *nowhere else* in the nation. One is much more likely to discover within regional culture distinctive arrangements of these national qualities. The civil religion of white southerners was thus distinctive without being "absolutely unique." The images themselves were found in other regions of the country, but the *configuration* of these images suggests a significant level of distinctiveness. One can highlight this distinctiveness by focusing on the different configuration of images of America held by Southern Baptists.

Southern Baptists' civil religion highlights both this distinctive configuration of images of America and the ambiguity of the South's relation to the nation. Such is possible because this public faith combined both national and regional images. Their more "American" images are most clearly projected in these southerners' reactions to the Communist threat.

The dualistic world view of American culture during the Cold War came clearly into focus on March 12, 1947. Concerned with Russian "meddling" in nationalist uprisings in Greece and Turkey, Truman feared that these two countries might go into the Soviet sphere. In a historic address to a joint session of Congress, the president enunciated what became known as the Truman Doctrine. America's security was involved wherever aggression imperiled freedom, and he called for quick action. "The earth," he warned, "is deeply divided between free and captive peoples.... And as much as we trust in God, while He is rejected by so many in the world, we must trust in ourselves."[16] Truman further described a fateful choice between two ways of life: "One way of life is based upon the will of the majority, and is distinguished by free institutions, representative government, free elections, guarantees of individual liberty....The second way of life is based upon the will of a minority forcible imposed upon the majority. It relies upon terror and oppression...and

---

[16.]Quoted in David Caute, *The Great Fear: The Anti-Communist Purge Under Truman and Eisenhower* (New York: Simon and Schuster, 1978) 30.

the suppression of personal freedoms."[17] A starkly dualistic picture of
the world was thus explicitly and officially drawn.

Response to Truman's speech was generally favorable, particularly in the South and Midwest. The *New York Times* celebrated "a
new and positive foreign policy of worldwide responsibility for the
maintenance of peace and order." Beyond the press response, Americans generally agreed with their president. Gallup polls showed that 75
percent of Americans knew of Truman's proposal and most of them
favored aid to Greece, while 47 percent supported a general policy of
helping governments put down such revolts.[18]

Neither the passage of time nor the change of presidential administrations changed these themes. Dwight D. Eisenhower painted a
picture of the world in hues more self-consciously religious than even
Truman had. In 1952 like uttered what has become the quintessential
expression of the American civil religion: "Our form of government
makes no sense unless it is founded in a deeply felt religious
faith—and I don't care what it is." As one scholar has noted, however,
this statement was part of a speech interpreting religious faith as the
key to the ideological war against Communism.[19] For Eisenhower as
for millions of Americans, anti-Communism essentially a religious
struggle: "What is our battle against Communism if it is not a fight
between anti-God and a belief in the Almighty? Communists... have
to eliminate God from their system. When God comes, Communism
has to go."[20]

Throughout these years political and religious leaders alike
described world events as a titanic rivalry between America and the
Soviet Union. In typically revivalistic and apocalyptic tones, evan-
gelist Billy Graham warned that "the day of opportunity is brief

[17]Quoted in Michael Parenti, *The Anti-Communist Impulse* (New York:
Random House, 1969) 146-47.

[18]The response to the Truman Doctrine is described in Richard J. Barnet,
*Intervention and Revolution: America's Confrontation with Insurgent Movements
around the World* (New York: Meridian Books, 1968).

[19]Patrick Henry, "'And I Don't Care What It Is': The Tradition-History of a
Civil Religion Proof-Text," *Journal of the American Academy of Religion 49* (March
1981): 35-45; see also "Eisenhower Calls for Strong Religious Faith," *AB 118* (January
8, 1953): 5. This article was a press release by the Religious New Service (RNS).

[20]"Presidential Candidates Stress Role of Religion," *Religious Herald 125*
(January 25, 1952): 3. (*Religious Herald,* published in Virginia, hereafter cited as *RH.*)

because the world is engaged in a struggle that will end in the death of Christianity or the death of Communism."[21] Thus American culture at large interpreted the world situation of the Cold War period as an apocalyptic dualism moving toward an Armageddon between the forces of evil and good.

Responding to the threat of Communism, southerners generally sounded the same notes as their Northern counterparts. In fact, they often opposed Communism more radically than did their compatriots. Regarding southerners' views on foreign affairs, Alfred O. Hero notes that at the beginning of the Korean War the South was the region most supportive of a "preventive war" against the Soviet Union.[22] The power of nationalistic and militaristic impulses over southern culture has had a long history and such responses came as little surprise.[23] This backdrop helps illuminate anti-Communist impulses among Southern Baptists. The essential dualism of non-southern response was likewise present among these southerners. This dualism, however, was founded on a mixture of the themes of America as a Christian democracy and as the defender of freedom. An analysis of these themes indicates the degree to which Southern Baptists' civil religious images of America mirrored those of the larger American culture.

Ideas of America's messianic chosenness permeated the comments of Southern Baptist leaders. In 1944, even before the Cold War era, the president of the Southern Baptist Convention asserted that in America's settlement and growth, "the divine purpose of the ages becomes clear. We are the acme of Christian civilization."[24] L. L. Gwaltney, who preceded Leon Macon as editor of the *Alabama Baptist*, attributed the whole of American history to the workings of Providence, which he believed had set America apart as the world's guardian of liberty. Anyone, he contended, who did not view

---

[21]Quoted in Reuben E. Alley, "I Will Build My Church," *RH 127* (January 28, 1954): 10.

[22]Alfred O. Hero, Jr., *The Southerner and World Affairs* (Baton Rouge: Louisiana State University Press, 1965) 108-10.

[23]The best discussion of this militaristic impulse in the South is John Hope Franklin, *The Militant South* (Boston: Beacon Press, 1956).

[24]Quoted in Harold E. Fey, "Decry Favoritism Toward Catholics," *Christian Century 61* (May 31, 1944): 672 and 678.

Providence at the center of his understanding of America would "prove himself to be a sorry historian."[25]

God's special choice laid on the nation a grave responsibility. America was to be the world's primary example and missionary for democracy. W. O. Carver, Professor of Missions at the Southern Baptist Theological Seminary, sounded this theme. He depicted America as history's highest representative of the democratic ideal. This was in part the consequence of the nation's status as a "world power." Beyond military matters, however, America was to be "the spokesman and protagonist of the democratic ideal for world order." Carver understood America not only as the embodiment of democracy, but also as "the prophet and missionary of democracy to mankind."[26]

Democracy as usually practiced in contemporary America would not suffice, however. The ideal for many Southern Baptists was "Christian democracy." Herbert Gabhart, then a pastor in Memphis, Tennessee, and later president of Nashville's Belmont College, understood Christian democracy to include certain important hallmarks: acceptance of God's sovereignty, belief in the sanctity of the human soul, individual freedom to choose, separation of church and state, and the belief that "righteousness exalteth a nation." He asserted that "Christianity gave birth to democracy....The greatest asset to the ideal democracy is a Christian citizen."[27]

Other Southern Baptists acknowledged that the United States and the Soviet Union constituted two "armed camps" in the world. They saw the American form of government as sanctioned by the Bible. From this assumption, W. I. Pittman, a layperson from Alabama, discussed the ideological foundation of the American political system. Our government, he believed, "was founded on a recognition of the dignity and rights of the individual. The recognition of the individuals' right to 'life, liberty, and the pursuit of happiness' stems from the teachings of Christ. Dictators know that, hence the diabolical efforts of Hitler, Stalin, Tojo and others to suppress Christianity."[28]

---

[25]"The First Year of the Last Half of the Twentieth Century," *AB 116* (January 4, 1951): 5.

[26]Carver, "America in a Triangle of Threat," 8.

[27]Herbert C. Gabhart, "Catholicism, Communism, and Christian Democracy," *WR 125* (December 20, 1951): 10.

[28]W. I. Pittman, "Brother Baraca," *AB 117* (July 4, 1952): 4-5.

Thus Southern Baptists' image of America as a Christian democracy laid great stress on America's role as the guardian of freedom and individual rights. For them this constituted the ultimate meaning of their nation. In 1952 the president of the Alabama Baptist Convention, John H. Buchanan, returning from a trip abroad, expressed his pride in America. "I have thanked God," he exulted, "for the heritage that has been mine—A land where the fullest measure of freedom enjoyed on this earth is a heritage of every citizen."[29] Whether or not *every* citizen experienced such freedom is questionable, but there was no doubt that Southern Baptists viewed individual rights as central to the meaning of America. Out of that image they warned of the Communist danger.

Over against godly America stood the Communist demon poised for attack. The Soviet Union was depicted by the State Department as an imperialistic power destined to swallow every nation in its way. The Soviet master plan was international domination, with an effort to line up Asia and Europe against the United States. Almost all Baptists agreed and called for the nation to be prepared. Gwaltney warned, "Let no one believe that if America assumes the qualities of a lamb and lies down before 'the bear that walks like a man' the bear will not eat the lamb."[30] Responding to the Korean conflict, Gwaltney's editorial successor, Leon Macon, viewed the Balkans, Iran, and Indochina as possible trouble spots unless some action were taken.[31]

Of course, overt acts of conquest were not the only cause for alarm. Internal subversion was another part of the diabolical Soviet strategy. Baptist leaders in the McCarthy period left virtually unchallenged the idea that Russian spies plied their trade within American borders. Reuel T. Skinner, editor of Kentucky's *Western Recorder*, was convinced that "fifth columns are now at work in this country" and warned that "America had better go on twenty-four-hour watch against the enemies within her gates—not just the FBI, but all loyal American citizens."[32]

Baptists perceived the Russian leaders, and to only a somewhat lesser degree the entire Russian people, as essentially evil by nature.

---

[29]"America At The Crossroads," *AB 117* (June 5, 1952): 4-5.

[30]"Focal Points," *AB 115* (January 26, 1950): 3.

[31]Leon Macon, "New Developments," *AB 115* (July 13, 1950): 3.

[32]"Russia Will Be Stopped Only by Christianity," *WR 124* (July 27, 1950): 8.

Their plans of conquest and subversion were but the outward expressions of their sinfulness. This understanding would by the 1980s help move most Southern Baptist conservatives into the political camp of President Ronald Reagan, who famously referred to the Soviet Union as an "evil empire." Georgia's Louie D. Newton, a former president of the Southern Baptist Convention, commented on the Russian proclivity toward violence, acknowledging that "the trigger puller, we will all agree, in matters of war, world economic stability, etc., is Russia."[33] Noting little difference between the Russian and other versions of Communist ideology, Skinner charged that Communism was always synonymous with "utter and complete cruelty."[34]

Because of such moral flaws, trusting such demonic enemies was a complete impossibility. To "the barbarians in the Kremlin" any talk of religion or ethics, or even coexistence, was useless.[35] For Southern Baptists this devilish ideology embodied the absolute antithesis of Christianity. This was the crux of its threat to America. Christianity stood for love, truth, and righteousness, while Communism was founded on hate, lies, and lawlessness. Another writer interpreted the atheistic foundation of Communism: "Communism is anti-God, anti-Christ, and anti-everything that tends toward progress and the upbuilding of a people's government."[36] More strident than any other Baptist paper, the [Texas] Baptist Standard rejected out of hand the possibility of cooperating with Communists. Communism and Christianity were utterly contradictory. No one with even a modicum of Christian maturity could think otherwise. The paper's editor, David Gardner, pronounced that "Communism was spawned in the pit of perdition. There is nothing about it that is compatible with the Christian religion."[37]

In essence these southern images of America accorded quite well with the images being drawn by the official shapers of American culture at large. Mark G. Toulouse suggests Secretary of State John

---

[33]"This Changing World," *CI 131* (April 12, 1951): 9.

[34]"Peace," *WR 217* (September 17, 1953): 4.

[35]"Focal Points," *AB 115* (May 11, 1950): 3-4; "Focal Points," *AB, 115* (March 23, 1950): 3.

[36]M. W. Rankin, "The Present and the Former Regime in China," *WR 124* (April 13, 1950): 3 and 27.

[37]"Christianity vs. Communism," *BS 65* (December 3, 1953): 2.

Foster Dulles as a significant influence on the American civil religion of this decade.[38] A Presbyterian with little southern exposure, Dulles described a dualistic world in largely civil religious terms. Nevertheless, his description found similar expression among Southern Baptists. At the very least, this points to a basic Americanness of these southern images. From a force so diametrically opposed to all that was right and good and Christian (not to mention American), the threat was obvious. Christian values and the American way of life hung in the balance. Before it was too late, therefore, America needed to act to counter the Communist threat. Another peril, however, lurked nearby.

Most historians' descriptions have accustomed us to interpreting the 1950s primarily in terms of the American-Soviet confrontation. For Southern Baptists, however, fear of the Communists was but half the story. Their worldview was triangular rather than exclusively dualistic, and they understood America as locked in mortal combat with the Vatican as well as with the Kremlin.

With his dualistic perceptions of America's Cold War struggle, Truman illustrated the difference between the views of general American culture and that of Southern Baptists. The president sought to persuade all American church groups to forswear petty disagreements and to unite in a "common affirmation of faith against Communism."[39] Truman particularly sought the aid of the Catholic Church because of its strong enmity toward Communism. Southern Baptists, however, would have none of it. An alliance with Catholicism was unthinkable, even in the face of the "Red Menace." Southern Baptists thus disdained Catholicism quite as strongly as Communism and described the two enemies as having similar agendas and methods.

Catholic assertiveness around midcentury significantly stimulated criticism from a large segment of American Protestantism. Rapid numerical growth and the increasing political power of the Catholic Church, asserts historian Roland Bainton, created a good deal

---

[38]See Mark G. Toulouse, *The Transformation of John Foster Dulles: From Prophet of Realism to Priest of Nationalism* (Macon, Ga.: Mercer University Press, 1985).

[39]Quoted by John J. Hurt, editor of Georgia's *Christian Index*, in "Without Hope," *CI 131* (November 11, 1951): 6.

of uneasiness even among liberal Protestants.[40] When the government began to make what seemed like concessions to the Catholics, Protestants grew even more restive. In 1947 the Supreme Court awarded a New Jersey board of education the right to reimburse parents for bus fare paid to transport their children to Catholic schools. Advocates of church-state separation were scandalized. Southern Baptists were particularly livid when Truman appointed an official ambassador to the Vatican in 1951.[41]

The perceived Catholic threat to separation of church and state was occasion enough for concern. But when the Catholic population in the postwar South began to increase dramatically, Southern Baptist concern almost turned to hysteria. The industrialization of the South brought significant numbers of Catholics into Dixie, raising their population to 1.5 million.[42] A wistful editor thus reminisced of a time when the South was composed of "good old Anglo-Saxon stock." The state of affairs had unfortunately "changed drastically *and* radically....The South will never be the same as we knew it a few years ago, either politically or socially."[43]

Baptists were even more distressed by the new Catholic aggressiveness in the South. In 1950 Catholics distributed a study, "A Survey of Catholic Weakness," which formulated a plan to strengthen Catholicism in rural areas of the country. Alarmed by such a possibility, one writer challenged his fellow Baptists to respond in kind: "Are we going to stand idly by while they build churches and schools in rural areas...? Is it not high time for us as Baptists to turn to our great stronghold, the rural areas of the southland [and]...win

---

[40]"Catholic-Protestant Relations in the United States," *Watchman-Examiner* 42 (October 14, 1954): 932-33.

[41]The Supreme Court decision was criticized by a resolution of the Richmond Dover (Virginia) Baptist Association. The Southern Baptist Convention later adopted this resolution. See Reuben E. Alley, "Concerning Decision of the Supreme Court," *RH 120* (April 24, 1947): 13. Editorials critical of the ambassadorial appointment were quite numerous. A good example of their argument is Reuel T. Skinner's "Things Are Reversed—Keep It Up," *WR 124* (May 18, 1950): 10. See also *Annual of the Southern Baptist Convention*, 1950, 37.

[42]Reuben E. Alley, "Look to the Homeland," *RH 126* (April 30, 1953): 10.

[43]David Gardner, "Election Reflections," *BS 64* (March 20, 1952): 2.

the country side to Christ? The time is now—it's later than you think!"[44]

Southern Baptists thus spoke of Communism and Catholicism in almost identical terms. Both posed grave danger to freedom and the American way of life. Some Baptists warned against allowing the fear of Communism to blind them to the threat that Catholicism posed to the American way.[45] Baptists warned of the Catholic peril in language quite surprising given the deep anti-Communist paranoia of American culture at large. Herbert Gabhart made a telling comparison: "*No power* is harder at work bidding for the supremacy of our free country than the Vatican-controlled Catholicism here in America.... The recent attempt to obtain an ambassador to the Vatican from America is but a part of the master plan"(emphasis mine).[46]

Had totalitarianism been the only sin of the Catholic Church, Baptist solicitude would not likely have been as intense. Southern Baptists were convinced, however, that the Vatican intended to subvert American freedom and values. They interpreted the ambassadorial appointment and the Supreme Court decision as actions designed to increase the Pope's power in America. Catholic subversion had particularly set its sights on the American public school system. David Gardner accused Catholics of creating a smoke screen in the current charge that the public schools were seedbeds of Communism. They sought to bring the system into disrepute "with the hope of getting control of our entire educational system, in order to force our government to use tax funds to pay for teaching their own anti-America ideology."[47]

Southern Baptists thus considered Catholicism to be as totalitarian, and as threatening, as Communism. America's mission was to seek equal rights for all people, and her policies must stand against totalitarianism in any form. Not surprisingly, in 1953 the Southern Baptist Convention adopted a resolution against Communism and

---

[44]Hugh A. Brimm, "Catholics and Their Two-hundred-Year Plan for Rural America," *BS 62* (December 7, 1950): 1 and 12. Cf. Also Leon Macon, "The South a Mission Field," *AB 118* (May 14, 1953): 3; Alley, "Look to the Homeland," 10; and "Urges Greater Catholic Efforts in the South," *BM 70* (May 7, 1953): 1.

[45]See Reuben E. Alley, "Exploitation and Fear," *RH 126* (June 11, 1953): 10-11.

[46]Gabhart, "Catholicism's Bid For Supremacy," *WR 126* (January 3, 1952) 3.

[47]"Coddling Communists," *BS 61* (April 28, 1949): 4.

other forms of tyranny.[48] In such actions Southern Baptists acted in accordance with their worldview. In such a framework of reality, their civil faith in America as a Christian democracy and as the protector of liberty virtually forced them to react fearfully and vigorously to the opposing forces in the "triangle of threat." To compromise with Catholicism, therefore, was as unthinkable as abetting the Communists. The only answer lay in redoubling their efforts to actualize their hopes of a Christian America.

Spiritual preparation was for Southern Baptists the critical element in American participation in the apocalyptic struggle. Baptist understandings of God's favor on America, coupled with Communist and Catholic threats to the American way of life, demanded that the nation be brought back to its divine calling. Whenever in American history evangelical sermons have addressed the *res publica*, they have always taken the form of the jeremiad. Such laments were plentiful in the Cold War period. If not a Jeremiah, a Baptist Hosea—John Eden—warned that America was an "unturned cake." He pleaded, "May we seek to be...what we yearn for our nation to become— Christian."[49] Southern Baptists agreed that America needed to actualize its potential as a Christian nation.

Sabbath breaking and laxity in "soul winning" also weakened the country. Having seen a highway crew working on Sunday, and incensed editor, A. L. Goodrich, trumpeted the gravity of such a state of affairs. In an editorial exaggeratedly entitled "Crisis in Mississippi" he wrote, "We sing 'God Bless America.' How can He? Such work is an open violation of the law."[50] Leon Macon of Alabama similarly warned, "We cannot long survive as a great nation with most of our citizens drunk, refraining from church attendance and turning the Lord's Day into a picnic."[51] Resorting to the customary Southern Baptist panacea, Reuel T. Skinner summoned his readers to greater evangelistic fervency. The destiny of the world depended on it: "Unless

---

[48]See Carver, "America in a Triangle of Threat," 8; L. L. Gwaltney, "Focal Points," *AB* (June 8, 1950): 3; Reuben E. Alley, "Methods Must Be Right," *RH 123* (August 10, 1950): 10; *Annual of the Southern Baptist Convention,* 1953, 55.

[49]John Eden, "America-God's Unturned Cake," *RH 124* (February 22, 1952): 4-5, 51.

[50]A. L. Goodrich, "Crisis in Mississippi," *Baptist Record 37* (July 29, 1954): 3.

[51]"Thanksgiving Day," *AB 118* (November 26, 1953): 3.

Christians in America become *Christian* we are doomed as a nation; unless Christians become missionary to the point of *sacrifice* the whole world is doomed to destruction."[52] Thus the final conflict with Communist and Catholic demons required the spiritual intervention of a truly godly nation. Only then might these southerners' vision of America be realized.

In his well known analysis, anthropologist Clifford Geertz holds that religious symbols serve to sum up what a people knows about its universe of meaning. Their world view reflects "both what a people prizes and what it fears and hates."[53] Southern Baptist anti-Communist and anti-Catholic rhetoric readily revealed both what they hailed as virtues and what they despised as vices. Inasmuch as these hates and loves pertained to the nation, they brought into focus their vision of America, and thus reflected their civil religion.

Whatever else may be said of this vision, it was a traditionally Protestant one. As to the vices they perceived, these Baptists rejected any ideology that restricted individual choice, except where blacks were concerned. They hated the regimentation of life and atheistic dogmas of Communism; they despised what they saw as the religious coercion of Catholicism. Wrote Leon Macon, "The beauty of being a Baptist is that one does not have to sacrifice his individuality to a system." He further asserted that "self-reliance is encouraged by Christ, and is essential in any part of our lives. When we lose that, we seek a Pope or Dictator."[54]

Southern Baptist conservatives naturally interpreted such individualism as the essential meaning of America. America had been created by rugged individualism and American democracy was shaped by it. Baptists understood American democracy, however, as Protestant democracy.[55] Evangelical Christianity had given birth to demo-

---

[52] "Russia Can Be Stopped Only by Christianity," *WR 124* (July 27, 1950): 8.

[53] *Interpretation of Cultures*, 127 and 131.

[54] "The Importance of Individuality," *AB 118* (April 23, 1953): 3 and "Self-Reliance," *AB 118* (April 30, 1953): 3.

[55] There has been a historic tendency among many Southern Baptists to refuse the appellation "Protestant." Such a perspective remained extant during the 1950s, as it does in some quarters to this day. Thus Southern Baptists did not use the term "Protestant democracy." My use of it merely acknowledges the consensus of historians that Baptists are Protestant, as were Christians' hopes for "righteous empire" throughout most of American history.

cracy. J. Howard Williams of Texas suggested that Evangelicalism's idea of individual responsibility was woven into the democratic form of government.[56] When coupled with emphasis on evangelism, these understandings suggested that the individual's right to experience, by individual choice to experience Christian conversion was the Southern Baptist *summum bonum*. America's role in the world was to protect that right for all people.

Thus Baptists interpreted Communism and Catholicism together as dangers to democracy and evangelical America. If American democracy were to be "submerged under opportunistic totalitarianism," state W. O. Carver, "our meaning in history will be lost."[57] Southern Baptist civil religion, therefore, cherished a traditional, almost nineteenth-century, vision of America. America was a chosen nation with an international role in the world, but to Southern Baptists that role was less secularly political than evangelically religious.

This suggests the obvious: that the homogeneous, highly evangelical South of the 1950s was only beginning to shift toward a more pluralistic society. In these early years of the decade, Southern Baptists imaged an America slipping away from its evangelical moorings and thereby failing in its responsibility to exemplify and protect individual freedom in the world. The images and hopes of black southerners, however, took a somewhat different form.

Although sounding many of the same religio-patriotic themes as Southern Baptists, the images of black Baptists adopted quite a different focus and goal. These distinctions raise a central question: Did blacks have different interpretations of images of America that they held in common with whites? A conspicuous indication of a different agenda among National Baptists is the relatively cool reception they gave the religious revival of the 1950s. These black Baptists did not spend much effort praising the religiosity of Dwight D. Eisenhower. When, on occasion, black Baptist leaders did congratulate the president, their encomiums were as fervent as those of Southern Baptists. Witness the statement of W. H. Jernagin: "I thank God for Dwight Eisenhower, who as President of the United States, led the nation in prayer when he took the oath of office. He is the first President in the history of this nation to take this significant step.

---

[56]"Baptists and Democracy," in *AB 117* (April 17, 1952): 6.
[57]Carver, "America in a Triangle of Threat," 8.

Since in office, he has endeavored to set an example for Christian laymen and other officials in Government, to seek God's guidance in world affairs."[58] In spite of such high praise for Ike, however, black Baptists noted or commended his piety much less frequently than did their Southern Baptist counterparts.

Another salient distinction among National Baptists was their tendency to defend their loyalty to America. Such a practice was hardly necessary among the red, white, and blue Americans like the Southern Baptists. The paranoia of the McCarthy era created the need for black Baptists to profess their faith in America. Blacks might, after all, have had reason for being disloyal to the nation. Since at least the 1930s, with the Communist Party's support of the Scottsboro boys, certain segments of white America had suspected foreign subversion in the struggle for racial equality. Thus African Americans had good reason to defend their Americanism. In addition, there were rumblings in certain quarters that blacks had become so embittered about America that they would no longer defend their country. Such was the view of performer and activist Paul Robeson, who had asserted that blacks would refuse military service in any war against the Soviet Union.[59]

J. Pius Barbour of the *National Baptist Voice* countered Robeson's remark with a declaration of NAACP chief Walter White that "the Negro is an American and in any Crisis he will perform his duty like any other American." Barbour argued that White more accurately represented the views of "the largest group of blacks, the church-going blacks who believe they can be integrated into American life."[60] In Mississippi, eminent Baptist pastor H. H. Humes agreed with Barbour, citing the blacks' bravery in every American war since the Revolution. He disqualified Robeson as the voice of American blacks and declared, "We can't afford to sweet heart with the Russian Government and Communistic Doctrine; we love America, the

---

[58]*Minutes of the National Baptist Sunday School and Baptist Training Union Congress,* 1956, 42. Quotation comes from the president's address.

[59]Noted in an editorial of J. Pius Barbour of the *National Baptist Voice,* (*NBV*) the official organ of the National Baptist Convention. See "Paul Robeson, Walter White, and Ralph Bunche," *NBV 32* (April 15, 1949):4.

[60]Ibid.

greatest country on earth. It is courageous in war and forgiving in peacetime. We love America!"[61]

Thus whatever necessitated their pledges of allegiance, black Baptists based their loyalty on an image of America as a Christian nation. Somewhat like their white counterparts, they envisaged a *potentially* Christian nation.

An important principle of doctrinal development in the patristic period of church history was that known as *lex orandi, lex credendi.* This idea suggested that the "law of prayer" helped determine the "law of belief." Practically, this meant that the deepest beliefs of a religious group would be reflected in its prayers. If so, a 1948 prayer meeting of hundreds of black preachers at the White House revealed some of what blacks believed about America. Gathering as the National Fraternal Council of Negro Churches, they prayed, "We come in sacred memory and deep gratitude for Thy goodness and mercy to us as a nation. Thou hast protected, and exalted this nation, and permitted it to grow and prosper and sit in high places among all the nations of the world....Help this Christian nation to glorify the things of the Spirit."[62]

On other occasions, however, black Baptists were not so certain that America was Christian. Arguing that Christians ought to be involved in politics, *American Baptist* editor William H. Ballew asserted, "We ought never to forget that ours is a Christian nation, at least in name, and that we have been and are being blessed above many peoples of the earth, and that because of this our responsibilities are greater."[63] Indeed, many black Baptist preachers doubted that America was Christian—particularly those who in this period began to address political and social issues.

Such doubt led many activist ministers to use the term "Christian nation" in an ambiguous manner. W. J. Hodge, a young pastor in Lynchburg, Virginia, claimed he never spoke of America in these terms. He nevertheless noted the ambiguity of American Christianity. While America had largely condoned slavery, it included, after all, *some* denominations that had rejected slavery and a government that

---

[61]"The Voices of a New Day," *NBV* 32 (August 1, 1949): 7.

[62]"Preachers Pray on White House Steps," *NBV* 32 (January 15, 1948): 1.

[63]William H. Ballew, "Religion and Politics," *American Baptist* 78 (March 16, 1956): 2. (Hereinafter abbreviated as *AmB.*)

eventually had outlawed that practice. Beyond this, he acknowledged that many black preachers of the period believed that America had the "greatest possibility for the fulfillment of the 'democratic idea.'"[64]

Ralph David Abernathy and Fred Shuttlesworth expressed similar understandings. Abernathy commented that he often preached that America was not a Christian nation, but rather a "hypocritical nation."[65] Shuttlesworth elaborated this theme: "America was *not* a Christian nation,...while it was founded upon Christian principles, Christian pronouncements, Christian platitudes, it had really never been a Christian nation...[T]here were creeds without deeds, slogans without programs....And I think God intended America to be a Christian nation."[66] Mid-twentieth black preachers echoed a major theme from the nineteenth century slave criticisms of white Christianity and the oratory of abolitionist Frederick Douglass, who made a powerful distinction between "slaveholding Christianity" and the "Christianity of Christ" in his appendix to his *Narrative of the Life of an American Slave*: "I love the pure, peaceable, and impartial Christianity of Christ: I therefore hate the corrupt, slaveholding, women-whipping, cradle-plundering, partial and hypocritical Christianity of this land. Indeed, I can see no reason, but the most deceitful one, for calling the religion of this land Christianity." Black Baptist preachers thus saw America as potentially Christian, even as did their white coreligionists. Their images were similar also in terms of what they understood as the nation's role in the world.

Recounting "the history of Christian America," rural Kentucky pastor R. L. Amos noted Americans' belief that their nation was the highest civilization known to humankind and the "epitome of freedom." For him America was the "citadel of the four freedoms."[67] Prominent pastor Sandy F. Ray of Brooklyn, New York, sounded this theme before a Senate committee in 1947. Speaking as the chairman of the National Baptist Social Service Commission, he averred that the nation was based on the principles of freedom and equality of opportunity. Beyond this, he spoke of America as a land of promise, with a special mission "in the realm of international reconstruction."

[64]Hodge, interview with author, April 2, 1984.
[65]Abernathy, interview with author, March 21, 1984.
[66]Shuttlesworth, interview with author, March 10, 1984.
[67]R. L. Amos, "We Would See Jesus," *AmB 79* (September 27, 1957): 2.

America had been called, he declared, to lead in the building of a stable world order.[68]

In light of such a responsibility, of course, America was obligated to serve as an example of stability and justice. Only so could the nation exercise its leadership. Consequently, black Baptists called on America to exemplify a tolerance that would facilitate the stable world order that Ray envisioned. Barbour saw such tolerance as a basic tenet of Americanism: "If we want to believe in and practice *class* intolerance, we should not be Americans, but Communists. But if we believe in Americanism, we must proclaim the doctrine that all men are created equal and must be so regarded."[69] Thus black and white Baptists largely agreed that their nation was the not-quite-Christian beacon of freedom in the world. The obvious distinction was what they saw as the key obstacle to America's actualizing its potential. In the eyes and the sermons of National Baptists, the problem was not a lack of piety or fervent evangelism, but rather America's mishandling of its own heritage of freedom.

Much as Southern Baptists, National Baptists perceived some serious threats to the fulfillment of America's destiny. As Baptists they agreed with their white counterparts concerning the dangers of Roman Catholic influence. In a number of articles, National Baptists articulated themes similar to those in Southern Baptist rhetoric. They expressed concern over the educational drive of Catholics in Baptist territory and Catholic political efforts. They also warned of the Catholic danger to church-state separation, citing both the Vatican appointment and the Supreme Court decision on transportation to parochial schools. Black Baptists even referred to the "subversive" and "un-American" activities of Catholicism in the United States.[70]

---

[68] Sandy F. Ray, Chairman of the Social Service Commission, National Baptist Convention, Pleads for Democracy at Home," *NBV 31* (July 15, 1947): 6. Although Ray ministered in New York, he had served as pastor of churches in Georgia and Arkansas before settling in the North. Having grown up in Georgia, he can be safely interpreted as representing the perspectives of Southern blacks.

[69] J. Pius Barbour, "Good and Bad Side," *NBV 32* (June 15, 1948): 1 and 13.

[70] See Barbour, "The Catholic Threat," *NBV 31* (August 15, 1947): 4; "The Catholics Are Coming," *NBV 32* (May 1, 1949): 4; Gerald Hamilton (Pastor, First African Baptist Church, Brunswick, Georgia) "It Seems to Me...," *NBV 31* (July 15, 1947): 5.

The Baptist heritage, with its strong advocacy of religious freedom and church-state separation, led black Baptists along with Southern Baptists to look askance at the inroads of Catholic power. Nevertheless, their concern did not remotely approach the near-hysteria of Southern Baptists. As good Baptists they feared what they perceived as a Catholic threat to religious freedom. As blacks, however, they had another interest. Thus, for National Baptists, America's was not an external struggle against a foreign power such as the Kremlin or the Vatican. It was an internal struggle within the American tradition. As Sandy F. Ray testified, "Our approach is from the Christian point of view. We have not, and shall not commit our convention to any Foreign or subversive ideology. The justification for our fight is within the framework of our constitution, and our accepted Christian principles. We are calling for a practical application of the principles of Democracy for all citizens of the United States."[71] In his occasionally sardonic manner, J. Pius Barbour sounded this theme more pointedly, asking, "Why all this upstir about Russia? Are the Russians wild animals or criminals? The Furore [sic] is a smoke screen to hide the inherent weakness of our Social system."[72]

National Baptists saw the inconsistency between American values and practices as the most significant hindrance to America's assuming its role in the world. In one of his annual reports to the National Baptist convention, Ray reflected the wonderment of many black Americans: "It is exceedingly difficult to see how America can have such far-flung world dreams and designs, and fail to take a forthright position regarding the fifteen million loyal citizens who are hobbling in the crippling shackles of segregation, discrimination, political, social, and economic slavery before their very eyes."[73] Certain black leaders argued that equality in America would help defuse the Communist threat. Convention president Joseph H. Jackson believed that amelioration of the race problem would remove the social conditions susceptible to Communist exploitation: "Communism appeals to the underprivileged, the oppressed, the persecuted, and the disinherited. Let us devise a method by which such elements are removed

---

[71] "Sandy Ray, Baptists' Social Mongul Speaks," *NBV* 32 (January 15, 1948): 8.

[72] "Jews, Negroes, and Russians Three Scapegoats," *NBV* 32 (March 15, 1948): 1.

[73] "Sixth Annual Report of the Social Service Commission of the National Baptist Convention, U. S. A., Inc.," NBV 24 (November 1, 1952): 12.

from our society, and from our world community, and thereby destroy the breeding place of the destructive germs that threaten our way of life, and endanger the peace of the world."[74]

Not surprisingly, therefore, even before Martin Luther King's rise to prominence, black Baptists passionately believed that America's very survival depended on correcting these wrongs. Black Baptists strongly sensed that America would be condemned before the bar of history because of this injustice. World public opinion would be brought to bear on this "American dilemma." R. L. Amos wondered how Uncle Sam might rationalize his great interest in freedom throughout the world when such liberty was denied to "millions of his nieces and nephews at home.[75] The black consensus on the actual threats to America's heritage and role in the world was summed up in W. H. Jernagin's president's address to the 1955 National Baptist Sunday School and Baptist Training Union Congress: "The solution of this problem [of segregation] may well decide the fate of democracy. Our way of life will rise or fall in the estimate of the majority of the people of the world on the basis of how this problem is solved."[76]

National Baptists, hence carried an image of an America intimidated more by its internal dilemma than by any external enemies. On this point their civil religion diverged significantly from that of their fellow Baptists in the South. Even more importantly, however, these two civil faiths differed in their hopes for America.

At the practical level, black Baptists seemed merely to hope for America to actualize its potential. Sandy F. Ray echoed the hopes of his fellow Baptists in his testimony before the Senate committee in 1947. He declared that having fought for America in the war, "now, we hope for the real America. The America of the Constitution. The America of the patriots' dream. The America which we are capable of becoming: 'One nation indivisible, with liberty and justice for all.'"[77]

The idea of America becoming true to itself found its most moving expression in the thought and work of Martin Luther King Jr. Delivering perhaps the greatest speech in twentieth-century American

---

[74]"The Importance of America's Defense," *NBV 26* (May 1954): 5.

[75]"A Paradox of Paradoxes," *AmB 79* (August 30, 1957): 2.

[76]*Minutes of the National Baptist Sunday School and Baptist Training Union Congress*, 1955, 40.

[77]"Sandy F. Ray, Chairman," *NBV 31* (July 15, 1947): 6 and 14.

history, King spoke of his dream: "It is a dream deeply rooted in the American dream that one day this nation will rise up and live out the true meaning of its creed—we hold these truths to be self-evident, that all men are created equal."[78] Yet this theme came to King not as much from his academic background as from his experience as a southern black and from the legacy of the black ministerial tradition.[79]

Thus King was less the originator of the idea of "the dream" than the articulator of it. King's thought gave theoretical development and emotional expression to the largely unarticulated, or at least unheard, hopes of black Baptists, indeed, of all black Americans. Thus, hints of "the dream" found expression among black Baptists during the early 1950s, yielding perhaps the clearest understanding of black hopes.

Ray's testimony in 1947 reflected the hopes of an older generation of black ministers. But the nation's becoming "the real America" can be viewed as merely a step toward a larger goal. William H. Ballew, another older minister, spoke of that goal in biblical terms. He interpreted the struggle for equality not merely as a social or even a moral issue, but as a striving toward the kingdom of God.[80] Black Baptist ministers had long included social justice as a component of the idea of God's kingdom. Martin Luther King inherited this tradition from his Baptist forebears. King articulated a note that had long been a part of his preaching. King's oratorical power enabled blacks to make his images their own largely because they had become familiar with these images, at least in rudimentary form, in their Sunday schools and churches.[81]

---

[78]"'I Have a Dream'" text of the speech printed in *A Testament of Hope: The Essential Writings of Martin Luther King Jr.* ed. James M. Washington (New York: Harper & Row, 1986) 217-20.

[79]The best recent historiography is currently emphasizing the black church as the most significant roots of King's thought and life. See for example James M. Washington's introduction to King's writings in *A Testament of Hope*, xi-xxvi; David J. Garrow, "The Intellectual Development of Martin Luther King, Jr.: Influences and Commentaries," *Union Seminary Quarterly Review* 40, no. 4 (1986); 5-20; Garrow, *Bearing the Cross: Martin Luther King Jr. and the Southern Christian Leadership Conference* (New York: William Morrow, 1987); *There Is a Balm in Gilead: The Cultural Roots of Martin Luther King Jr.* (Minneapolis: Fortress Press, 1991).

[80]"Thanks," *AmB 78* (March 9, 1956): 2.

[81]Washington, interview with author, March 14-15, 1984.

Ralph David Abernathy echoed this assessment. Reminiscing about the preachers of his youth, he noted the long-standing theme of liberation within the black religious tradition:

> The pastors would always talk about fighting for the rights of mankind and the day when justice would come into being for all people. For all people, not just the black people but the oppressed people. Unlike so many that believed that blacks were satisfied with segregation, that is not true. They always looked forward to a better day. My grandfather, who was a great philosopher and taught me and the people in the community, would always talk about the "bottom rail coming to the top."[82]

As for King's own perspective, Kenneth Smith and Ira Zepp have argued that he first formulated the major motifs of the "I Have a Dream" speech during the pastorate of the Dexter Avenue Baptist Church in Montgomery, Alabama.[83] Moreover, the impulse to formulate those motifs, indeed the incipient form of those motifs, came from the religious culture in which King was nurtured. King's idea of the "dream" can thus be interpreted as the clearest expression of black Baptists' hopes for America. King understood America itself as the unfulfilled dream of a land where persons of every race, nationality, and creed might live as brothers. King found divine sanction for the dream in the self-evident truths of the Declaration of Independence—"that all men are created equal, that they are endowed by their Creator with certain inalienable Rights, that among these are Life, Liberty, and the pursuit of Happiness."[84]

---

[82]Abernathy, interview with author, March 21, 1984. The importance of the liberation theme within the black tradition is well established. See E. Franklin Frazier, *The Negro Church in America* (New York: Schocken Books, 1964); Mathews, *Religion in the Old South*; and Wilmore, *Black Religion and Black Radicalism*.

[83]Kenneth L. Smith and Ira G. Zepp. Jr., *The Search for the Beloved Community: The Thinking of Martin Luther King, Jr.* (Valley Forge, Pa.: Judson Press, 1974) 125-26.

[84]Martin Luther King Jr. "The American Dream," *Negro History Bulletin 31* (May 1968); 10. This article is a transcript of King's June 6, 1961, commencement address at Lincoln University.

In more concrete terms, King and his fellow Baptists hoped for a nation with truly equal opportunity for all persons and where national resources might be used to serve the rest of the world. King expressed these hopes thus: "We will be able to bring into being a new nation where men will live together as brothers; a nation where all men will respect the dignity and worth of the human personality; a nation in which men will not take necessities from the many to give luxuries to the few; a nation in which men will live by the principles of the fatherhood of God and the brotherhood of man."[85] King understood America as the place where the "beloved community," his vision of a completely integrated society of love and justice, might be actualized. In essence King dreamed that America might become such a community. If this were accomplished, America would become a caring community, with persons regarding others as created in the image of God and sacrificing for the common welfare.[86] The ultimate goal for America, toward which King and his fellow Baptists (along with many others) worked, was "genuine intergroup and interpersonal living."[87]

In King's thinking, the New Testament concept of *agape* (selfless love) undergirded this vision of America. In such a dream, the nation would be characterized by a willingness to let *agape* direct all individual and social relationships. This would involve viewing humanity as a unity and understanding that "whatever directly affects one person affects all indirectly." Americans ought to concern themselves with injustices done to any American, for this vision leaves no room for the idea of an "outside agitator."[88] Rather, King's "dream" required that America develop a global consciousness. "[We] must develop a world perspective if we are to survive," King said. "The American dream will not become a reality devoid of the larger dream of a world of brotherhood, and peace, and good will....[W]e must all

---

[85]King, "A View of the Dawn," *Interracial Review* 30 (May 1957): 85. See also "The Rising Tide of Racial Consciousness," *YWCA Magazine*, December 1960, 3, quoted in Smith and Zepp, *Search for the Beloved Community*, 126.

[86]For an excellent discussion of the character of the "beloved community," see Ansbro, *Martin Luther King Jr.* 187-92.

[87]Martin Luther King Jr. *Strength to Love*, 2d ed. (Philadelphia: Fortress Press, 1981) 34.

[88]Ansbro, *Martin Luther King Jr.* 34-35.

learn to live together as brothers, or we will all perish together as fools."[89]

Thus, in terms similar to Robert Bellah's hope for a world civil religion, King articulated the inchoate hopes of black southerners, and black Baptists in particular, that America would live up to its calling to embody and exemplify to the world an ideal brotherhood. America had a special role in creating the brotherhood, noted Fred Shuttlesworth, for "once we got all the melting pot together here, and the hardest bite was to assimilate the blacks into it, then we could be an example for the world."[90] Such were blacks' images of and hopes for America, not only before 1954, but throughout the civil rights struggle of the 1950s and sixties.

Summary

In the South prior to 1954 the American civil religion manifested itself in two related but distinct versions. Both versions were American in that they centered on myths or images of America's religious meaning. In their version black Baptists focused single-mindedly on the meaning of the nation. Such would be expected as the federal government had historically, albeit to varying degrees, protected black rights from more regional efforts to truncate those rights. In addition, southern blacks had no tradition of loyalty to any sort of southern nationalism.

Black Baptists saw America as the potentially Christian nation, called to embody the principles of democracy and equality. The major impediment to America's becoming the "real America" was an internal problem—the "Negro problem." While acknowledging the presence of external foes, National Baptists greatly minimized the danger of their subverting the divine purpose for America. External threats could be rendered harmless, they argued, if America would come to itself and treat its black citizens fairly. Such would give the divided and dangerous world an example of how to live together as a brotherhood. The image of America among black Baptists which

---

[89]King, "The American Dream," 11-12.

[90]Shuttlesworth, interview with author, March 10, 1984. See also Andrew M. Manis, *A Fire You Can't Put Out: The Civil Rights Life of Birmingham's Reverend Fred Shuttlesworth* (Tuscaloosa: University of Alabama Press, 1999).

constituted their hopes for the nation was thus a pluralistic one. Best expressed in Martin Luther King's idea of the "beloved community," black hopes awaited an America that would be a "city set on a hill" to model for the world how to live with its pluralism.

Pluralism found a different place within the Southern Baptist version of the American civil religion. As whites steeped in the southern way of life, Southern Baptists focused dually (pluralistically?) on both America and the South. Thus, in accordance with the South's historic relations with the nation, this version of the civil religion was ambiguous. It was American, yet distinctively southern.

One indication of this distinctiveness was the intensity of Southern Baptist paranoia concerning Catholicism. Richard Hofstadter has described the "paranoid style" of mind as one of exaggeration, suspicion, and conspiratorial fantasy, expressing itself with the fear that its way of life is in jeopardy.[91] This mentality prevailed much more Southern Baptist literature than in Northern or southern black periodicals. While some non-southern papers, for example, linked McCarthy with Catholicism, they were much less prone to reject McCarthy's tactics because of any purported similarity to those of the Catholic Church. In short, Southern Baptists were paranoid on a wider, vaster scale and more likely to describe the Catholic threat in conspiratorial terms. Such an aversion to Catholicism was hardly matched by the larger American culture of the day.

This suggests one other note of distinctiveness. Most historians have interpreted the civil religion of the 1950s as watered down, domesticated faith, shorn of Protestant particularities. But the nationalistic religion of Southern Baptists was anything but post-Protestant, as indicated by the Baptist editor who criticized Eisenhower for not making his inaugural prayer "in Jesus' name."[92] Ike may not have cared which particular "deeply felt religious faith" provided the basis for American life, but conservative Southern Baptists apparently did. Unlike that of black Baptists, the civil religion of Southern Baptists ideally envisioned not a religiously pluralistic nation, but a homogeneously Protestant one. To these Southern Baptist eyes, such a

---

[91]Richard Hofstadter, *The Paranoid Style in American Politics and Other Essays* (Chicago: University of Chicago Press, 1979) 3-4.

[92]Finley Tinnin, "President Eisenhower's Prayer," *BM 70* (February 12, 1953):2.

nation was under severe attack during the postwar era and would continue to be through culture wars and into the twenty first century.

Thus, Southern Baptists' perceptions of the "triangle of threat" pitting America against the Kremlin and the Vatican suggests the images of a distinctively southern version of the American civil religion. When coupled with its equally hysterical anti-Catholicism, the exaggerated fervor of Southern Baptists' anti-Communism made their civil religion significantly different (i.e., more Protestant) than the standard, watered down religion-in-general that scholars have come to associate with the America of the 1950s. It was this different, even if not unique, arrangement of national traits that set the civil religion of white Southern Baptists apart.

Southern Baptists' images of America generally agreed that America's role in the world entailed serving as the example and protector of individual rights and freedom. They also agreed that the world situation had placed such freedom in serious jeopardy. The threats they perceived, however, were mainly external. Communism was the diabolical enemy; Catholicism was equally dangerous. Other than a lack of piety or evagelism, few if any internal problems seemed to threaten America's vaunted role in the world. Consequently, it is hardly surprising that Southern Baptist editor O. P. Gilbert wrote that the dual danger from Moscow and Vatican City, rather than "the Negro problem," constituted the real "American dilemma."[93] During the stormy years after *Brown v. Board of Education* the South and the Southern Baptists would at least begin to question that assessment.

---

[93]"The American Dilemma," *CI 127* (April 8, 1947): 3.

3

DESEGREGATION AND SOUTHERN HOPES
IMAGES AFTER 1954

The year 1954 ended the hesitant silence of the white South and re-
placed its apprehension with controversy and reaction. That crucial
year also saw black paeans to the traditions of the American civil religion increase in frequency and fervor. No one event affected these
developments as much as the United States Supreme Court's landmark
Brown v. Board of Education decision. Unanimously declaring that
separate facilities in public education were "inherently unequal," the
Court ruled segregation unconstitutional. If storm clouds were gathering in the early postwar years, the lightning began to flash with the
Brown ruling. The predictable rumblings of southern thunder were
soon to follow.

Without question 1954 was a crucial year for blacks and whites
in the South. Certain scholars view the year as the beginning of the
end for the "southern church." The civil rights movement, and, later,
the social unrest of the sixties enabled the southern church to feel the
significant movements of the twentieth century in unprecedented
ways.[1] Similarly, the events beginning with the *Brown* decision
created a new perception among southern blacks that they could work
to change their current status in America. From the black point of
view, the Supreme Court decision opened a beneficent Pandora's box
in American life.[2]

---

[1] Wallace M. Alston, Jr., and Wayne Flynt, "Religion in the Land of Cotton," in
You Can't Eat Magnolias, ed. H. Brandt Ayers and Thomas H. Naylor (New York:
McGraw-Hill, 1972) 111-12.

[2] Washington, interview with author, April 14-15, 1984.

Of course, the stormy aftermath of 1954 also affected the civil religions of Southern and National Baptists. Beginning with *Brown*, a swift succession of important events served to shift Southern Baptist civil religious images more toward southern traditions. The same events, however, caused black Baptists to appeal ever more militantly to the American tradition of freedom and equality. The process by which civil religious images in the South increasingly moved in opposite directions thus revealed the character of these civil religions in conflict.

The refocusing of Southern Baptist civil religious images, however, reflected the ambiguity of the South's relations with the nation. As projected by Southern Baptists in the 1950s, these images cannot be interpreted unambiguously as a *southern* civil religion. To understand these images as exclusively southern is to duplicate a significant weakness of Charles R. Wilson's analysis. It would disregard an "interactive" perspective that could underscore the conflicting loyalties of white southerners to both America and the South. That perspective suggests that the American and southern civil religions increasingly interacted during these years, and that Southern Baptists interpreted American civil religious images through the traditions of the southern civil religion. More simply put, Southern Baptists fused their images of America into a civil religious syncretism that included both American and southern elements.

For southern blacks, on the other hand, the events after 1954 did not shift their civil religious images as much as intensify their appeal to them. Encouraged by the decision of the Supreme Court, black Baptists more publicly and more militantly demanded the end of racial segregation and discrimination. This they did by more fervent appeals to the oldest and most central themes of the American civil religion.

Further, events from 1954 through 1957 made the issue of desegregation a central element in the religio-patriotic sentiments of both these sets of southerners. Silence was impossible after *Brown*. One could not address civic issues in the South or the nation without reference to the problem of desegregation. At the same time, one could not analyze the idea of integration without relating it to the meaning of the nation. Thus desegregation became a crucial symbol within the civil religions of these southerners. Inasmuch as southerners' images of America embodied their central hopes for the nation, desegregation as a civil religious symbol related directly to the possibility of actualizing these hopes. For most National Baptists, desegregation functioned as the hope of actualizing their images of America. For more reactionary Southern Baptists, however, the specter of desegregation symbolized the nonfulfillment of their images. Thus, as it functioned in these civil religions, desegregation came to symbolize the fulfillment of blacks' hope and the disappointed hope of many southern whites.

Initial Reaction to the Storm

In light of the widely divergent racial contexts in the South, it is no surprise that the reactions to the key events of this period were also quite different. The 1954 Supreme Court decision, the Montgomery bus boycott, and the debacle in Little Rock brought the idea of desegregation (or integration) from the realm of anticipation into stark reality. Beyond this, these key events crystallized the idea of desegregation as a symbol within southerners' civil religions.

The event that began the "Second Reconstruction" was the Supreme Court's 1954 decision against segregation in public schools. Since 1950 the NAACP had been challenging the policy of segregation in various parts of the country. The Court considered five cases from Kansas, Virginia, Delaware, and Washington, DC, collectively; on May 17, 1954, it delivered the historic ruling overturning the "separate but equal" doctrine.

The unanimous decision held that separate schools were "inherently unequal," inasmuch as they created within minority students a sense of inferiority. As such, the Court ruled that segregated schools denied black students equal protection under the law. The ruling postponed the question of implementation pending further study of local conditions. A year later the Court acknowledged the difficulty of local problems and set no specific time frame for implementation other than to call for desegregation to be accomplished by local school boards "with all deliberate speed." Thrown into the South's volatile racial context, the initial ruling of the Supreme Court could not but precipitate a vociferous response from both races. If the desegregation process was to be deliberate, the reaction of both black and white Baptists was quite speedy.

National Baptists generally greeted the Court's ruling with a euphoria tempered with realism. Ralph David Abernathy recalled exulting over the decision with the words "Hallelujah, 'tis done!"[3] William H. Ballew saw the edict as the most important declaration in the United States since the Emancipation Proclamation, noting that it was well past time that Americans' consciences should be "prepared for this hour."[4] At the 1954 meeting of the National Baptist Convention, the director of the organization's Social Service Commission rejoiced with this declaration: "The greatest legal mandate of the twentieth Century was issued on May 17, 1954. The Social Gospel of Jesus received its endorsement by the Highest Court of the nation."[5] National Baptists also celebrated the decision through public ritual. Within a month of the decree, National Baptists joined with the National Fraternal Council of Negro Churches to plan a Thanksgiving pilgrimage to the Lincoln Memorial. There they hoped on hundred thousand blacks would gather to celebrate the first Emancipation Proclamation and to give thanks for the *Brown* decision.[6]

At the September meeting of the National Baptist Convention president Joseph Jackson made two significant proposals relative to the Supreme Court's decision, both of which were adopted by the Convention. He first suggested that a day of mourning, thanksgiving, prayer, and fasting be planned for the second anniversary of the *Brown* decree. At various places throughout the country, Jackson hoped, National Baptists and persons of all faiths might gather to give thanks for the long overdue breakthrough for justice. When May 17, 1956, arrived commemorative services were held in every region of

---

[3] Abernathy, interview with author, Atlanta, Georgia, March 21, 1984.

[4] William H. Ballew, "Let's Think and Talk Sense," *AB 76* (May 28, 1954): 2.

[5] Claude L. Frazier, Report of the Social Service Commission of the National Baptist Convention, U. S. A., Inc., *Annual of the National Baptist Convention*, 1954, 334.

[6] "One Hundred Thousand Colored Americans Will Go on a Thanksgiving Pilgrimage to Lincoln Memorial, Washington, D. C.," *NBV 26* (June 1954): 12. The National Fraternal Council of Black Churches, U. S. A., was an interdenominational fellowship of black denominations and Christians. The meeting was advertised in the *NBV* throughout the summer and autumn of 1954.

the nation, including the southern states of Alabama, Arkansas, Kentucky, Louisiana, Virginia, Mississippi, and Tennessee.[7]

Second, Jackson proposed that the Convention ask Congress to set aside May 17 as a legal holiday celebrating the victory of the Constitution and American democracy. The National Baptist Convention made its request through prominent pastor Adam Clayton Powell of New York, who was also a member of Congress, Powell introduced to the House of Representatives in January 1955 a bill that would have made the day of the *Brown* decision a legal holiday known as Anti-Segregation Day. The bill died in the Judiciary Committee, but nevertheless indicated the importance black Baptists placed on the Court ruling.[8]

At a more personal level the decision generated a sense of euphoria and hopefulness within the black community. In a 1955 Emancipation Day speech at Birmingham's Sixteenth Street Baptist Church, Fred Shuttlesworth interpreted the Court's decision, advising his hearers that there was no longer any reason for not pressing for their full rights. Transcending the practical consequences, however, was the pathos of Shuttlesworth's initial reaction to the ruling: "I had felt like a man when I passed the newspaper stand and saw 'Supreme Court Outlaws Segregation.' I... had then, second only to when I was converted, the second greatest feeling in my life, really. I felt like I was a man."[9]

In a sermon originally preached at Dexter Avenue Baptist Church, Martin Luther King Jr. as is traditional in the black church, described this great event using the image of the Exodus. As King understood it, the Supreme Court had "opened the Red Sea and the forces of justice are moving to the other side.... This decision is a great beacon light of hope to millions of disinherited people. Looking back, we see the forces of segregation dying on the seashore. The problem is far from solved and gigantic mountains of opposition lie ahead, but at least we have left Egypt, and with patient yet firm determination we shall reach the promised land."[10]

---

[7] Jackson, *Unholy Shadows*, 78; Jackson, *Christian Activism*, 288-308; William H. Ballew, "A Day of Repentance, Fasting and Prayer," *AmB* 78 (April 13, 1956): 2.

[8] Jackson, *Unholy Shadows*, 79; *Christian Activism*, 287-88.

[9] Shuttlesworth, interview with author, March 10, 1984.

[10] King, *Strength to Love*, 81-82.

Speaking at the annual meeting of black Baptists in Mississippi, state convention president H. H. Humes praised the ruling but warned of racial misunderstandings in the nation. Admitting it was "hard to be a Negro in America," he said that "every race of people that came to America are accepted more freely than the Negro." He strongly rejected segregation, which he believed "should not be on the status [statute] books of a Christian government."[11] Given Hume's great popularity in Mississippi, his sentiments concerning the ruling were quite representative of black Baptists throughout the South.[12]

Beyond the hopefulness was a stimulus to greater activity among blacks to press for their rights. King believed that *Brown* marked the beginning of the third great period of race relations in America, the "period of complete and constructive integration."[13] Shuttlesworth testified that this event "created in me a desire to push, perhaps more than usual, because I had always had these feelings [of inferiority and a desire to change the status quo]. But here was now... the legal opportunity and basis to give expression to them. More than that... I had the feeling it would make America to be what she said she was. And that if America was to lead the world, we ought to be straightening up the house here, within."[14]

Few black leaders believed the struggle was over, however. In Kentucky, R. L. Amos admonished his readers not to be so foolish as to rest their efforts: "Our battle cry now must be, 'We have just begun to fight.' After it became obvious that the enemies of democracy were not going to accept the mandates of the Supreme Court, without a fight, it became imperatively necessary that we double our efforts and continue our fight."[15] In sum, black Baptists viewed the *Brown* ruling as a divine sign of coming liberation and as a summons to further action for the realization of their rights.

---

[11] J. Pius Barbour, "Humes Triumphs in Mighty Struggle," *NBV* 26 (July 1954):2.

[12] Ibid. Barbour defended Humes's position as a leader of Mississippi blacks (not just black Baptists) despite a challenge to Humes's presidency at the July 1954 convention. Humes won reelection by an eight-to-one margin. According to Barbour the election solidified Humes's position as "the unchallenged leader of the Mississippi Delta where over a half Million Negroes live."

[13] King, "A View of the Dawn," 85.

[14] Shuttlesworth, interview with author, March 10, 1984.

[15] "How and When Will It End?" *AmB* 79 (February 1, 1957): 2.

To probably no one's surprise, a Gallup poll in July 1954 discovered that the South overwhelmingly disapproved of the *Brown* decision. The same poll found that every other region of the country, and an overall 57 percent of Americans, favored the ruling.[16]

Such a regional distinction renders plausible Ulrich Bonnell Phillips's dictum that the central theme of southern history has been a resolve that the South "shall be and remain a white man's country."[17] Inasmuch as the South certainly cannot be considered the sole preserve of American racism, the hardest edge of the Phillips thesis, that white supremacy is the hallmark of the South, probably requires significant softening. There is little doubt, however, that more than any other factor the historic necessity of white southerners to relate personally to the presence of large numbers of blacks helped determine the southern ethos. Throughout American history, in various times and places North or South, white Americans forced by circumstance to share geographical space with African Americans have almost always sought to establish cultural and political dominance over them. If whites in the South have seemed more committed to white supremacy than white Americans in other regions, that reality is traceable to greater numbers of blacks rather than to a greater degree of racism.

If one's experience contributes to the formation of his or her individual self, collective experience also helps shape a people's sense of selfhood. The South's distinct regional identity has been shaped by a historical experience that has itself been shaped by the presence of the black American. Thus, despite its great diversity, the South has long exhibited, as at least one scholar has argued, an inner cohesiveness related to the black presence.[18]

May 17, 1954, put in grave jeopardy a cornerstone of the southern way of life. And the southern church, so often the custodian of southern culture, found itself caught between Christian principles and institutional success—and many other scholars have, one might add, been caught between two versions of the American civil religion. Numan V. Bartley has noted that the response of the southern churches

---

[16] Cited in Muse, *Ten Years of Prelude*, 75.

[17] Ulrich Bonnell Phillips, "The Central Theme of Southern History," *American Historical Review 34* (October 1928): 30-43.

[18] James W. Vander Zanden, "The Ideology of White Supremacy, *Journal of the History of Ideas 20* (June-September, 1959): 385.

was varied and complex. Southern Baptist response reflected this complexity. Certainly a diversity of racial opinion existed within this mammoth southern denomination. Not all Southern Baptists took reactionary positions in the issue of desegregation. Even the majority who agreed with the basic perspectives surveyed in this chapter did not express them vocally or as violently as the representatives of the far right.

Indeed, this analysis shows the significant effort of a "progressive elite" that attempted to move the denomination slowly toward an acceptance of the *Brown* decision. But their calls for justice were weakened by their concern to hold together a denomination largely dominated by segregationist sentiment. The resulting response of the progressives to the issue of civil rights, in Bartley's apt description, "buried the principle of the *Brown* decision in evasive pronouncements or drowned it in silence."[19] Surveying Southern Baptists' more reactionary responses to *Brown*, one can understand why this was so.

The most immediate response came in the editorials of the various state newspapers. Few commended the decision. All wrote of the difficulty of implementing it in the South. Most echoed the sentiments of an editor who saw segregation as rooted in social custom and resistant to change.[20] Calling for calm and clear thinking, David Gardner of Texas advised his readers to adjust themselves to the problem as "good citizens and loyal Americans."[21]

Others evidenced deep concern that the decision might irreparably disrupt southern life. Leon Macon of Alabama believed the decree "jarred to the foundation a southern institution," warning that the South had not faced so serious a difficulty since Reconstruction. The Louisiana editor viewed the ruling as ill-advised. He further pointed out that Northern pressure groups for years had agitated for such an action. Noting their great progress since Reconstruction, he believed southern blacks generally viewed race mixing as unwise.[22]

---

[19] Bartley, *Rise of Massive Resistance*, 304.

[20] S. H. Jones, "Segregation and the Schools," *Baptist Courier 86* (June 3, 1954): 2. (*Baptist Courier* hereafter cited as *BC.*)

[21] David M. Gardner, "Segregation's Problems," *BS 66* (June 10, 1954): 2.

[22] Macon, "The Supreme Court Decision," *AB 119* (May 27, 1954): 3; Tinnin, "Non-Segregation," *BM 71* (June 3, 1954): 2.

The reaction of local pastors received little notice in the state newspapers. Quite pointed criticisms of the Court by two highly respected ministers, however, did receive significant publicity. John H. Buchanan, pastor of Birmingham's Southside Baptist believed the decision "complicates and damages relations between races in the South. Much progress has been made under [the] decision of 1896. The present court from its cloistered chambers has overlooked the reality of the situation."[23] W. A. Criswell, pastor of First Baptist Church of Dallas, Texas, and popular Bible conference preacher throughout the Convention, remarked on the decision in a 1956 foray into South Carolina. At that state's evangelism conference, Criswell harshly denounced the Supreme Court's ruling. So impressed was Governor George Timmerman that he invited Criswell to address a joint session of the South Carolina legislature on February 22, 1956. Availing himself of the opportunity, the preacher issued a rather uncivil denunciation of those who favored integration, particularly the Supreme Court: "Let them integrate. Let them sit up there in their dirty shirts and make all their fine speeches. But they are all a bunch of infidels, dying from the neck up."[24] Many Southern Baptists heartily approved of Criswell's scathing repudiation of the *Brown* ruling. Support for Criswell was mixed, but probably leaned more toward qualified approval. Among editors, only Finley Tinnin of the Louisiana paper criticized Criswell (most others did not mention the address) but only for his speech's "cheap and tawdry language." Of eight letters responding to Tinnin's editorial, five defended Criswell. Of the three letters critical of the Texas preacher, two objected mainly to the tastelessness of Criswell's address, not its substance.[25] That the 1954 Southern Baptist Convention did not issue a similar rejection of the ruling is therefore quite surprising.

---

[23] "Southern Baptist Leaders Call for Calm Appraisal of Court Ruling," *BR* 37 (May 27, 1954): 1.

[24] "Dallas Pastor Stirs Controversy with Statements on Integration," *BM* 33 (March 1, 1956): 1. See also James E. Towns, ed., *The Social Conscience of W. A. Criswell* (Dallas: Crescendo Publications, 1977) 222-34, for an introduction to and the text of Criswell's speech. Criswell did, however, publicly change his views on segregation in his 1970 sermon, "The Church of the Open Door"; see Towns, 157-71.

[25] Cf. Finley Tinnin, "Dr. Criswell's Remarks," *BM* 73 (March 15, 1956): 2; Correspondence *BM* 73 (March 15, 1956): 2; Letters to the Editor, *BM* 73 (March 29, 1956): 3.

The Convention addressed itself to the decision by way of the report of the Christian Life Commission. As to the Court decision, the commission recommended that Southern Baptists recognize the ruling as "in harmony with the constitutional guarantee of equal freedom to all citizens, and with the Christian principles of equal justice and love for all men." It further commended the Court for delaying its ruling on implementation and urged Christians to conduct themselves in the spirit of Christ.[26] When the report came up for adoption, there was a motion to eliminate the commissions recommendation concerning *Brown*. Time for discussion of this amendment was extended for five minutes, but a motion to extend discussion for ten additional minutes failed. The motion to eliminate the recommendation failed, as did an effort to adopt the recommendation seriatim. Finally, after twenty minutes of discussion, the commission's report and all its recommendations, including the one concerning the Supreme Court's decision, were adopted. Negative votes numbered about fifty, though that number was "but a fraction of those who had been applauding opposition speeches."[27]

Editors of the state newspapers minded their reportorial responsibilities in the aftermath of the Convention's action. Among them, only Mississippi editor A. L. Goodrich rejected the Christian Life Commission's report outright, ostensibly because he viewed it as a political issue outside the concern of the Convention. Seeing the report as a violation of church-state separation, he called it the "lowest point of the whole convention."[28]

Goodrich's criticism primed the pump for a flurry of denunciations of the Supreme Court's ruling in the pages of the Mississippi paper. On June 9, the First Baptist Church of Grenada, Mississippi, unanimously passed a resolution repudiating the Southern Baptist Convention's "endorsement of the Court's ruling." The church further resolved that "in the future any messengers sent from this Church to the Southern Baptist Convention are hereby requested to vote against things political; matters that pertain to the State; anything that smacks

---

[26] *Annual of the Southern Baptist Convention*, 1954, 407.
[27] See "Ruling on Segregation Endorsed," *CI 133* (June 10, 1954): 9; Leon Macon, "Convention Issues," *AB 119* (June 17, 1954): 3; and *Annual of the Southern Baptist Convention*, 1954, 55-56.
[28] "The SBC Convention," *BR 37* (June 10, 1954): 3.

of socialism, modernism, or Communism, and other resolutions that may cause strife, arguments and civil disorders among members of this Church or other brethren throughout the South."[29] A week later Goodrich noted that he had received enough letters concerning *Brown* to last three months, and almost all of those he printed rejected it.[30]

In Georgia, little criticism of the decision surfaced in the *Christian Index*. One pastor, however, was fired and asked to resign by each of his two part-time churches for publicly supporting the Court's decision.[31] The Georgia Baptist Convention expressed a similar viewpoint when it met in November. The messengers (delegates) adopted a resolution calling for "justice and calmness" with regard to the race problem. In actuality, the Convention tried to remain neutral on the propriety of the *Brown* decree.

Before the vote was taken, however, a minor *cause celebre* was kindled as a messenger from Augusta stood to discuss the resolution. He was opposed to the report, as were, he believed, the majority of Baptists in Georgia, because it approved of the Supreme Court decision. He also praised the efforts of Georgia governor Herman E. Talmadge, who had vowed to close the public schools if integration were attempted.[32] The messenger argued that to approve the report was to repudiate the governor's policy.

Responding to these charges, prominent pastor James P. Wesberry of Atlanta arose to defend the report. Noting his friendship with the governor, he declared that he did not view the report as a rejection of Talmadge's program.[33] Wesberry's defense of Talmadge apparently had significant effect, for the committee's report was passed unanimously. The vote was unanimous, however, largely because Wesberry was able

---

[29] "Grenada First Dissents," *BR 37* (June 17, 1954): 4.

[30] Our Readers Write, *BR 37* (June 24, 1954): 4-5; Our Readers Write, *BR 37* (July 8, 1954): 4.

[31] "Pastor Fired Again," *BS 67* (January 1, 195): 6-7.

[32] Georgians, a majority of whom were Baptists, voted for a constitutional amendment to abolish the public schools in the face of an integration order. This referendum passed despite the criticism of Georgia Baptist leaders, most of whom opposed the measure. See Len G. Cleveland, "Georgia Baptists and the 1954 Supreme Court Desegregation Decision," *Georgia Historical Quarterly 59* (Supp., 1975) 107-8.

[33] "Justice, Calmness Keynote Plea of Commission on Racial Issues," *CI 133* (November 25, 1954): 19.

to convince the messengers that their governor's perspective on the issue of desegregation was not being repudiated.

That an influential denominational leader felt it necessary to defend the governor's position strongly suggests that Talmadge's hard-edged segregationist line was quite representative of the views of a great many Georgia Baptists. Beyond this, Talmadge repeatedly garnered strong support from his fellow Georgians, most of whom were Baptists. Indeed, Talmadge himself as a Baptist layperson, a member of a Southern Baptist church in Hampton, Georgia.[34]

In many ways, therefore, Talmadge's book *You and Segregation* revealed some of the more reactionary Baptist attitudes toward the *Brown* decision. In it he suggested that the Court's ruling misinterpreted the Constitution. He stated that "the Supreme Court is teaching error, and its rulings should be sternly disapproved by both officials and the general public. Such a decision is not 'the law.' It is simply an enforceable or unenforceable pronouncement of the Court."[35]

Producing an even more hysterical diatribe against the Supreme Court ruling was another Baptist layperson, circuit court judge Thomas P. Brady of Brookhaven, Mississippi. His book *Black Monday* expressed southern racism in its most virulent form and in the process revealed the attitudes of the most reactionary elements in Southern Baptist life.[36]

---

[34] Talmadge was listed as a Baptist in *Who's Who in the South and Southwest* (Chicago: A. N. Marquis Co., 1950) 729-30. In addition, according to James Wesberry, Talmadge was and remains a member of Hampton Baptist Church, Hampton, Georgia. He never joined a church in Atlanta while serving as governor. Wesberry, telephone interview with author, May 4, 1985. Another indication of the governor's popularity among Georgia Baptists was the *Christian Index* printing of Talmadge's 1949 New Year's message. See "Governor's New Year Message," *CI* 129 (January 6, 1949): 3 and 19.

[35] Herman E. Talmadge, *You and Segregation* (Birmingham: Vulcan Press, 1955) 75.

[36] As a deacon and men's Sunday school teacher in First Baptist Church of Brookhaven, Mississippi, Brady was a much more active Baptist than Talmadge. He can thus be legitimately studied as an example of far right-wing Southern Baptist perspectives. Information on Brady's churchmanship comes from the following correspondence with the author: letter from Robert E. Self, pastor of First Baptist Church, Brookhaven, April 24, 1984, and letter from Talmadge E. Smith, Director of Missions, Lincoln Baptist Association, Brookhaven, Mississippi, May 1, 1984.

Appropriating a term that was being used to sloganize the date of the *Brown* decision, Brady expressed his unqualified distaste for the Court's decision:

> Black Monday ranks in importance with July 4th, 1776, the date upon which our Declaration of Independence was signed. May 17th, 1954, is the date upon which the declaration of social-istic doctrine was officially proclaimed throughout this nation. It was on Black Monday that the judicial branch of our government usurped the sacred privilege and right of the respective states of this union to educate their youth. This usurpation constitutes the greatest travesty of the American Constitution and jurisprudence in the history of this nation.[37]

Sensing in the Court's decree a grave threat, he wrote his book as a summons to battle—for the southern version of the American way of life: "It is written to alert and encourage every American, irrespective of race, who loves our Constitution, or Government and our God-given American way of life.... It is dedicated to those who firmly believe that socialism and Communism are lethal messes of porridge for which our sacred birthright shall not be sold."[38]

Thus, the angry and defiant words of Talmadge and Brady express the sentiments of the South's most rabid segregationists. Their perspectives, however, represented a strain of thought that was shared by a large segment of Southern Baptist conservatives, but which only occasionally appeared in Southern Baptist literature, typically filtered out by the always-mediating policies of the state newspaper editors. Beyond this, as will be seen later, these reactionary spokespersons expressed important images of America during this stormy era.

On December 1, 1955, a black seamstress named Rosa Parks refused to give her seat on a Montgomery, Alabama, bus to a white passenger. Her incarceration led an organization of black ministers later known as the Montgomery Improvement Association to use the incident as a test case for challenging Jim Crow. Led by the young pastor of the Dexter Avenue Baptist Church, the Reverend Martin

---

[37] Tom Brady, *Black Monday* (Winona MS.: Association of Citizens Councils, 1955) foreword.
[38] Ibid.

Luther King Jr. the black citizens of the Cradle of the Confederacy resolved to boycott the bus line and challenge the city's segregation code. Before the yearlong moratorium was over, the effort had made King into a national figure and served notice to the South the era of gradualism was ending. More importantly, the event galvanized large segments of the southern black community for a civil rights offensive that it would not "let nobody turn them around."

To discuss National Baptist *support* for the boycott may be superfluous inasmuch as its two most vocal leaders were National Baptist pastors. Martin Luther King Jr. and Ralph David Abernathy did, however, receive strong support from their National Baptist brethren. Convention president Joseph H. Jackson claimed King as one of his own, his eventual antagonism toward King not having surfaced by 1955. Interpreting the boycott as an extension of the civil rights emphasis of the National Baptist Convention, Jackson encouraged the work of the Montgomery Improvement Association. He offered to have the Convention buy a bus to help with transportation during the boycott, but ultimately gave money instead. Jackson also wrote to National Baptist state leaders urging them to send gifts directly to Montgomery and led his own Olivet Baptist Church in Chicago to give one thousand dollars to the cause.[39]

In a more institutional show of support, the 1956 meeting of the National Baptist Convention celebrated the boycott, featuring the leaders of the Montgomery Improvement Association on the program. Also, the Convention's Sunday School and Training Union Congress of that year asked Ralph Abernathy to be the devotional speaker for each morning session.[40]

The leaders of this movement were thus highly regarded by their black Baptist constituency. The degree to which local pastors, usually in conjunction with the local chapter of the NAACP, supported the boycott financially testifies to this. That the National Baptist Convention showcased the leaders of the boycott on a national scale suggests that King and the others had greatly stimulated the pride of the entire black community. William Ballew's encomium of King accurately expressed the sentiments of many black Baptists: "Those leaders

---

[39] Jackson, *Unholy Shadows*, 76-77.

[40] *Minutes of the National Baptist Sunday School and Baptist Training Union Congres*, 1956, 22-26, 31.

and people, such as the Rev. Martin Luther King Jr. and his followers are to be congratulated for their methods of procedure, dominated by heroic courage, the highest type of culture, and the noblest spirit of Christian Brotherhood."[41]

As to the boycott itself, King believed that God was using the conflict to presage the eventual triumph of justice in America. He saw no better place for beginning that ultimate victory than the city that symbolized the Old South. "It is one of the splendid ironies of our day," he noted, "that Montgomery, the Cradle of the Confederacy, is being transformed into Montgomery, the cradle of freedom and justice."[42]

Others agreed that the boycott marked a significant change in black consciousness and in the status of blacks in America. Ballew believed the boycott "foreshadowed a new epoch in the history of a long dejected minority group that has suffered long and much."[43] Fred Shuttlesworth interpreted the boycott as the logical end of the Supreme Court ruling and as the sign that emancipation was being actualized.[44] The comment of Theodore J. Jemison, who had led the Baton Rouge bus boycott, succinctly summed up blacks' sense of the importance of the Montgomery struggle: "Well, it's going to spread all over the South now."[45]

The year between the *Brown* decision and the Court's implementation decree gave southern white reaction time to solidify. Immediately after *Brown*, a sense that the integration of the South was inevitable prevailed in most quarters. By the next year, however, the Citizens Councils had mobilized sentiment into a defiant refusal to comply.[46] Discussion of these issues in Southern Baptist sources,

---

[41] William H. Ballew, "Have You a Constructive Offer?" *AmB 79* (January 18, 1957): 2.

[42] King, *Stride toward Freedom*, 70.

[43] "Right Will Win" *AmB 78* (March 30, 1956): 2.

[44] Shuttlesworth, interview with author, March 10, 1984.

[45] Jemison and Jones, interview by Barton, transcript, 32. Johnnie Jones, a member of Jemison's church and the attorney who gave legal counsel to the leaders of the Baton Rouge boycott, saw their 1953 effort, and by extension the Montgomery boycott, as signaling the beginning of black demands for justice: "After '53 when we came on with the boycott, that's when blacks started demanding. That was the inception of demanding something. Up until then you always asked" (p. 39).

[46] Martin, *Deep South Says "Never"*, 30-31.

however, suggested a studied effort to mute the furor. This is particularly noteworthy in light of efforts like the Montgomery bus boycott by blacks in the South. Again, the progressive elite seemed to desire above all to keep the volatile situation under control. One sure way to accomplish this was virtually to ignore the boycott. Thus one finds little comment on the event in Southern Baptist sources.

At the 1955 session of the Southern Baptist Convention, the report of the Christian Life Commission made no major mention of the segregation issue and was adopted without incident or significant discussion.[47] The November 1955 session of the Alabama Baptist State Convention was not able to keep as silent on the matter. The Alabama Christian Life Commission report questioned the wisdom of the Citizens Councils and their tendency to polarize opinion rather than offer constructive answers. Nevertheless, the report did not pass moral judgment on the Councils, possibly indicating some sensitivity to the support that the Councils were garnering among the people.[48]

By the next year, the new militancy of both blacks and reactionary whites precipitated some oblique references to the racial issue. The Christian Life Commission report of the Alabama Baptist Convention noted the intense reactions in the state caused by the enrollment of the first black student at the University of Alabama. The report called Autherine Lucy "a seeming tool of the NAACP." In addition, the commission made the only specific mention of the Montgomery boycott to be found in the literature, noting only that the boycott had raised tensions in the old southern city. The commission stated that it could not view a policy of forced integration as "the will of God for our state in 1956." Finally, the commission called for "the more independent negro ministers" to meet with white ministers to find a way to reduce tensions. These meetings, they advised, should consist of no ministers holding membership in either the Citizens Councils or the NAACP.[49] Unfortunately they underestimated the difficulty of finding leaders in the black community who were not affiliated, at least in spirit, with the latter organization.

That events like the bus boycott and the rise of the Citizens Councils solidified southern reaction can also be seen in the 1956

---

[47] *Annual of the Southern Baptist Convention*, 1955, 56.

[48] *Annual of the Alabama Baptist State Convention*, 1955, 125.

[49] *Annual of the Alabama State Convention*, 1956, 134-35.

meeting of the Georgia Baptist Convention. At that session the Convention's Social Service Commission made five recommendations, one of which was "to accept the Supreme Court decision as the law of the land and acknowledge that it is in harmony with the Constitution and our fundamental democratic concepts and with the principles of our Christian religion."[50] The commission also recommended (1) that churches help create an atmosphere in which public school administrators could comply with the *Brown* ruling and (2) that the Convention and its churches support any organization of interracial cooperation. All of these recommendations were defeated by a vote of three to one.[51]

One can adduce little direct evidence that the new militancy of the black community, as reflected in the Montgomery bus boycott, hardened Baptist reaction. The mediating denominationalists who largely controlled the state papers and national agencies, and who above all else sought to keep peace in the denomination, largely ignored King and the boycott. The evidence is clear, however, that a hardening occurred, for the Baptist state conventions that in 1954 had been relatively compliant with the Supreme Court decision had become more vocally critical of it by 1956.

The white Baptists of the Deep South had thus grown significantly more critical of the Court decision by their conventions of 1956. In 1954 and 1955 they generally limited themselves to statements of concern about possible problems, but tended to view integration as inevitable. In 1956 these same conventions defeated efforts to accept *Brown* as "in harmony with the Constitution." By the next year, the reaction would become still more hardened.

In early 1957, the Little Rock Board of Education had developed a plan for token integration in that city's Central High School. Working with civic groups, the board sought quietly to implement the plan so as to stir up as little controversy as possible. Just before the beginning of the school session, however, the Capital Citizens Council of Little Rock mounted a quick campaign to stop the integration of the school. Both sides appealed to Governor Orval Faubus, who in reality wanted to stay out of the matter.

---

[50] "Social Service," *CI 135* (November 15, 1956): 3.

[51] Ibid.; see also "Messengers Ban Specifics in Racial Issue," *CI 135* (November 22, 1956): 4.

At the opening of the school session, amid rumors of possible violence, Faubus mobilized the Arkansas National Guard, ostensibly to prevent any incidents. Segregationists rejoiced, but only temporarily. When the federal district court so ordered, Faubus complied and removed the guard. By this time, however, the spotlight had been focused on Central High, and a mob of citizens gathered to prevent the nine black students from entering. At that point, President Eisenhower reluctantly entered into the situation, sending the 101st Airborne Division to Little Rock to keep the peace. Arkansas and Faubus immediately became the symbol of southern racist reaction.[52]

Perhaps not surprisingly, this event created little stir among blacks. By 1957 the incipient civil rights movement was well under way, and the SCLC had already been formed. In addition, by this time blacks in America had already experienced a full term of an Eisenhower administration and were considerably less than delighted. Ike seemed oblivious to the stubbornness of southern reactionaries and had not publicly defended the *Brown* decision. Martin Luther King Jr. by then the unrivaled leader of southern blacks, was dissatisfied with Eisenhower's lack of leadership on the issue of civil rights, particularly evident in his lackadaisical support for and enforcement of the 1957 Civil Rights Act.[53]

Thus black reaction to the Little Rock debacle focused more on the inaction of Eisenhower than the action of Faubus or the mob. The governor's role was expected, but the tardiness of presidential leadership infuriated blacks. As William Washington recalled: "They felt that Eisenhower was condoning [segregation] when he was so long in sending the 121st Airborne [*sic*] to enforce the court order....They took Faubus to be, excuse the expression, another Red Neck, and he was acting natural. But [in] the president of the United States we always expected a man with more character."[54]

King saw the incident in Arkansas as "a tragic revelation of what prejudice can do to blind the vision of men and darken their under-

---

[52] This survey of the Little Rock incident is taken largely from Waddy William Moore, "Arkansas," in *The Encyclopedia of Southern History*, ed. David C. Roller and Robert W. Twyman (Baton Rouge: Louisiana State University Press, 1979) 73.

[53] Stephen B. Oates, *Let the Trumpet Sound: The Life of Martin Luther King, Jr.* (New York: Harper & Row, 1982) 121-22.

[54] Washington, interview with author, March 14-15, 1984.

standing." Further, it indicated that persons of goodwill had been silent while the recalcitrant opposition had organized.[55] Much lesser known black preachers agreed with King. R. L. Amos of Kentucky argued that Little Rock had brought disgrace and shame to the name of America: "America is receiving a black eye from the world as a result of the flaunting of the Constitution of the United States and the Supreme Court's decree on school integration."[56]

Another Kentucky pastor, C. N. King, turned the tables on the southern reactionaries by identifying their defiance of the Court with Communist subversion. "It is an open threat to overthrow the government of the land," he suggested. "Perhaps, and it could be possible, that behind...the leaders of the White Citizens' Councils may be Communist money. It is a certainty that by their divisive tactic and defiance of established courts, they are playing into the hands of Communism."[57]

Thus black Baptists were far from surprised by the events in Little Rock. They were accustomed both the intransigence of southern reactionaries and to the relative indifference of the president of the United States. Needless to say, however, the event had a much more significant effect on Southern Baptist.

Following the lead of white southern culture at large, the hardening of Southern Baptist reaction, well under way in 1956, accelerated significantly in the aftermath of Little Rock. The event heightened racial tensions and stiffened southern resistance to the encroachments of the federal government. A thoughtful Little Rock resident correctly noted that the city had become an emotional symbol of an impending attack on a sacred southern tradition. In addition, white southerners, he declared, interpreted the sending of federal troops as "a threat to [the South's] future and violation of its rights."[58] The reaction of the white South was, not surprisingly, a virtual call to arms.

Southern Baptist reaction followed suit. In May 1957, an organization known as Baptist Laymen of Alabama was created avowedly to

---

[55] Oates, *Let the Trumpet Sound*, 124.

[56] R. L. Amos, "Little Rock in a Big Role," *AmB 79* (October 25, 1957): 2

[57] C. N. King, "Wake Up, America!" *AmB 79* (November 15, 1957): 2.

[58] Robert R. Brown, *Bigger Than Little Rock* (Greenwich, Conn.: Seabury Press, 1958)< 129.

foster white supremacy and to fight "philosophies foreign to our beliefs as Christian white men." Numbering only about 160 members in nine Alabama counties, most of whom lived in the Montgomery area, the group nonetheless illustrated the ongoing hardening of racial attitudes.[59] The events in Little Rock built on this hardening foundation.

Southern Baptists essentially responded in three ways. Some tried to remain neutral, venturing only to repudiate the violence of the crisis. Such was the approach of the editor of the Georgia newspaper, who underscored that he was making no pronouncements on the background issues. "This," he assured his readers, "is a condemnation of mob violence; nothing more and nothing less."[60] Another response focused on a perceived abuse of federal authority. Leon Macon of Alabama noted the long-standing drift toward the centralization of government power. Greatly alarmed by that trend, he called the sending of federal troops an abhorrent sight. While stating his belief in law and order, he viewed the issue as one of "too much authority in the federal government."[61]

Two events in Little Rock itself illustrate a third, more reactionary, response. During the second weekend in October, citizens of that city were offered a choice of two prayer services for peace regarding the segregation issue. One was planned by the Little Rock Ministerial Association. An ecumenical affair, these services were to be held in various churches throughout the community and advised peaceful compliance with the desegregation order. The other, held at the Central Baptist Church, was planned by a group of segregationist ministers who were prepared to that the segregated status quo might be maintained. The latter meeting was attended by a higher percentage of church members, and its sponsors were delighted with the turnaway

---

[59] "Alabama Baptists Hit New Lay White Supremacy Group," *BR 80* (May 30, 1957): 1. Leaders in the Alabama Baptist State Convention criticized this group for using the word "Baptist" in their name, and stated that the organization was not an official agency of the Convention. While such actions implicitly criticized the purpose of the group, the Baptist leaders did not publicly criticize their racism. Interestingly, the article describing the group and the Baptist rejection of it did not appear in the *Alabama Baptist.*

[60] John J. Hurt, "It Can Happen Here," *CI 136* (October 3, 1957): 6.

[61] Leon Macon, "Time for Meditation," *AB 122* (October 3, 1957): 3.

crowd. By contrast, the ecumenical meetings, which attracted a much lower percentage of attendants, were a disappointment to their hosts.[62]

The second event was the Arkansas Missionary Baptist Association's adoption of a resolution underscoring God's preference for segregation and voicing its opposition to "any force within or without our country, whether Communistic, socialistic or other, which seeks to destroy our democratic and American way of life." [63]

Admittedly, these actions were not taken by leaders of Southern Baptist churches. Most knowledgeable interpreters of Southern Baptist life would agree, however, that the rank and file rarely distinguish between Southern and the more independent, fundamentalist type of Baptists. The cultural fundamentalism endemic to southern culture, as well as the strong fundamentalist strain within Southern Baptist life, make such distinctions difficult for the laity. They also suggest that the views of the Arkansas Missionary Baptist Association probably had strong influence on the views of Southern Baptist laity, as well as a good many of the clergy. Ernest Q. Campbell and Thomas F. Pettigrew have argued that the segregationist ministers "encouraged partially latent but very powerful sentiments present in every congregation in the city [of Little Rock]."[64] Thus, these ministers very likely represented Southern Baptist reactionary perspectives more closely than the more moderate Southern Baptist leadership.

The events in Little Rock, therefore, strengthened the hand of Southern Baptist reactionaries and created more vocal criticism of the denomination's integrationist impulse. The state conventions of Alabama and Louisiana passed resolutions explicitly endorsing segregation.[65] In Georgia, a strong contingent of Baptists pressed for a resolution arguing that segregated facilities were in the best interest of both races. That resolution was defeated, but only after intense

---

[62] Campbell and Pettigrew, *Christians in Racial Crisis*, 25-34. The segregationist group consisted mainly of Missionary Baptist ministers, but included one Southern Baptist, the Reverend Wesley Pruden, who was later elected president of the Capital Citizens Council.

[63] Ibid., 38-39.

[64] Ibid., 36-37.

[65] "Alabama Baptists Ask Continued Public School Segregation," *AB 122* (November 28, 1957): 4; "Race Question Gets Attention," *CI 136* (November 28, 1957): 3.

debate.[66] The prosegregation resolution was brought to the Convention by a layman from Camilla, Georgia. A vague statement by the Georgia Baptist Social Service Commission, which called for "fitting poise, dignity, and balance in these times of tension," had been adopted the previous day. Thus, the resolutions committee, essentially controlled by two pastors, recommended that the Con-vention not take further action. The incident again highlights the significant schism between the views of the Southern Baptist laity and much of the ministerial leadership. Also just before the Convention, the Colquitt County Baptist Association unanimously adopted a reso-lution "protest[ing] any invasion from any source," criticizing the political expediency of the Supreme Court and endorsing segregation as Christian. South Carolina Baptists withstood a strong effort to criticize the Southern Baptist Christian Life Commission for its pronouncements on the race issue.

Such actions by the state conventions suggested that three years of mobilization since *Brown* had strengthened the more reactionary elements within Southern Baptist life. The numbness of the immediate response to *Brown* had been transformed into the angry reaction to Little Rock. The events of 1954 and after, therefore, reawakened the southern loyalty latent within Southern Baptists' civil religion. For National Baptists, loyalty to the values of the American civil religion were heightened. Thus there arose two interpretations of desegregation within two contrasting sets of images of America.

Desegregation as Fulfilled Hope: A Black Response

As Leonard I. Sweet has noted, citizens black and white have long had a providential understanding of American history, with the United States viewed as playing a special role in the advancement of human-kind. Within the designs of Providence, however, black leaders often discovered a particular role for the black community—that of testing America's commitment to its avowed values of equality and freedom. This conception, notes Sweet, permeated the views of nineteenth-century black leaders. By comparing white ideals to black realities

---

[66] "Segregation Showdown Rejected," *CI 136* (November 21, 1957): 8. "Colquitt Takes Segregation Stand," *CI 136* (November 7, 1957): 16.

these intellectuals put the nation's loyalty to its values to the test.[67] Both the providential understanding of American history and the particular role of black America within that history were greatly revitalized during the 1950s. Together these elements hint that the growing black movement constituted a heightening of the American civil religion among southern blacks. As the focal point of that heightened civic fervor, desegregation was increasingly interpreted as the fulfillment of these blacks' hopes for America.

In describing the movement that began in Montgomery, Martin Luther King Jr. admitted that the people accepted nonviolence not primarily because they believed in it as a philosophy of life, but because they were convinced that it was a "simple expression of Christianity in action."[68] This suggests that the motivating force behind the incipient civil rights movement was black Christianity, rather than an explicitly civil religion. Civil religious attitudes and values, however, were at least implicit in King's theology and his appeal to his followers. He and the African American activist ministers of the SCLC used the exodus images of Christianity to inspire and galvanize the black masses in the civil rights struggle. King's use of civil religious themes not only inspired his own people, however. It also served important strategic uses with whites in power, as he sought to convince them that rather than being influenced by foreign subversion, the civil rights agenda was "deeply rooted in the American dream." Beyond that, judging from his images of America, King can easily be classified as a prophet of the American civil religion.

In March 1957, on returning from a trip to Africa, King assured his followers that his interest was not in any "Back to Africa" movement. Claiming that as American citizens blacks deserved their rights in the nation, King professed his faith in America: "I feel that God has marvelous plans for this world and this nation and we must have the faith to believe that one day these plans will materialize."[69]

King's rhetoric appealed to civil religious images not only because he spoke of God's purpose for America, but also because he preached of America's fulfilling its own purpose. By relating the growing black movement to the possibility of the nation's actualizing its meaning in

---

[67] Sweet, *Black Images of America*, 2-3, 161-63.

[68] King, *Stride toward Freedom*, 89.

[69] Quoted in Oates, *Let the Trumpet Sound*, 118.

the world, King specifically functioned as a prophet of civil religion. Thus he saw the movement as an attempt to call America back to its essential meaning. The black community would provide "a new expression of the American dream that need not be realized at the expense of other men around the world, but a dream of opportunity and life that can be shared with the rest of the world."[70]

Ralph Abernathy similarly reflected this understanding of the related roles of America and its black citizens. The Negro's role in America, he averred, was to demonstrate "that with whole and absolute freedom, he is, can be, and always will be a pillar of strength upon which America can lean to prove to the world that Democracy is a living, God-granted and God-guided actuality."[71] These views indicate the practice, common among leaders of the movement, of fusing images of the American civil religion with the call for civil rights.

King's attack on segregation expressed the most significant themes of the black religious tradition—the themes of the Exodus and deliverance from bondage. King often criticized southern segregationist "pharaohs" who employed legal maneuvers, economic reprisals, and physical violence as means of keeping blacks in the "Egypt of segregation." He also spoke frequently of the "promised land" of freedom and justice.[72]

These images, however, have never belonged exclusively to black Christianity in America. James H. Smylie has correctly argued that the Exodus motif has historically been quite influential on American culture at large. White Americans, he maintains, have understood themselves as a chosen people and interpreted America as a Zion in the wilderness. Further, the image of Israel's deliverance at the Red Sea was almost chosen by the federal constitutional convention as the scene to be engraved on the Great Seal of the United States. That King spoke in an idiom so meaningful to white Americans is, to Smylie, a

---

[70] King "A Testament of Hope," *Playboy*, January 1969, 234, quoted in Smith and Zepp, *Search for the Beloved Community*, 127.

[71] Ralph David Abernathy, "The Role of the Church and the Minister in Helping End Segregation" (Speech to the Greater Atlanta Council on Human Relations, July 22, 1963) 7-8. Manuscript on file in the SCLC Collection at the Martin Luther King Jr. Center for Nonviolent Social Change, Atlanta, Ga.

[72] Ansbro, *Martin Luther King Jr.* 278.

significant irony.[73] At the very least, however, King's use of these themes shows the close relation between civil religion and civil rights within the movement.

Thus the black Baptist leaders of the burgeoning civil rights movement spoke unanimously that their efforts were not subversive or un-American, but were rather in the best of the American tradition. Disavowing any Communist associations, Fred Shuttles-worth noted his usual response to that charge: "I'm too American black to be Russian red, and it didn't take a Communist to tell me how to read the Constitution....We didn't need anybody to tell us how to interpret the Constitution, we knew how to read and write. It didn't take Communism, or Russia, or anybody else to tell us what equality and freedom meant."[74] Echoing King's view, Ralph Abernathy interpreted the black movement as an extension of the American tradition: "Actually, we are experiencing the climax of the continuing social revolution in the United States which began with out Declaration of Independence and our war to throw off colonial rule.... The present revolution is an attempt to gain the rights guaranteed all citizens in this Declaration of Independence, the Constitution and the amendments to the Constitution. So the present struggle is in the best American tradition."[75]

Even Joseph H. Jackson argued that the movement arose from the civil tradition of the nation. In his 1956 statement "The Negro's Declaration of Intention," Jackson asserted that "with love for our nation, good will towards all, utter devotion to the Federal Constitution, and undying faith in God; we intend to continue our struggle for the complete victory of freedom on every front, and the preservation of the soul of the nation whatever the cost."[76] Within such a generally held perspective, black Baptists, not surprisingly, understood the idea of desegregation as a step toward actualizing their images of America.

---

[73] James H. Smylie, "On Jesus, Pharoahs, and the Chosen People," *Interpretation* 24 (January 1970): 74-75.

[74] Shuttlesworth, interview with author, March 10, 1984.

[75] "Accepting the Challenge of This Age," manuscript, 3, SCLC Collection, Martin Luther King Jr. Center for Nonviolent Social Change, Atlanta, Ga.

[76] *AmB 78* (April 20, 1956): 1.

Black Baptists agreed that America had been called to the high purpose of helping democratize the world by its example. By the mid1950s these southerners became convinced that the hour was crucial for America to deal with the question of racial justice and its failure to live in harmony with its democratic principles. Since the most significant impediment to the full democratization of the nation was the practice of Jim Crow, the concept of desegregation represented for blacks the crucial first step in fulfilling the American purpose.

Commenting on the practice of segregation, Nannie H. Burroughs, president of the National Baptist Women's Convention argued that efforts to "build a democracy out of race attitudes left over from slavery" would render America unable to realize its original dream.[77] Stating the problem more positively, King noted that "segregation and discrimination are strange paradoxes in a nation founded on the principle that all men are created equal." He further interpreted the issue of racial desegregation as a critical choice between democracy and fascism. In a passage replete with images of America's purpose and destiny, King enunciated his country's dilemma:

> History has thrust upon our generation an indescribably import-ant destiny—to complete a process of democratization which our nation has too long developed too slowly....The future of America is bound up with the solution of the present crisis. The shape of the world today does not permit the luxury of a faltering democracy. The United States cannot hope to attain the respect of the vital and growing colored nations of the world unless it remedies its racial problems at home. If America is to remain a first-class nation, it cannot have second-class citizenship.[78]

Joseph Jackson sounded a similar note, identifying racial segregation as the "last frontier" of democracy. For him it was a frontier that had to be conquered if democracy were to survive. He warned that "if this sacred cause is lot, we shall see the hallowed flag of this great Republic lowered to the dust of shame....[T]he battle to destroy

---

[77] Nannie H. Burroughs, president's address, Women's Convention Auxiliary to the National Baptist Convention, *Annual of the National Baptist Convention,* 1954, 411.

[78] *Stride toward Freedom,* 191, 196-97.

segregation and discrimination, and to give full and unrestricted freedom to every deserving person under the stars, is America's battle; and we are fighting today on this last frontier."[79] Thus, in spite of their significant differences, King and Jackson agreed that segregation was irreconcilable with the purpose of the nation and, conversely, that desegregation was a sign of the fulfillment of that purpose.

Another way black Baptists identified desegregation as the fulfillment of the American purpose was by equating it with "true Americanism." For one writer, the willingness to live with the integration of the races constituted the essence of Americanism. Said Kentucky editor William Ballew: "This thing of integration will mark the blessed and the cursed; it will distinguish the good citizen from the rebel; the American from the un-American."[80]

Thus, in the view of southern blacks, the segregationist mentality seriously misconceived America's meaning for the world. Black Baptists argued this in two related ways. Appropriately enough, they first appealed to the declaration of Independence. Frequently sounded by King and Abernathy, this note was heard from lesser known black Baptist leaders as well. Ballew argued that by limiting civil rights to their own race or class, many Americans had forgotten the meaning of the Declaration. Expounding that document, he noted that inalienable rights belong to citizens "in the same way that their arms and legs do," and underscored the universality of the phrase "all men." He posited that these elements marked the message of the Declaration of Independence and announced: "We want the world to know it. We want every nation to know that America is a country which lives by these Christian truths."[81]

Thus, to grant *all* citizens, including black Americans, their civil rights was for America to "live out the true meaning of its Creed." For black Baptists in the South, not surprisingly, this granting of their constitutional rights came to be symbolized, in the abolition of racial segregation. In appropriating the power of the Declaration of Independence, these preachers invoked the sanctity of the nation's

---

[79] "A Pleas to the White Citizens' Councils of the South," *Annual of the National Baptist Convention*, 1956, 50-51.

[80] "America's Challenge," *AmB 79* (April 19, 1957): 2.

[81] "The Declaration of Independence Something to Live By," *AmB 69* (June 27, 1947): 2.

"sacred document." By appealing to that particular document they reentered the "sacred time" that had given birth to America and its myth.[82] With varying degrees of self-consciousness, black preachers appealed to America's myth of origin and thus asserted: This is how our nation began. The values embedded in our "sacred document" define what we are as a people. Since those values are inconsistent with the practice of Jim Crow, desegregation fulfills the mythic meaning and the universal purpose of America.

Second, black Baptists also used the concept of American pluralism to argue that desegregation fulfilled the American purpose. Blacks' most basic image of America was of a melting pot composed of immigrants from every nation of the world. The pluralistic diversity of the world existed in microcosm in America. Moreover, the nation was called by God to be an exemplar nation, revealing to other nations how to live together in global community.

From this perspective, desegregation was naturally viewed as a further step toward the actualization of the hoped-for state in which America itself might come to terms with its pluralism. Only if its disparate ethnic groups were to learn to live in harmony could America fulfill its exemplary role in the divided world. Relating desegregation to the issue of pluralism, W. J. Hodge noted, "We live in a pluralistic society, and if people are ever to get any basic understanding of each other and have reasonably and creatively harmonious relationships, we just can't keep them apart. There has to be some way that people and children...can grow up together."[83] Fred Shuttlesworth stressed that America's living with its pluralism required the desegregation of the races. In his usual blunt manner, this Baptist firebrand took an uncompromising stand: "I say America either means integration or we might as well dismantle our concept [of America]. We might as well send the Germans back to Germany, and the Italians back to Italy, and everybody back where they came

---

[82] The concept of "sacred time" is common within the history of religion's approach to the study of religious experience, particularly in the work of Mircea Eliade. See especially *Patterns in Comparative Religion* (Cleveland: Meridian Books, 1963) and *Myth and Reality* (New York: Harper & Row, 1963). Among scholars of American religion, Catherine L. Albanese has used this approach most provocatively. See her *Sons of the Fathers: The Civil Religion of the American Revolution* (Philadelphia: Temple University Press, 1976).

[83] Hodge, interview with author, April 2, 1984.

from, and give the country back to the Indians. America means integration or it means nothing."[84]

Thus, in a nation falling far short of blacks' mythic images of its own pristine ideals, blacks understood desegregation as the fulfillment of their hopes for the country they loved. For them desegregation was no panacea; they understood that mere "de-segregation" alone could not actualize the America for which they hoped. In their understanding of the nation, in their civil religion desegregation functioned as a symbol of hope that America might fulfill its promise and they as black Americans might "overcome someday."

Desegregation as Disappointed Hope: A White Response

To some significant degree—what degree is still a debated point among southern historians—the central theme of southern history *has* been the South's desire to preserve itself as a white man's country. This is not to accuse that region of being intrinsically more racist than other sections of the nation. It is rather to argue that it has been more overtly racist because it has more directly and to a greater degree known the presence of black Americans. Further, the central events of southern history, the events that have largely determined the self-image of white southerners, have been related to that presence.

In light of such a historical experience, which has been the primary shaper of southerners' appropriation of the American civil religion, one could hardly expect the majority of white southerners to view desegregation as did their black counterparts. To average southern white, desegregation connoted a sense of dire threat, hence their highly defensive reactions to it. In, with, and under the threat of desegregation, however, was a symbol of hope for an America they feared would never be actualized. The civil religion of southern whites, as represented by Southern Baptists, tended generally to include desegregation as the symbol of a disappointed hope.

Having receded into relative hibernation since World War I, the southern civil religion was reawakened by the foreboding sounds of the *Brown* decision. The religion-like loyalty to Dixie that had been so much a part of southern culture in the aftermath of the Civil War and

---

[84] Shuttlesworth, interview with author, March 10, 1984.

Reconstruction came again to the fore. Whites' responses to the central events of the decade clearly expressed their religious loyalty to the South. The object of the southern civil religion was not, however, solely the South. The distinctiveness of the southern civil religion was the way in which southern loyalty combined with American loyalty. Such was the nature of the southern civil religion that was reborn in the mid-1950s.

That very old and very southern ideas were recycled was evident from some of the reaction to the Supreme Court's desegregation decision. In the *Richmond News*, editor James J. Kilpatrick retrieved the antebellum concept of interposition as the central means of opposing the Supreme Court's ruling. Similarly, using the language of the South's earlier conflict with the nation, Senator Harry F. Byrd of Virginia called the desegregation order "the most serious crisis that has occurred since the War Between the States."[85] Herman Talmadge, whose views were often quite attractive to Baptists in his state of Georgia, exhibited a renascent sectionalism in his reaction to a voter registration drive by the NAACP: "The die is cast. The challenge has been issued by the NAACP leaders. We must meet this challenge head-on or submit meekly and undergo a mid-Twentieth Century reconstruction period."[86]

James McBride Dabbs correctly noted that these reactions and the emotions tapped by the symbol of segregation were reminiscent of the sentiments of post-Civil War devotees of the Lost Cause. The reactions of these white southerners were emotionally connected to the Old South. In such an outlook, Dabbs believed, segregation "is the only thing we have left, the last beleaguered fortress of the Lost Cause. If we surrender it, who will remember what the Old South was?....We

---

[85] Both the Kilpatrick and Byrd reactions are cited in Bartley, *Rise of Massive Resistance*, 110. The doctrine of interposition originated with a combination of the political thought of Thomas Jefferson and John C. Calhoun, and, in its twentieth-century version, sought to "interpose" the sovereignty of the state between federal courts and local school boards. This concept held that in joining the federal union, the states had surrendered only those powers specifically listed in the Constitution. All other responsibilities, including public school policy, remained in the states' possession. See Bartley, who views this tactic as an obfuscation designed to "lift the debate from sectional racism to more defensible 'higher ground' of state sovereignty" (pp. 126-32.)

[86] Talmadge, *You and Segregation*, 25.

defend it, therefore, as patriots who love their native land, as pious men who will not deny their past."[87] These actions and reactions of "patriots" and "pious men" strongly suggest a renascent southern civil religion.

This emotional defense of the southern past, however, disclosed a southern public faith that fused southern with American symbols. The historical experience of the white South had thus created a hybrid civil religion composed of both the southern creed and the American creed. Campbell and Pettigrew have noted the white South's tendency to "'wrap itself in the Constitution,' when defending customs and interests in relations between the races."[88] Gunnar Myrdal agreed that even conservative southerners adhered ambivalently to the ideals of equality, justice, and fair opportunity: "The conservative southerner is not so certain as he sometimes sounds. He is a split personality. Part of his heart belongs to the American Creed."[89] The civil religious images of these southerners indeed reflected the ambivalence and the mixed symbolism of a renascent southern civil religion.

One evidence of a mixed symbolism regards the warm greetings southerners gave presidential candidate. Eisenhower on a campaign trip through the Deep South. Extremely popular (at least until the Little Rock debacle) because of his piety, his military experience, and his conservatism, Ike was welcomed by hundreds of thousands of people wherever he traveled. Leon Macon of Alabama noted that some had likened his popularity in the South to that of Robert E. Lee.[90] If, as Catherine Albanese has suggested, the person of George Washington became a symbolic *theos aner* (divine man) for Revolutionary Americans, for southerners that role could only be assumed by Lee. For any American figure to have compared favorably in the southern mythic mind with Lee is at least suggestive of a significant degree of symbol mixing.

Herman Talmadge similarly fused the patriotic symbols of southernness and Americanness. Protesting that America ought not be concerned about providing "grist for the Communist propaganda mill," the Georgia governor noted the heroic examples of George

---

[87] *Haunted By God*, 128-29.

[88] Campbell and Pettigrew, *Christians in Racial Crisis*, 57.

[89] Myrdal, *American Dilemma,* xliv, 461-62.

[90] "New Developments," *AB 117* (September 11, 1952): 3.

Washington, Thomas Jefferson, and Patrick Henry, who were quite unconcerned about the opinion of foreign powers. Further, admonishing his fellow southerners to fight to preserve the southern way of life, he appealed to the sacred memory of the saints of the American civil religion: "It will take courage...of the kind our forefathers showed when they signed the Declaration of Independence, the kind of courage they showed at Valley Forge,... at Gettysburg, and during the Reconstruction Era after the War Between the States."[91]

Viewing the possibility of perilous changes in the southern status quo, and desiring to maintain it, segregationists warned that only by preserving the southern way of life could the American way of life survive. Thus in terms that echoed the Cold War fervor of the Dulles State Department of the McCarthy crusade, these Baptists identified the integrationist impulse as Communist inspired. The well-known allegations concerning the Communist associations of Martin Luther King began in this period, as evidenced by a comment by Leon Macon. In what was perhaps a veiled reference to King during the Montgomery bus boycott, the Alabama editor wrote of the strong possibility that "the Communists are aggravating the [segregation] problem here in our own state."[92] Never hesitant about finding subversive influence in the black movement, circuit court judge Tom Brady warned his readers that "Communist Russia's aim is the establishment of a beachhead through the negro in these United States. To alienate racial groups against racial groups,...negro against white, is what Russia desires."[93] Thus, the perspective of reactionary Southern Baptists had a significant element of implicit Americanism within its explicit southernism.

Nevertheless, "Yankee hating," perhaps the *sine qua non* of the southern civil religion, remained a prominent component of the Southern Baptist reaction. A virulent southernism manifested itself in a great fear of things Northern. One writer accused those Baptists who had supported the Supreme Court decision of having lined up with the National Council of Churches and "the radicals of the North."

---

[91] Talmadge, *You and Segregation*, vi-vii, 76.
[92] "The Segregation Problems," *AB 121* (March 8, 1956): 3.
[93] Brady, *Black Monday*, 54.

Another opined that the southern racial disturbances "must be gratifying to many Northern politicians."[94]

In his 1956 speech before the South Carolina legislature, W. A. Criswell, one of the most influential Southern Baptist ministers of the twentieth century, violently articulated this enmity against Northerners. Those who criticized segregation he castigated as "good-for-nothing fellows who are trying to upset all of the things that we love as good old southern people....They are not our kind, I say. They don't know us and I'm glad. Let them stay where they are, wherever they are, but leave us alone."[95] He said, moreover, that "they are not our folks. They are not our kind. They are not our stripe. They don't belong to the same world in which we live."[96]

Such anti-Northern feeling, constant within the mind-set of southern whites, surfaced in the mid-1950s with an intensity unmatched since the Reconstruction. Beyond the criticisms of the North, however, was a manifestation that went to the heart of southern identity. Sociologist John Shelton Reed, perhaps the preeminent student of southern sectionalism, has closely associated that identity with a "sense of ill-treatment at the hands of the rest of the country."[97] The events of this period, particularly after those in Little Rock, created such a sense of grievance among a great many southerners.

At the November 1957 convention of Alabama Baptists, the Christian Life Commission report provided a salient example of the South's martyr complex. The report asserted that the recent events had aggravated the South's fear of arbitrary government. Accompanying this fear, however, was the plaintive cry of the persecuted South:

> Never in the history of the nation has a federal government by judicial decree attempted to enforce a law against the overwhelming and persistent opposition of the majority of the citizens of an area, as is being presently the case in the south. Then to add agony to pain the thoughtful Christian realizes that what is being

---

[94] T. J. Preston, "Baptists and Segregation," *CI 134* (January 6, 1955): 6; Finley Tinnin, "A Sane View on Segregation," *BM 73* (September 27, 1956): 3.

[95] Criswell, in Towns, *Social Conscience of W. A. Criswell*, 232.

[96] Ibid., 228.

[97] John Shelton Reed, *Southerners: The Social Psychology of Sectionalism* (Chapel Hill: University of North Carolina Press, 1983) 70.

called 'the law of the land' has never been passed by the lawmaking agency of the government.[98]

Thus, the Americanism and the southernism in the rhetoric of reactionary Southern Baptists suggest a strong reawakening of the southern civil religion. This civil religion fused its southern images with a robust Americanism. Closely reflecting the images of the "religion of the Lost Cause," this reprise also included significant southern hopes for America.

By formulating a vision of a homogeneously and evangelically Protestant American, the white South hoped to re-create the nation in its own image. Any recrudescent southern civil religion in the mid-twentieth century was obliged to sound the ancient rallying cry of the Lost Cause: "Save the South to save America."

Samuel S. Hill has correctly noted that southern churches, considered by many white southerners to be the purest in all Christendom, were deemed the universal ideal. Hill stated that since Reconstruction southern church leaders have compared southern religious life to that in other regions, always to find the southern pattern purer. Such assessments usually implied or asserted that "their brand [of Christianity] was the hope of the world."[99] Southern Baptist images of America and the South in this period revealed just this sort of triumphalism.

Alabama pastor A. L. Strozier applauded Southern Baptists as the strongest denomination in the South, which he viewed in turn as the "population seedbed for the entire nation." He argued that migration of southerners to other regions had helped keep urban populations stable. He stated that Southern Baptists were in a strategic position within God's purpose, warning, "The future of our denomi-nation, our nation, and perhaps the world depends on our stewardship of the gospel now.[100]

By making the South responsible for the nation's (and the world's) survival, these Baptists implied that America could be salvaged only if it became southernized. The likeness in which they would have re-fashioned America included the South's political or ideological

---

[98] *Annual of the Alabama Baptist State Convention,* 1957, 128-30.

[99] Hill, "The South's Two Cultures," 36 and 43.

[100] A. L. Strozier, "The Battle of the Giants," *AB 120* (July 14, 1955): 8 and 16.

attitudes, as well as its religious outlook. Senator James O. Eastland of Mississippi clearly sounded this note before Congress, asserting that the South had a vital role to perform in thwarting the Communist threat. "The future greatness of America," said Eastland, "depends on racial purity and maintenance of Anglo-Saxon institutions, which still flourish in full flower in the South."[101] Although the senator was a Methodist, his words found agreement among his Southern Baptist friends.

W. I. Pittman, of Birmingham, Alabama, saw the South and Southern Baptists as bulwarks against radicalism, whether Northern or foreign. He was convinced that other denominations envied Southern Baptists "simply because we have stoutly held the line against undemocratic and subversive influences."[102] Judge Tom Brady, though apprehensive about the infiltration of radical ideas into southern churches and denominational colleges, nonetheless averred that the southern churches were much less tainted with the blight of socialist revolution.[103] Extolling the South as the bastion of democracy, Judge Brady "exposed" a Soviet plot to subvert his beloved region. "The Communists of America," he alleged, "have been trying since 1936 to destroy the South. The bait which attracts them is the negro population. Hate campaigns against the southern States were conducted in the North. Abuse and falsehoods were flagrantly utilized. Counsel and advice were given the negro leaders.... It was and is being done on behalf of Communist Russia. If the South, the stronghold of democracy, could be destroyed, then the nation could be destroyed."[104]

To say, therefore, that Southern Baptist segregationists hoped for a homogeneous, evangelical America is another way of saying that they hoped for a southernized America. To their minds, America could survive only if the South remained an incorruptibly pure remnant within the nation. If, however, the issue went beyond survival to the question of their ideal hopes, those hopes could be fulfilled only if America became more like the South. Thus, if America were to be southernized, it would have to remain a segregated society.

---

[101] From the *Congressional Record*, 83d Cong., 2d sess., May 27, 1954, 7257, quoted by Bartley, *Rise of Massive Resistance*, 118-19.

[102] Pittman, "Brother Baraca," 4-5.

[103] Brady, *Black Monday*, 53, 60-61.

[104] Ibid., 60-61.

In this brand of civil religion, the concept of desegregation could serve only to symbolize the nonfulfillment of this image of America.

In his insightful analyses of southern religion and culture, Samuel S. Hill has noted "the tendency to identify 'American' as Anglo-Saxon" as a salient element of the southern way of life.[105] The accuracy of Hill's assertion is evidenced by the values reflected in a statement by Brady that "the loveliest and purest of God's creatures, the nearest thing to an angelic being that treads this terrestrial ball is a well-bred, cultured southern white woman or her blue-eyed, golden-haired little girl."[106]

The civil religion of these Southern Baptist segregationists, which would include a southernized image of America and a corresponding system of values, could never abide the threat of desegregation. The integration of the white and black races, even more than the possible onslaught of non-Protestant, non-English-speaking immigrants, symbolized in an ultimate way the nonfulfillment of their hopes for America.

More than entailing nonfulfillment, segregationists felt strongly that desegregation would completely destroy American culture and civilization.[107] This perspective began by branding the desegregation impulse of the civil rights movement as an alien ideology. These views surfaced fairly often in the Southern Baptist state newspapers, despite the editors' general efforts to maintain a mediating position. H. T. Sullivan considered the civil rights movement as synonymous with socialism, Communism, and the impending destruction of the social order. To him the proponents of desegregation were "exploiting a helpless race to advance their own selfish political purposes and to force socialism upon a free people. How can a loyal American sit... idly by while the 'Termites,' and the evil, filthy 'Vermin of Communism' eat up the foundation of the social order."[108]

Why did these Baptists make the connection between the desegregationist impulse and Communist subversion? Largely because they

---

[105] Hill, "The South's Two Cultures," 45.

[106] Brady, Black Monday, 45.

[107] See Billy Don Sherman, "Ideology of American Segregationism" (Th. D. diss., Southwestern Baptist Theological Seminary, 1967).

[108] H. T. Sullivan, "The Christian Concept of Race Relations," BM 74 (October 10, 1957): 1 and 4.

combined the cultural paranoia(s) of their context. As Americans living in the Cold War era, their ultimate threat was "international Communism." As southerners in close touch with their history and traditions, they viewed the ultimate threat as interracial marriage. Given the subliminal fearfulness that affected American culture during the 1950s, these southerners, not surprisingly, fused their fears into one great bogeyman.

Reactionary Baptists like Brady could thus argue that "the Communist leaders of this world are not fools. They know a mongrelized race is an ignorant, weak, and easily conquered race.[109] Consequently, the logic that began by warning of foreign subversion ended with unvarnished, not to say unreconstructed, racism. The destruction of American civilization would occur not directly because of a Soviet conquest. Rather, it would come because racial amalgamation world irreparably weaken the Anglo-Saxon race and thus render America incapable of staving off the Communist threat. History itself could prove the point. Brady began his racist diatribe with the theory that all the great civilizations of both Western and Eastern cultures had decayed because of intermingling with the black race. Marshalling his "evidence," Brady judged that the cultures of Egypt, India, Burma, Siam, Greece, Rome Spain, and Central America had all been destroyed by "negroid amalgamation."[110]

To southerners with such a system of values, and with such lily-white images of America, the concept of desegregation symbolized an absolute threat. The founder of the Citizens Councils, Robert Patterson, succinctly summed up this perspective: "We just felt like integration would utterly destroy everything that we valued."[111] Thus, in the views of reactionary Southern Baptists, desegregation would render impossible the fulfillment of their hopes for America.

---

[109] Brady, *Black Monday*, 67.
[110] Ibid., 1-6.
[111] Quoted in Martin, *Deep South Says "Never"*, 3.

Summary

The momentous events of the mid-1950s began a process that eventually changed the face of the South and all America. They also made unmistakable the divergent images of the nation that were available to the civil religious consumption of southerners, white or black. Given the general direction of the *Brown* decision, the Montgomery bus boycott, and the Little Rock affair, the concept of desegregation (or integration) became the fork in the road for southerners. Forced to put a moral evaluation on the issue of desegregation, black and white southerners increasingly parted company with one another.

In doing so, they found themselves hoping for the actualization of different Americas. Most black Baptists held the vision of a pluralistic society giving justice and equal opportunity to all its citizens and showing the entire world how to live together. Moreover, in their civil religious system, God had called America to this task and would judge the nation by its fidelity to its original values. For blacks this task represented America's religious meaning and purpose, indeed its *raison d'etre*. Desegregation for these southerners embodied the hope that they could finally be accepted into the melting pot. Only through the first step of desegregation could America come to terms with its pluralism and assume its exemplary role in the pluralism of the global village.

For the reactionary whites of the South, the images were of a much different nation. They hoped for a homogeneous, Protestant, Anglo-Saxon America that would defend individual liberty in the world. Increasingly forced to curtail their own liberty to segregate black southerners, they viewed desegregation as a religious symbol, a token that their hope for America would go unfulfilled. To these patriotic Americans—and no one would doubt their patriotism—desegregation became a symbol of the ultimate threat. The telling statement of Robert Patterson epitomizes their sense of foreboding: "Integration represents darkness, regimentation, totalitarianism, Communism, and destruction. Segregation represents the freedom to choose one's associates, Americanism, state sovereignty, and the survival of the white race. These two ideologies are now engaged in

mortal conflict and only one can survive....There is no middle ground."[112]

The South in the 1950s was thus a region neither simply given to displays of patriotic fervor and civil religion nor simply caught in the throes of racial conflict. It was rather a region divided by its civil religions or, perhaps more accurately, divided by greatly differing versions of the American civil religion. Desegregation became a religious symbol within these two civil faiths and crystallized the interaction between them. The hope and the specter of desegregation thus became the focal point of the South's conflict of civil religions.

---

[112] Quoted in Kelsey, *Racism and the Christian Understanding of Man,* 105.

4

THE SOUTH IN THE CIVIL RIGHTS ERA:
CONFLICT OF CIVIL FAITHS

For southerners in the civil rights era divergent images of America created correspondingly divergent views of desegregation. Had the events of the decade not forced the racial issue, these divergences might merely have continued to travel parallel paths. The announcement of *Brown v. Board of Education*, however, and the consequent "massive resistance" of the white South forced whites and blacks onto a symbolic collision course. In the course of very human and very controversial events, divergent images of America became civil religions in conflict. As a result, this clash of American public faiths turned the South of the civil rights era into the battleground of a civil religious holy war.

Focusing on the conflict of these two civil religions raises a number of questions relative to the way this clash affected southern society. How did southerners of both races respond to the choice between two starkly different visions of America? More basically, how did they respond to the fact of choice? And what changes did the fact of choice stimulate in the institutional framework of the South? Interpreting the civil rights era as a prelude for a civil religious holy war can at least suggest some possible answers.

In that decade, however, the black freedom struggle was still in its early stages of development. Violence had begun to break out, though not to the degree that would prevail during the 1960s. The violence that began in the 1950s at least partly grew out of the South's civil religious conflict. Religious violence often arises when one group persistently violates the sacredness of another group's system of meaning. With respect to the nation, civil religion serves as just such a system of meaning. Different perspectives between southern blacks and whites precipitated more than the mere breaking of social custom. They constituted virtual profanations of one another's sacred worlds. In other words, the civil religions of white and black Baptists violated the "sacred legitmations" of one another.

Civil Religion and Sacred Legitimation

John F. Wilson has noted the link between the sociological concept of civil religion and systems of meaning. Every collectivity possesses cultural materials that provide its sense of meaning. When these materials place the social system within a larger framework of meaning and seek to justify the national status quo, they function as a civil religion.[1] By connecting the concept of civil religion to that of meaning systems, Wilson hints at the legitimating function of civil religion. Legitimations are generally understood as explanations that give moral sanction to the prevailing social order. The sociological theories of Peter Berger and Thomas Luckmann, however, help elucidate the concept of legitimation more specifically.[2]

Berger has argued that every society imposes a framework of meaning on discreet human experiences. This framework of meaning is called a "symbolic universe" and encompasses the institutional order in a symbolic totality.[3] By fitting everything thought to be part of reality into this symbolic universe, a society explains and justifies that reality to its members. By supplying an ordered framework of meaning for "reality," the symbolic universe legitimates the institutional arrangements of the social order. Legitimation is thus the process of explaining and justifying that order.[4]

Berger also suggests that because of its ability to ground reality in sacredness, religion has historically been society's most potent legiti-

---

[1] Wilson, *Public Religion in American Culture,* 26-27.

[2] The theories upon which my analysis is based are found in two important works: Berger and Luckmann, *Social Construction of Reality,* and Berger, *Sacred Canopy.*

[3] *Social Construction of Reality,* 95. Berger also calls this framework of meaning the "nomos," by which he means a body of taken-for-granted knowledge that is shared by members of society. The nomos fits discreet human experiences into a meaningful order. See Berger, *Sacred Canopy,* 21-25.

[4] Berger and Luckmann, *Social Construction of Reality,* 93.

mating instrument.[5] By fitting social realities into a sacred cosmos, religious legitimations grant to human institutions a certain inevitability, because they "are understood as but manifestations of the underlying structure of the universe.... [T]hey are now grounded in a sacred time within which merely human history is but an episode. In a sense, then, they become immortal."[6]

Religious legitmations justify institutional roles as well as institutions. These roles become ways of participating in the symbolic universe that includes the institutional order. Specific ways of behaving are thus deemed normative because they are located within a cosmological and sacred framework of meaning. Of particular importance is the capacity of the symbolic universe to assign ranks in a hierarchy of being to various phenomena. Berger and Luckmann believe that different types of persons can be similarly ranked, such types often "defined as other than or less than human"[7]

This approach to the legitimation of social institutions and roles underscores societies' tendencies to speak of their arrangements in semidivine terms. Thus, when the social structure is explained in terms of a general framework of meaning, it comes to be seen as divinely sanctioned, sacred, and inviolable. Civil religion characteristically functions in this manner with regard to national reality, and during the civil rights era it legitimated the segregated status quo in the South. A significant difficulty developed, however, when another version of the civil religion, another symbolic universe that legitimated the destruction of segregation became available for southerners' consumption.

Popularly and insufficiently understood merely as differences between social groups, pluralism properly refers to the "division of a society into subsocieties with more or less distinct cultural traditions."[8] Sociologist Phillip E. Hammond believes that the concept is best discussed in terms of multiple belief systems. As a competition between idea systems, pluralism raises important questions regarding

---

[5] Berger, *Sacred Canopy*, 32, 35-36.

[6] Ibid., 37.

[7] *Social Construction of Reality*, 96-97, 102.

[8] James Davison Hunter, *American Evangelicalism: Conservative Religion and the Quandary of Modernity* (New Brunswick, N. J.: Rutgers University Press, 1983) 12.

legitimation. Hammond suggests that a plurality of meaning systems in a society jeopardizes its status as a society; it can virtually cease to be a society. What is more likely, however, is that the society will work toward a "new, more generalized, common meaning system."[9] Pluralism thus makes maintaining the legitimations of the social order much more difficult.

World maintenance becomes difficult when the symbolic universe itself becomes questioned. This can occur when a deviant version of the symbolic universe is shared by a sub-group within the society. This deviant version becomes a reality in its own right and "becomes the carrier of an alternative definition of reality."[10] Human beings need their beliefs about reality to be confirmed by other persons with the same beliefs. To be maintained indefinitely a meaning system thus requires a network of persons who share that particular system of meaning.[11] Berger calls these networks "plausibility structures." Pluralism multiplies the number of competing plausibility structures in a society. As a result, the original meaning system loses its taken-for-granted, objective status and is increasingly viewed as "rooted within the consciousness of the individual rather than any facticities of the external world."[12] Thus pluralism weakens the original plausibility structure because its symbolic universe, stripped of its objective and monopolistic character, has become more difficult to believe, or has become implausible. This is because it no longer seems "God-given"; instead it looks merely like one of many "man-made" belief systems.

Pluralism also removes the monopoly status of the religious system. As its most significant result, creates a market situation for the original religious tradition. In that situation the dominant definition of reality can no longer be authoritatively imposed. Instead, it must be marketed. Consequently, in a pluralistic milieu "religious

---

[9] Phillip E. Hammond, "Pluralism and Law in the Formation of American Civil Religion," in Bellah and Hammond, *Varieties of Civil Religion,* 142-44.

[10] Berger and Luckmann, *Social Construction of Reality,* 106-7.

[11] See Peter L. Berger, *The Heretical Imperative: Contemporary Possibilities of Religious Affirmation* (Garden City, N. Y.: Doubleday & Co., 1979) 18-19; McGuire, *Religion: The Social Context,* 30-33; and Berger, *Sacred Canopy,* 45-18.

[12] Berger, *Sacred Canopy,* 151-52.

traditions become consumer commodities" and the sub-societies that believe in them become "marketing agencies."[13]

The pluralization of meaning systems carries with it a fragmentation and a weakening of every system of belief and value. The modern situation, with its attendant pluralism, therefore creates a world of choice, and the "necessity of choosing reaches into areas of beliefs, values, and worldviews." This necessity is what Berger has termed "the heretical imperative."[14] During the civil rights era such an imperative was increasingly brought to bear on the South.

The fervency with which black and white Baptists disagreed on the question of desegregation suggests that sacred legitimations were being invoked on both sides. Moreover, only in the 1950s did the modern situation of pluralism begin to become a southern reality. Religious pluralism was a late development for the South. Samuel S. Hill has noted that the South was only forced to come to terms with religious pluralism during the 1960s, and then through "an abrupt and wrenching social revolution."[15] While the religious homogeneity of the South has been often overemphasized, scholars for some time now have been applying an important corrective, highlighting the South's religious diversity.[16] Nevertheless, while diversity marked the southern religious landscape before this period of incipient change, the perspectives of the diverse groups always remained very much minority views.

Beyond that, the preexisting religious diversities seldom took serious issue with the social order. Presenting a minority perspective on certain religious questions, they most often accepted the status quo. In the 1950s, however, this began to change. Writing in the mid-1960s, when the South's changes had become more fully developed, Hill aptly described the southern situation: "The South today is in crisis. For a surprisingly long time it was able to retain its accustomed ways, while

---

[13] Ibid., 138-39.

[14] *Heretical Imperative*, 19, 27-28. The term comes from the Greek verb *hairein*, "to choose." "Hairesis" originally meant the taking of a choice, with a heretic being one who picks and chooses from the authoritative religious tradition instead of accepting it as a whole.

[15] Hill, "Strange Career of Religious Pluralism," *Bulletin of the Center for the Study of Southern Culture and Religion* 4 (July 1980): 19.

[16] See David Edwin Harrell, ed., *Varieties of Southern Evangelicalism* (Macon, Ga.: Mercer University Press, 1981).

the world about it underwent radical change; now it finds itself beset
by ideas, social forces, and human groups which cannot be prevented
from altering regional folkways. This will doubtless be true of every
aspect... of life in the South, for the whole culture is experiencing the
dynamic impact of the revolution in progress." [17] Harbingers of
impending change appeared when a significant and indigenous group
within the society began to question the status quo from its peculiar
religious perspective and to legitimate social change on religious
grounds.

Southern blacks presented, in Berger's terms, a deviant definition
of reality. The black Baptists' divergent symbolic universe, when more
narrowly focused on national reality, created a version of the American civil religion that countered that of most whites. These civil religions held significantly different interpretations both of America's
calling and destiny as well as of the question of desegregation. The
dominant (white) definition of American reality obviously legitimated Jim Crow, while the deviant (black) version legitimated social
change.

The presence of an alternative and threatening definition of reality, supported by a large and increasingly militant group of believers
(a plausibility structure), shook the foundations of southern society.
In response southern society began to grope toward a new, more
generalized, system of meaning that included blacks. This new system
of meaning, which still has not yet become taken-for-granted reality
in the contemporary South, began to be constructed as southern
society began to adjust to a new racial situation. More pertinent to
this study, it developed out of these two civil religions and their
conflicting sets of sacred legitimations.

Dixie's Sacred Legitimations

The American South has made defending its social order and its world
view a long-standing historical tradition. Most often, southern clergy
have been the staunchest and most effective defenders of the southern
status quo. From Richard Furman's defense of slavery and the Lost
Cause evangelism of J. William Jones to the midcentury segregation-

---

[17] Samuel S. Hill, Jr., *Southern Churches in Crisis* (New York: Holt, Rinehart
and Winston, 1966) xi.

ists, preachers have sought to give divine sanction to the southern social order and maintain its socially constructed world.

One scholar has described southern religion's role in world maintenance by focusing on the preaching of southern preachers from 1830 to 1900. V. P. Loefflath-Ehly specifically used the theories of Berger and Luckmann to analyze the relation between religion and culture in the South. He noted that the church has been the institution chiefly responsible for preserving a society's symbolic universe. Functioning in the role of what Berger and Luckmann called "universal experts," preachers have often claimed "expertise in the ultimate definitions of reality." Thus, says Loefflath-Ehly, as expressing southern sermons, "the southern symbolic universe...was held together by the keystone of 'God is on our side.'"[18]

Such a perspective is the quintessential religious legitimation, and its use by southern clergy continued into the crisis of the Second Reconstruction. As in most wars, holy or otherwise, both sides claimed the favor of God. Beyond this, both groups of civil religionists found divine sanction for their views and actions. Black Baptists legitimated social change, while their white counterparts legitimated the Jim Crow social order.

Reactionary southern whites rejected segregation partly because it violated their sense of sacredness. Conversely, they attempted to justify that social arrangement by grounding it in sacred reality. Specifically, they legitimated segregation by appealing both to the American civil tradition, indirectly interpreted as sacred because of America's chosen status before God, and to the more direct sacredness of the law of God. This dual source of sacred legitimation is illustrated by the initial clauses of what Ernest Campbell and Thomas Pettigrew have called the "creed of segregation":

Americans should establish their own racial policies based on God's Will. It should not be determined by the African, Russian, or Asiatic peoples nor by their reactions to it.

---

[18] Victor Paul Loefflath-Ehly, "Religion As the Principal Component of World-Maintenance in the American South from the 1830s to 1900 with Special Emphasis on the Clergy and Their Sermons: A Case Study in the Dialectic of Religion and Culture" (Ph.D. diss., Florida State University, 1978) 31 and 153. See also Berger and Luckmann, Social Construction of Reality, 117.

Forced...racial desegregation is un-Constitutional since it violates traditional American freedoms of self-determination and local autonomy.

Racial integration cannot be American since segregation is pleasing to the Lord and America is a Christian nation.[19]

Both the southern preacher and politician appropriated this fusion of civil and religious legitimations. From the civic direction, integration was rejected because its enforcement violated the sacred tenet of states' rights. Herman Talmadge argued that the United States Constitution formulated the "American concept of a national government with limited powers." He asserted that only by preserving the rights of the states could the rights of the people be defended.[20]

Alabama Baptists agreed with the Georgia governor, fearing what they viewed as the excessively centralized power of the federal government. After the Little Rock incident, the Christian Life Commission report to the 1957 Alabama Baptist State Convention declared, "Historically Christians... have never fared so well when all government was concentrated into one excessive central power.... Currently there are portents which may indicate the gradual end of state government as a full partner within the American system. More and more power is being assumed by the central government in Washington. Less and less is being retained by the sovereign governments of the forty-eight states."[21] To be sure, these rationales may have been merely efforts to obscure the real issue of racism, but they did indicate that southern whites defended segregation by underscoring its legitimacy within the American constitutional tradition. In this instance, the tradition of states' rights served as the bulwark of another sacred legitimator of segregation, individual freedom.

Alabama pastor John H. Buchanan described America as a "noble experiment" to create a government that would protect the individual's rights to pursue liberty, prosperity, and happiness. He exulted that in the God-blessed land of America "the individual can come to his finest fruition when he is left free, untrammeled, unregimented,

---

[19] Campbell and Pettigrew, *Christians in Racial Crisis*, 60.

[20] Talmadge, *You and Segregation*, 13.

[21] *Annual of the Alabama Baptist State Convention*, 1957, 129.

uncontrolled by the statism that held mankind in partial slavery for six thousand years."[22]

W. A. Criswell tied segregation more specifically to the American right to choose. For him the right to segregate in the rearing or religious training of children represented the essence of America. "That's America," he preached. "That's freedom. That's a spiritual democracy." The glory of a democratic society was the right to choose one's friends, companions, and mates.[23] Thus the Dallas pastor raised the question of the (inter)marriage of southern daughters. Noting his concern for his own daughter, Criswell concluded his South Carolina speech with this plea: "Don't force me by law, by statute, by Supreme Court decision,... don't force me to cross over in those *intimate things* where I don't want to go.... Let me have my friends. Let me have my home. Let me have my family. And what you give to me, give to every man in America and keep it like our glorious forefathers made it—a land of the free and the home of the brave."[24]

The traditions of states' rights and individual freedom were, therefore, the civil instruments by which southern reactionaries legitimated the prevailing order. Segregation violated these derivatively "sacred" traditions, for to these southerners God had chosen America and had thus sanctioned its constitutional arrangements. Thus the "creed of segregation" can be understood by the following syllogism:

> Major premise: Segregation is pleasing to the Lord.
> Minor premise: America is a Christian nation.
> Conclusion: Racial integration cannot be American.

Legitimating Jim Crow by grounding it in the "traditional American freedoms," the segregationists justified Jim Crow largely in terms of their minor premise. As such, they invested it with an indirect sacredness borrowed from the essential sacredness of the entire "American experiment." Criswell's worries about "those intimate things," however, moved the argument toward the issue of interracial

---

[22] John H. Buchanan, "America at the Crossroads," *AB 117* (June 5, 1952): 4.

[23] W. A. Criswell, "Segregation in Society," in Towns, *Social Conscience of W. A. Criswell*, 228-30.

[24] Ibid., 234.

marriage and the segregationist's major premise. In so doing, they advanced a more direct religious legitimation of the status quo.

Southern segregationists consistently charged that the integrationist impulse sought the goal of intermingling and intermarriage between the races. Talmadge considered this the ultimate objective of the efforts of the NAACP, citing as evidence the Supreme Court's rulings against miscegenation in California and Virginia. Moreover, he viewed the marriage of NAACP president Walter White to a white woman as a further indication of that organization's plans. The governor interpreted the Supreme Court rulings as actions of the NAACP because those cases were handled by lawyers of the organization. By contrast, black leaders consistently denied that inter-marriage was a significant part of their civil rights efforts. King and Shuttlesworth often said that the black man wanted to be the white man's brother, not his brother-in-law. The president of Mississippi's black Baptists, H. H. Humes, added: "There are some white citizens in Mississippi who are preaching that the Negro is seeking integration, inter-marriage and social intermingling, which is not true. And those who are preaching this kind of propaganda know this isn't true.... The Negro is not fighting the separation of the races, but he is dissatisfied with discrimination." [25]

Responding to what they saw as an effort toward intermarriage, reactionary southern whites believed "that any biological mixture of a superior and an inferior race is certain to downgrade American culture." Consequently, they legitimated their views with both the civil tradition and explicitly religious language.[26] The Citizens Councils interpreted themselves as the South's answer to the "mongrelizers." Stating their pride in their white heritage in the pamphlet bearing their organization's name, they legitimated segregation by appealing to America's civil saints: "If we are bigoted, prejudiced, un-American, etc., so were George Washington, Thomas Jefferson, Abraham Lincoln, and other illustrious forebears who believed in segregation. We choose the old paths of our founding fathers and refuse to appease anyone."[27] Similarly, Tom Brady challenged the enemy: "We have,

---

[25] Talmadge, *You and Segregation*, 42-43. See also "The Voices of a New Day," *National Baptist Voice 32* (August 1, 1949): 7.

[26] Quoted in Sherman, "Ideology of American Segregationism," 87.

[27] Quoted in Carter, *The South Strikes Back*, 43.

through our forefathers, died before for our sacred principles. We can, if necessary, die again. You shall not show us how a white man 'may go through the guts' of a negro. You shall not mongrelize our children and grandchildren."[28]

The taboo against interracial marriage was thus identified with sacred principles from the civil tradition and suggested as implicitly religious legitimation. Many southern preachers were willing to make that sanction explicit, however. In a radio message to blacks, the Reverend Bob Jones Jr. advised them to be thankful they were in America where "you have your own schools and your own churches and your own liberties and your rights, with certain restrictions that God Almighty put about you-restrictions that are in line with the Word of God."[29] For the recalcitrant, he added, "If you are against segregation and against racial separation, then you are against God Almighty because He made racial separation."[30]

Many, if not most, Southern Baptists agreed. An Alabama layman pressed an argument denying that God had given blacks the same rights as whites. He stated that if God had given blacks "the inalienable right to social equality and intermarriage," then logic dictated that God had also granted them the right to destroy the white race. He condemned those who sought "a mongrel America," and concluded that "there is nothing unamerican and unchristian in racial segregation. God expects us to preserve the color line. It is high time we Baptists concern ourselves about his business in that respect."[31]

A full-fledged and highly representative legitimation of the Jim Crow system was presented by a pastor in Dallas, Texas. On the Sunday morning after the *Brown* decision, the Reverend Carey Daniel, minister of the First Baptist Church of West Dallas, preached a sermon entitled "God the Original Segregationist." The son of

---

[28] Brady, *Black Monday*, 89.

[29] Quoted in Robert Sherrill, *Gothic Politics in the Deep South* (New York: Grossman Publishers, 1968) 227. While Jones was not a Southern Baptist, there is little question that his brand of independent Baptist fundamentalism was and continues to be influential upon rank-and-file Southern Baptists. Indeed, like-minded Southern Baptists were easy to find.

[30] Ibid.

[31] Horace C. Wilkinson, "This Matter of Segregation," *AB 113* (February 5, 1948): 8.

Southern Baptist missionaries and a graduate of Baylor University and Southwestern Seminary, Daniel used the traditional southern argument for segregation, tracing God's segregation of the races to the divisions between Noah's sons after the Flood. His proof text? Gen. 10:32: "These are the families of the sons of Noah...in their nations: and by these were the nations divided in earth after the flood."[32]

Daniel also appealed to a popular text from the New Testament. Acts 17:26 also proved that God was a segregationist: "And [God] hath made of one blood all nations of men for to dwell on all the face of the earth, and hath determined the times before appointed, and the bounds of their habitation." Since, said Daniel, "the Bible word for race is always 'nation,'" the preacher's segregationist sermon was certainly based on solid, authoritative ground: God himself had segregated the nations, i.e., races.[33] If this authority were not sufficient, Daniel added that all the central custodians of his hearers' sacred tradition—Abraham, Moses, Nehemiah, Habakkuk, Jesus, and Paul—had been segregationists.[34]

A symbolic universe includes all of a society's "knowledge." Its taken-for-granted character dictates that when the keepers of the status quo appeal to it for legitimation, they rarely do so consciously or describe it *in toto*. Consequently, the defenders of Jim Crow did not articulate every element to their symbolic universe. They merely justified the social arrangement currently under attack by grounding it in what they understood as ultimate reality. By interpreting segregation as the work and will of God—understood in biblicist, fundamentalist terms—they related their humanly constructed reality to universal and sacred reality.

Southern segregationists viewed the Jim Crow system, appropriately placed within their universal and sacred framework of meaning, as inviolable. The difficulty arose, however, when another group of southerners began more vigorously to challenge this order

---

[32] The full text of the sermon is found in Holland, *Sermons in American History*, 513-22. For an analysis of what has been called "the Ham myth," a study using an approach similar to this chapter, see Thomas Virgil Peterson, *Ham and Japeth: The Mythic World of Whites in the Antebellum South* (Metuchen N. J.: Scarecrow Press, 1978).

[33] Ibid., 513.

[34] Ibid., 515-19.

with a conflicting definition of reality and its own particular legitimations.

Southern blacks' legitimations corresponded to those of southern whites in at least one respect. They were grounded in both the American tradition and a more explicitly religious perspective. Both sides of the civil religious conflict claimed both the derivative sacredness of the American heritage and the direct sacredness of "God's work in the world." Invoking both these types of legitimations, National Baptists justified their challenge of the southern status quo by claiming God's participation in it. Specifically, they expressed their legitimations in three lines of reasoning.

The first and most obvious appeal was to the sacred American perspective of equality as a God-given and inalienable right. Throughout the 1950s and into the civil rights struggle of the 1960s, blacks pointed to this American tradition as the justification for their criticism of Jim Crow. For them there was no question that that system was irreconcilable with the nation's sacred purpose.

In 1950 J. Pius Barbour, editor of the *National Baptist Voice*, printed a front-page editorial, "The Death Knell of Liberalism," which included an appeal to the sacred value of equality. America, the author asserted, had been created as an "innovation in the history of nations," as a nation whose government's first principle was "to protect [the citizens] from invasion of their *God-endowed* rights" (emphasis mine). The God-granted quality of American's rights was underscored by a lengthy quotation from Alexander Hamilton: "The Sacred rights of mankind... are written... by the hand of the Divinity itself, and can never be erased or obscured by mortal power. That is what is called the law of nature, which, being co-equal with mankind, and dictated by God himself, is, of course, superior in obligations to any other. It is binding over all the globe, in all countries, and at all times. No human laws are of any validity, if contrary to this."[35]

This theme literally pervaded the movement for civil rights, as any hearer of King's "I Have a Dream" speech could testify. King was not alone in this approach, however. Indeed, almost all black preachers, from the bona fide activists like King, Abernathy, and Shuttles-

---

[35] "The Death Knell of Liberalism," *NBV 32* (June 15, 1950): 1. This editorial was borrowed from John W. Bradbury, *Watchman-Examiner 38* (May 29, 1950): 660-61.

worth to the less prominent ministers who wrote for the black Baptist newspapers, almost all black preachers cited the tradition of the Declaration of Independence: "We hold these truths to be self-evident, that all men are created equal, that they are endowed by their Creator with certain inalienable Rights, that among these are Life, Liberty, and the pursuit of Happiness." Here then was a line of reasoning that adduced legitimations mainly from the American civil tradition.

A second argument arose from a more "sectarian," less deistic, African American theological perspective, which found God himself at work in the black freedom movement. The activist-preachers believed that God had chosen the black people as his special instruments in America. Ralph Abernathy testified to this particular sense of chosenness: "We felt God had chosen black people to save the soul of America, and to do it through nonviolence....We had to be the teachers of America and straighten America out."[36] King also saw a special place for blacks in enabling the nation to achieve moral maturity. "Let us therefore not think of our movement as one that seeks to integrate the Negro into all the existing values of American society," he wrote. "Let us be those creative dissenters who will call our beloved nation to a higher destiny, to a new plateau of compassion, to a more noble expression of humaneness."[37]

Perhaps the clearest expression of these Baptists' sense of calling was their tendency to describe the goals of their movement in millennial terms. Challenging an audience to press for passage of the 1964 civil rights bill, Abernathy said, "I call upon...men and women, boys and girls of all faiths and religions to join forces and rid our nation of the evil system of segregation, discrimination, racial injustice and human inequality. If we will accept the challenge, then 'every valley will be exalted'...and not only will black and white people live together, but 'the lion will lie down with the lamb'...and men will 'study war no more.'"[38] By relating the struggle to three biblical passages (Isa. 40:4, 11:6, and 2:4) commonly classified by scholars as messianic,

---

[36] Abernathy, interview with author, March 21, 1984.

[37] Martin Luther King Jr. *Where Do We Go from Here: Chaos or Community?* (New York: Harper & Row, 1967) 133.

[38] Abernathy, "Accepting the Challenge of This Age," manuscript, 6, SCLC Collection, Martin Luther King Jr. Center for Nonviolent Social Change, Atlanta, Ga.

Abernathy figuratively associated the attainment of civil rights with the advent of an earthly golden age of justice.

Given their sense that God had issued them a specific millennial call, blacks' tendency to interpret their struggle as a movement of Providence is no surprise. William H. Ballew admonished his readers that liberating the underprivileged of the world necessitated that America's own house be put in order. Believing this process to be well under way, he confessed, "We are persuaded that what is happening in America and abroad is neither an accident nor a mere incident, but the ripening and fruition of Divine Providence."[39] From such a vantage point, Ballew implicitly appealed to what has been called "the Gamaliel argument": "If God is in it, you better not fight it!" Fighting against desegregation was to fight against the inevitable. "There is a rising tide of fellow feeling and brotherly love, in the thinking of Christian America,... and despite the clannish concepts of rebel fossils, the evils that have been thrust upon minority groups... shall vanish, and we shall be seen as people, created by God with free and equal rights to live and enjoy the blessings of God's world."[40]

For black Baptists, the events of the black movement proved God's participation in their struggle. An event near the end of the Montgomery bus boycott serves as an example of their faith. In November 1956, Montgomery attorneys asked a local judge to issue an injunction against the car pool that enabled the city's blacks to boycott the buses. They claimed the pool was a "public nuisance" and "a private enterprise" operating without a franchise. If successful, the ploy would effectively have ended the boycott, and King feared the worst.

In court on November 13, King recalled, "The clock said it was noon, but it was midnight in my soul." But at the midday recess, an Associated Press reporter rushed into the courtroom with a news release stating that the Supreme Court had ruled unconstitutional Alabama's state and local laws segregating the buses. In the elated commotion of the courtroom, a pious bystander shouted, "God Almighty has spoken from Washington, D.C.!!"[41] Black Baptists thus

---

[39] William H. Ballew, "A Sane Approach," *AmB* 76 (July 2, 1954): 2.

[40] William H. Ballew, "Self-Distruction" [sic], *AmB* 77 (December 9, 1955): 2.

[41] Oates, *Let the Trumpet Sound*, 102-3.

saw God himself as an active participant in their struggle for civil rights.

Black legitimations of their movement for social change, and consequently of their view of desegregation, leaned heavily on identifying God and/or Providence with their struggle. So insistent were black Baptist convictions of God's favor that they hardly needed to make direct scriptural legitimations of integration. When they bothered to do so, however, they ironically appealed to the same New Testament passage as the segregationists, Acts 17:26. William Ballew chided Southern Baptists after "black Monday," noting that "it is upon them that the responsibility rests, to be first to put into practice the unmistakable teaching...that 'out of one blood, God made all nations to dwell upon the face of the earth.'"[42]

Hence, both groups of southerners sought to legitimate their views of segregation by investing them with a sense of sacredness. White reactionaries divinized the status quo, while black activists sanctioned a challenge to the social order. These conflicting sets of legitimations helped shape the character of the South during the 1950s.

The 1950s: Prelude to Holy War

Perhaps the classic biblical proof text for the ideology of holy war is Deuteronomy 3:22: "You shall not fear them; for it is the Lord your God who fights for you." The latter clause of this text articulates the primary defining characteristic of a holy war—the conviction and the claim that "God is on our side." Perhaps the former clause enunciates a corollary that since God is on their side, the combatants respond with such fanatical devotion that they fear no enemy. If these are the traits of holy war, the Baptists of the South, both black and white, served as the war's worthy combatants. A significant question arises, however: Was this a holy war of civil religions?

Contemporary culture often assumes that wars of religion have been relegated to a close-minded and primitive past. Loefflath-Ehly correctly questions this view, asserting "that the necessity of world maintenance and the growth of conflicting reality definitions have

---

[42] William H. Ballew, "Southern Baptists Endorse Desegregation," *AmB* 76 (June 11, 1954): 2.

been and remain matters of life and death."[43] Inasmuch as civil religion is a definition of reality relative to the nation, the situation of the South during the 1950s can readily be interpreted as a holy war of civil religions.

Sydney E. Ahlstrom wrote that civil religion is more deeply felt "if nourished by a rich culture and a long tradition, and still more deeply if threatened by enemies, in which case a resort to violence or war may ensue."[44] All three of these conditions obtained in the South of the 1950s. The historical experience, culture, and tradition in the South, affecting in divergent ways both white and black communities, nurtured the kinds of images that in this study have been described as civil religions.

Beyond this, a sense of conflict and of threat developed between these two sets of images. White images of America were severely threatened by the images of black southerners, and more so by the assertiveness with which they were articulated. Thus, both groups of Baptists evidenced this conflict. The drawing of the battle lines by the Citizens Councils indicates as much, as articulated in Robert Patterson's war cry: "These two ideologies are now engaged in mortal conflict and only one can survive.... There is no middle ground."[45] As Robert Sherrill suggested, one reason why the problems that confronted the South in the civil rights era constituted a Second Reconstruction "is that these southerners are not just aging a political and economic war against change, but [are fighting] a religious war."[46]

Similar perspectives were found also among southern blacks, as evidenced by Martin Luther King Sr., when he wrote of the racial situation of the late 1940s: "Not only my sons were going to be needed in an ongoing, ever difficult, battle but the sons of everybody in this nation who wanted to see America grow beyond what it had become....A Civil War that had never really ended would now be fought on several fronts: moral, legal, social, and political."[47] Perhaps the war

---

[43] Loefflath-Ehly, "Principal Component of World-Maintenance," 103.

[44] Sydney E. Ahlstrom, "Civil Religion," in *Eerdmans' Handbook to Christianity in America*, ed. Mark A. Noll et al. (Grand Rapids, Mich.: William B. Eerdmans Publishing Co., 1983) 434.

[45] Quoted in Kelsey, *Social Ethics among Southern Baptists*, 105.

[46] *Gothic Politics*, 217.

[47] King, *Daddy King*, 129.

King described was fought on the civil religious front as well. Clearly, southerners white and black were prepared to "go to war" to defend or propagate their images of America.

The civil religious character of this conflict may be most clearly seen in comparison with a contemporary parallel. Sociologist Meredith B. McGuire has discussed the strife between Protestants and Catholics in Northern Ireland as a conflict of civil religions. Her provocative analysis argues that the theological differences between these groups are but a small part of the struggle. Different perceptions of the nation identity (or images of the nation) constitute the chief division. These opposing visions of the nation were shaped by the peculiar histories and cultural differences between the two factions. Thus, says McGuire, "the history of 'our nation' is remembered differently by the two groups. Events centuries past are the basis for two completely opposing sets of myths, legends, and heroes."[48]

These sets of myths also include different symbols. Each group has its own flag, language, and songs. In addition, both national identities carry a highly religious nature, complete with the imagery of chosenness and a strong sense of "us" versus "them."[49]

Every component that McGuire suggests as an indicator of a civil religious struggle in contemporary Northern Ireland has a strong parallel with two civil religions in the mid-twentieth-century South. Both groups in the South, white and black, had different histories and cultural traits, all of which helped shape their distinct religious understandings of America. Each group had its own flag, "language" (in a sense of dialect and terminology), songs, and heroes. Finally, both groups used the language of a "chosen people," as well as the us-them polarity.

For these reasons, this conflict can appropriately be viewed as civil religious in nature. Thus, during the early years of the black revolution in America and the South, the civil religions of Southern and National Baptists clashed. These Baptists' images of America, their hopes for America, the symbolic meanings they attached to desegregation, and the sacred legitimations by which they supported those meanings all opposed each other with great intensity. By the 1960s the

---

[48] McGuire, *Religion: The Social Context,* 171.
[49] Ibid., 168-78.

conflict would express itself in violence. In the 1950s, however, the conflict was a prelude to holy war.

The divergent sacred legitimations of blacks and whites in the midcentury South created a pluralism of symbolic universes. The previously dominant segregationist definition of reality was increasingly challenged by the change-oriented perceptions of the black community. Despite accusations that the trouble stemmed from "outside agitators," the indigenous, southern character of the challengers weakened the plausibility structure of the reactionary civil region.

As a result, the rise of black assertiveness created a subgroup within southern society that defined national reality in a manner different from the dominant view. In addition, by justifying their views of America and desegregation with legitimations just as sacred as those of their opposition, blacks de-objectified the status quo. Consequently, the black civil religion made the reactionary view seem less inevitable and thus more difficult to believe.

The results of this encounter of symbolic universes were twofold, with one set of results for the combatants at the poles of the conflict and another for the "bystanders" in between. As to the combatants, inasmuch as the reactionary proponents of segregation attempted to defend an increasingly precarious status quo, the results quite naturally affected them more than their black opponents

Some scholars have associated civil religion with the concept of ideology because of its efforts to explain, legitimate, and unify the nation.[50] Assuming this association, one can fairly argue that the civil religion of white reactionaries was often expressed in ideological pronouncements. Anthropologist Clifford Geertz has argued that such pronouncements fit a context of "socio-psychological disequilibrium" and represent a kind of flight from social anxiety. Geertz believes such flight begins with social friction that creates a "chronic malintegration of society." In such a context, the standard defenses (legitimations) of the society become impotent to provide security for the members of the society. Ideological pronouncements thus "provide a 'symbolic outlet' for emotional disturbances generated by social disequilibrium."[51]

---

[50] Christenson and Wimberley, "Who is Civil Religious?" 82.

[51] Clifford Geertz, "Ideology as a Cultural System," in Geertz's *Interpretation of Cultures*, 201-4.

Ideology alleviates such emotional disturbances chiefly by providing what Geertz calls "cathartic explanations" of the social strain. This instrument is another name for the scapegoat theory, by which sociopsychological pain is eased by providing "legitimate objects of hostility." Needless to say, white reactionaries responded to social strain by focusing on the "enemies," which included both black activist-preachers and "outside agitators." Further, the cathartic explanations of white southerners contributed to a wider "solidarity explanation," which powerfully knitted reactionary whites together as a social class. Thus, Geertz himself suggests that "the South would not be The South without the existence of popular symbols charged with the emotions of a pervasive social predicament."[52]

Geertz's theory elucidates the social situation in the South of the 1950s. When one adds to this the powerful threat of sacred legitimations that were being challenged, the violence of the next decade is more easily explained. To be sure, the violence was in great part attributable simply to virulent racism. But the unrepentant—and, to the reactionaries, justifiable—violence might also be explained as a reaction to the profaning of the reactionaries' sense of sacredness. As earlier noted, these combatants feared no enemy because the Lord fought with them. Thus, they engaged in "holy war" in an attempt, in Peter Berger's words, "to kill off or quarantine the deviant world."[53]

Conversely, the tenacity with which blacks pressed their claims was supported by their civil religious images of America and their sacred legitimations of desegregation. Their near-fanaticism about actualizing their hopes for the nation constituted a kind of "violence." The rank and file of the black movement were constantly tempted to resort to literal violence and, had their leaders not committed the movement to nonviolence, they would likely have succumbed to the temptation more often than they occasionally did. Thus legitimating their respective symbolic universes with divine sanction, these groups engaged each other in a "violent" holy war of civil religions.

This civil religious conflict also affected the bystanders caught between what most white southerners saw as the two extremes. While the Citizens Council or Klan mentality had an influence on southern whites in general, and on Southern Baptists in particular, most were

---

[52] Ibid., 204-5.
[53] Berger, *Sacred Canopy*, 49.

not members and rejected the violence they advocated. But neither did
the majority support the views of the upstart ("uppity") black
ministers. If, as Gunnar Myrdal suggested, white southerners were
ambivalently committed to both the American creed and to segregation, they can be seen as caught between both civil religions.

In Berger's terms, these bystanders were presented with two distinct definitions of American reality. The pluralism of their symbolic
universes created for them a market situation that made choosing an
imperative. Before them stood the options of believing in the America
of the Citizens Councils or the America of the NAACP. Caught
between both these civil faiths, the bystanders in a real sense tried to
believe in both Americas. In that marketplace of American definitions
of reality, these customers had difficulty deciding which to buy. Their
tortured resolution was a decision not to decide.

Thus, the majority of southern whites—aptly represented by the
leadership of the Southern Baptist Convention—manifested their indecision through mediating, paralyzed "silence" on the race question.
"Silence" in this usage refers not to a complete failure to address the
South's "great matter." Rather, it describes a situation in which public pronouncements, so encumbered with the need to mediate, were
perceived merely as vague and vacuous platitudes.

Examples of such statements abound. From the incessant calls for
"calm and clear-thinking" to the 1956 president's address at the
Southern Baptist Convention, in which C. C. Warren advised one
extreme to slow down and the other to speed up, the response was a
mediating "silence."[54] Beyond this, in the conventions of certain Deep
South states the silence was more literal. Christian Life Commission
reports from South Carolina and Louisiana from 1954 through 1957
focused almost completely on the issues of alcohol, gambling, television, and juvenile delinquency. The only reference to the race issue

[54] See Robert L. Hartsell, "A Critical Analysis of Selected Southern Baptist
Convention Presidential Addresses, 1950-1970," (Ph.D. diss., Louisiana State
University, 1971) 262-65; Gardner, "Segregation's Problems," 2; and *Annual of the
Southern Baptist Convention*, 1956, 72.

came in the report of the Louisiana commission and merely suggested that Baptists face the problem with prayer and the spirit of Christ.[55]

No doubt this mediating paralysis was traceable in part to other more obvious factors. Chief among these was the desire for the institutional survival of the denomination and the social order. This concern for survival contributed to a sense that peace, at almost any price, was necessary for the denomination's well-being. This led even the progressive elite of the Southern Baptist Convention to phrase their pronouncements in a studied vagueness, always with an eye toward the constituency.

Given the institutional realities of a conservative denomination in a conservative culture, perhaps another explanation can shed additional light on the milieu of the South during the 1950s. Two civil religions, two definitions of national reality, competed for the civil allegiance of the bystanders in the middle. One version of the civil religion pulled them toward the status quo and the segregationist tradition. The other pulled them toward a millennial America where "all men are created equal."

These civil religions interacted by pulling the majority in different directions—one more southern, the other more "American." The frequency with which these middle-of-the-roaders said integration was inevitable but cautioned, "Not yet," testified to their dilemma. Forced by social circumstance and the historical process to choose between two versions of sacred reality, these southerners answered the "heretical imperative" first with indecision and finally with immobilized silence.

Thus the conflict of civil religions in the South affected both the "extremists" at opposite poles and the bystanders in between. Armed with their sacred legitimations, both extremes fought the good fight with God on their sides. Their clash ultimately expressed itself in physical violence. In the early years of the conflict, however, the violence was largely symbolic, expressing itself in the fanaticism and tenacity appropriate to holy warriors. The onlookers confronted a civil religious choice that left them torn between loyalties to both versions of America. Thus, during the civil rights era the South heard

---

[55] *Annual of the Louisiana Baptist Convention*, 1954, 73-74; *Annual of the Louisiana Baptist Convention*, 1957, 22-23; *Annual of the South Carolina Baptist Convention*, 1955, 23-24; *Annual of the South Carolina Baptist Convention*, 145-46.

the ominous strains of a prelude to holy war. Ultimately the victims included both the combatants and the bystanders.

5

CULTURE WARS:
THE SOUTHERN THEATER

Judging from the most significant fruits of their recent labor, historians of American religion apparently have tried to live and work by the commandment "Thou shalt not ignore pluralism!" Yet those scholars who have entered the labyrinthine study of civil religion have occasionally been tempted to circumvent this all-important dictum. The rationale for that attempt is understandable enough. Civil religion purports to be that all-American religion-in-general historically entrusted with the task of unifying American society by explaining the nation's religious meaning. Any admission of multiple manifestations of the American civil religion would naturally weaken its unitive power and thus confuse the issue.

Another historiographical commandment, albeit one or more recent provenance, holds, "Thou shalt not ignore the South's pluralism!" The idea of a "solid South" until quite recently had permeated not only that region's political history, but also its religious history. To be sure, homogeneity has been the hall mark of southern history. The pockets of dissent, however, have been increasingly noted as a significant part of the historical and the religious landscape.

The two versions of the American civil religion that affected the South during the 1950s underscored the divisive capabilities as well as the unitive power of civil religion. Such a discovery was not inappropriate to the South's cultural milieu during this period. For in those years the issue of race and the possibility of desegregation created both a division and a solidarity—division over the question of desegregation, solidarity among those who chose one side of that issue or the other. Thus, to write of civil religion in the South during the civil rights era is to write of *two* civil religions and, beyond that, of conflict between them.

The subject of civil religion in the South is not new. Numerous studies of southern nationalism have been written, and given the highly religious character of southern culture, that nationalism has always included a certain religious ardor. Moreover, the religious component of southern cohesiveness has long been noted, implicitly in the work of Samuel S. Hill and explicitly in the more recent work of Charles R. Wilson. While Wilson insightfully described the religion of the Lost Cause as a specifically southern civil religion, he neglected the degree to which the southern version interacted with the phenomenon known as the American civil religion. In fact, the 1950s comprised an epoch in which the central social issue of the day catalyzed a discussion in the South of America's religious meaning. Thus, the question of desegregation revealed a conflict of civil religions in the South.

The two largest religious groups of the South, Southern Baptists among whites and National Baptists among blacks, have served as case studies by which to analyze this conflict. The more reactionary elements of Southern Baptist life and the dominant strain of National Baptist perspective provided clear representatives of these two civil religions. Among Southern Baptists influenced by the Citizens Councils and among National Baptists led by Martin Luther King Jr. were found respective statements concerning America's religious meaning and purpose. Significantly, the interaction between these two civil religions revealed both similarities and conflicts.

Most obvious of the similarities was the shared sense of America's chosenness among the nations of the world. Both National and Southern Baptists understood American history as a kind of movement of Providence. Both versions also believed God had blessed America and had called the nation to a special work in the world. In addition, both groups shared certain civil religious symbols. Both attempted to further their social agendas by appealing to the American civil religious tradition. Both professed their loyalty to and love for their country. Both civil religions claimed to represent more fully the true America and the traditions of the nation's sacred documents, the Declaration of Independence and the Constitution. Though arguing in different directions, both these Baptist groups commonly cited the patriotically sacred examples of America's civil religious saints and called for freedom. Finally, both civil religions claimed divine sanction for their own activities.

Their similarities notwithstanding, these civil faiths conflicted at certain important points. While both invoked the vaunted value of freedom, their understandings of it were quite divergent. For reactionary Southern Baptists, freedom constituted individual liberty or choice. From this perspective they condemned any sort of regimentation or coercion, which they perceived in unwanted actions like the *Brown* decision. Given their dominant status, these southerners understandably defined freedom so as to perpetuate their choice to segregate blacks and thus protect their own dominant status. On the other hand, the dominated status of blacks dictated a definition of freedom as democracy and equality. For to an oppressed segment of society, freedom was impossible apart from equality.

As a result of this distinction, these groups' images of America differed significantly. For Southern Baptists, America's meaning was to protect individual liberty in a world of grave threat. Such threat came from two sources, the Kremlin and the Vatican. Both these threats were external and, from the Southern Baptist perspective, antagonistic toward true religion. Southern Baptists envisioned a traditional, homogeneous, and evangelically Christian America. God had called America to become such a nation and to protect these values for all nations.

For black Baptists, however, America was only a potentially Christian nation, yet called to embody their version of freedom, democracy, and equality. External threats were insignificant compared to the internal threat of hypocrisy with respect to the nation's deepest values. In this civil religion America was less the protector of individual liberty than the exemplar of brotherhood in a nationally divided world. Most clearly articulated in King's concept of the "beloved community," this image of and hope for America was essentially pluralistic. For as National Baptists perceived matters, only a truly pluralistic nation would ever accept them as equals.

When these respective images of America encountered the possibility of significant social change after 1954, the expected result was a vastly divergent interpretation of the idea of desegregation. In both of these civil religions desegregation functioned as a symbol that impinged upon their hopes for America. Envisioning the actualization of different Americas, these Baptists interpreted desegregation opposite ways.

Black Baptists, with their hopes for a truly pluralistic America, understood desegregation as a necessary first step toward America's coming to its true self. Fred Shuttlesworth's provocative remark aptly summed up their perceptions: America meant integration or it meant nothing at all. Hence, in this version of the civil religion, desegregation symbolized the fulfillment of black hopes.

Reactionary Southern Baptists, on the other hand, hoped for an America that would become increasingly like the South—homogeneous, Protestant, and Anglo-Saxon. They desired an America that would uphold individual rights both at home and around the world. Seeing their individual right to segregate blacks coming increasingly under attack, they despaired of the future of freedom as they understood it. As a result, they interpreted desegregation as a symbolic reminder that their hopes for America would go unfulfilled. Desegregation in this civil religion was, therefore, the symbol of a disappointed hope.

Judging then from its civil religious pluralism, the South of the civil rights era was a battleground for an incipient holy war of civil faiths. The sacredness of these civil religions led the warriors to invoke their tribal god and quote their scripture: "The good news of the [American] kingdom of God is preached, and every one enters it violently" (Luke 16:16). The violence that developed later during the civil rights movement of the sixties, did so partly because both groups claimed to be fighting for God's will. Fighting for the sacredness of a holy war thus legitimated the violence, whether literal (that of the Citizens Councils) or figurative (the tenacity of the civil rights preachers).

The sacredness also, in a sense, paralyzed those in the middle, making them choose not to choose between the available definitions of American reality. Faced with a market situation that offered two different images of America, southerners found they believed in both Americas. These "customers," unable to decide between products, began the slow process of developing, in Phillip E. Hammond's words, a "new, more generalized, common meaning system."[1] That process remains yet incomplete in the South and, increasingly, in America as a whole.

Inasmuch as America is still attempting to move, ever so haltingly and with frequent reverses, toward an approximation of King's dream of a "beloved community," certain general implications of this study might be suggested. The first relates to the inherent ambiguity of civil religion. In numerous responses to critics of his controversial thesis, Robert Bellah has consistently argued that civil religion is always capable of being perverted into intolerance and jingoism. Distinctions must always be drawn between the varieties of civil religion. One of the most useful of these distinctions is that between the priestly and the prophetic forms. The civil faiths that opposed one another in the South of the 1950s were classifiable within these two categories. One version idealized an exclusivist America, sanctified in priestly fashion that status quo, and justified the Jim Crow system. The other hoped for a pluralistic America that would be true to its best self and prophetically called for change.

All of this strongly confirms that civil religion per se is a neutral concept, taking a priestly or prophetic form depending upon factors extrinsic to the concept itself. The crucial factors in determining the particular form are many, but the example of the mid-twentieth-century South suggest that the form largely depends on the social status of the individual enunciator. Though there have been significant exceptions, when the chief spokesperson of the American civil religion is the president of the United States or someone else who speaks from the dominant class, the form will usually tend toward the priestly. When a spokesperson from the dominated class, such as King articulates it, the form is more likely to be prophetic.

This should remind anti-civil religionists that blanket denunciations of civil religion reveal a superficial understanding of the general concept. It underscores what so often and eloquently had been "preached" by Bellah—that "every movement to make America more fully realize its professed values has grown out of some form of public theology, from the abolitionists to the social gospel and the early socialist party to the civil rights movement under Martin Luther King

---

[1] Philip E. Hammond, "Pluralism and Law in the Formation of American Civil Religion," in Bellah and Hammond, *Varieties of Civil Religion*, 142-44.

and the farm workers' movement under Cesar Chavez. But so has every expansionist war and every form of oppression of racial minorities and immigrant groups."[2]

Another distinction between the various forms of civil religion—namely, Bellah's distinction between archaic and modern civil religions—has relevance for the two forms that were manifested in the South of the civil rights era. The particular form of civil religion takes is shaped by the nature of the society in which it is found. An archaic (traditional) society is characterized by hierarchy, while a modern society is marked by equality. "This contrast is rooted not just in political ideology but in fundamental conceptions of the nature of reality," Bellah observes. "It will therefore affect the nature of civil religion in the contrasting cases. Indeed, hierarchy or equality may be at the core of the respective civil religions."[3]

Part of the reason why equality is associated with modern societies is the differentiation and pluralization endemic to modernity. Largely the result of industrial development, the modern situation brings persons of different backgrounds together as they press for economic advancement. Understandably, religious perspectives and/or world views become pluralized, lose their givenness, and become matters of private conscience.[4] In a pluralistic setting these world views, stripped of their taken-for-granted status and thus their inevitability, become more or less equal competitors in the modern market situation. Hence, equality (at least in the ideal) is a characteristic of modern society.

Such a categorization fits the southern situation during the civil rights era. By these definitions, the civil religion propagated by the national Baptists was more modern in character by virtue of its acceptance of religious and cultural pluralism, and its call for freedom. Southern Baptist reactionaries enunciated a civil faith rendered

---

[2] Robert N. Bellah, "Religion and the Legitimation of the American Republic," in Bellah and Hammond, *Varieties of Civil Religion*, 15.

[3] Bellah, "Civil Religion in Comparative Perspective: The American and Japanese Cases," in Bellah and Hammond, *Varieties of Civil Religion*, 28. Bellah realizes that the distinction may not be so clearly manifest in historical actuality: "We might wish to consider that the contrast hierarchy/equality is a polarity or a continuum rather than an absolute antinomy" (p. 30).

[4] See Luckmann, *The Invisible Religion*.

archaic by virtue of its celebration of homogeneity and an essentially hierarchical social structure.

Bellah ordinarily attributes the jingoistic, nationally self-worshipping form of civil religion to a reversion to an archaic form. While the civil religion of the Citizens Councils may have fit the description of an archaic civil faith, it did not arise from a reversion. This extremist manifestation arose from a background of homogeneity which, supported by sacred legitimations, rejected the South's growing pluralism. This absence of pluralism helps explain the incivility of this civil religion.

In his offbeat discussion of American civil religion, John Murray Cuddihy defined the phenomenon as "the religion of civility." He did not interpret civil religion in the accustomed sense, as a general religious system that politely and platonically exists "alongside" the denominations. Rather, he described it as "activist, aggrandizing, subversive, intrusive, [and] incivil," inasmuch as it penetrates and civilizes the churches and their theologies.[5]

An expression of America's religious pluralism, civil religion, Cuddihy argues, teaches Americans ways of being "religiously inoffensive, of giving 'no offense,' of being religiously sensitive to religious differences."[6] Thus, Cuddihy's ironic implication is that civil religion is incivil because it penetrates the particularistic theologies of the denominations and forces them to be civil toward one another.

Given the link between religion and ethnicity in America, one might appropriately add that the American situation teaches a civility with respect to cultural as well as religious pluralism. This being so, this implication may be applied to the southern situation. When, on a larger scale than ever before, cultural pluralism appeared on the southern scene during the postwar era, its encounter with the South's homogeneity loosed a torrent of incivility among reactionary whites. Without a strong tradition of pluralism, and without these southerners ever having been taught how to behave in a civil manner, such a response came as no surprise.

On the other hand, National Baptists were much more accustomed to pluralism. Southern blacks who sought an education had long learned to migrate northward for their training. Most often, of

---

[5] Cuddihy, *Civil Religion and Protestant Taste*, 1-2.
[6] Ibid., 2.

course, they had little choice. That Northern exposure did not eclipse the southernness of these blacks, but it did force them to confront rival perspectives and learn to live with them. Widespread migration of blacks to the North after 1900 furthered this development. In addition, unlike the Southern Baptist Convention, the National Baptist Convention was a more solidly national denomination, thus including more people who were accustomed to pluralism. Finally, the black experience itself created a higher tolerance for pluralism, for blacks knew that they would be completely accepted as equals only in a truly pluralistic society. Not surprisingly, then, the black Baptists' version of the civil religion was more civil than that of Southern Baptist reactionaries.

Although the South did not undergo archaic reversion, contemporary American culture probably has. The version of the civil religion expounded by Reagan Revolution or the conservative resurgence, while ostensibly exalting the virtues of American pluralism, continues to express itself in more traditional, homogeneously Protestant, even fundamentalist, images. Add to this its perceived bias against the Third World and insensitivity to the plight of blacks and one suspects that a reversion to archaic civil religion—and its inherent incivility—is still in process.

Another implication of this study pertains to the civil religious tradition that was best expressed by Martin Luther King Jr. Since his assassination, King has become the latest member of America's civil religious pantheon of heroes. John Dixon Elder correctly noted that King revivified and extended the American civil religion.[7] He revitalized the concept of American chosenness, not in terms of domination and power, but in terms of America's exemplary role in the world.

King's work is a very real sense expressed the attitudes and situation of southern blacks. King also articulated the dreams of the southern black church. Ideas paralleling those of King commonly appeared in the preaching of lesser-known black preachers. Coupled with King's almost immediate acceptance as a black (Baptist) leader, this suggests that King is best understood as an expression of the black church in the South. Martin Luther King Sr., saw both his activist

---

[7] Elder, "Martin Luther King and American Civil Religion," 17-18.

sons (Martin and A. D.) as "southern men."[8] W. J. Hodge, a clerical contemporary of King, believes that interpreters of King have not sufficiently emphasized his heritage as a black Baptist from the South. He noted that "people made much, and he did himself, about Mahatma Gandhi's philosophy of nonviolence, but I always remind people that when Martin marched they weren't singing no Indian songs, they were singing black spirituals. And it was out of that context [that he preached]."[9] Although he severely devalues Gandhi's influence on King, Hodge's perspective nonetheless accurately describes King's continuity with the larger tradition of the black church.

Leonard I. Sweet has argued that throughout the nineteenth century, black leaders emphasized black America's specially chosen role as that of testing America's fidelity to its central values.[10] The tradition of the black church, which has always been the most prominent element in American black leadership, continued to function in that role during the 1950s.

Beyond this, however, it may be that the black community in America will assume that role indefinitely. One can certainly see a revitalization of the King tradition in contemporary black America. Cornel West, noting a lull in that vibrant tradition during the late sixties and early seventies, identified Jesse Jackson's 1984 presidential campaign as just such a renascence: "The Jackson campaign has brought together the broadest united front in black America since the days of the great Martin Luther King Jr. This display of black unity has been incredible and impressive—and has had an immeasurable symbolic effect on black Americans, especially poor black Americans."[11]

Although the Jackson campaign was an openly political movement, one would be hard pressed to divorce it from the tradition of the black church. Given its religious ideas and rhetoric, that political movement strikingly resembles a kind of civil religion. Further, although their political agenda has developed beyond the mere hope for desegregation, National Baptists' former images of America remain

[8] King, *Daddy King*, 127.
[9] Hodge, interview with author, April 2, 1984.
[10] Sweet, *Black Images of America*.
[11] Cornel West, "Black Politics Will Never Be the Same," *Christianity and Crisis* 44 (August 13, 1984): 304.

the hopes of blacks for America today. Thus the call to "keep the dream alive" is more than a mere slogan; it is for African Americans a sacred and civil religious call to arms.

The desire of southerners to be loyal to both their region and their country lies at the heart of the South's historically ambiguous relationship with the larger nation. In the 1950s, reactionary voices fervently asserted that one best honored America by honoring the traditions of the South. Dewey Grantham has accurately suggested that the South has never been able to repudiate its Americanism, even during its most passionate waves of Yankee hating.[12]

The ambiguity of that relationship extends to the question of southern identity. Arguably the most distinct region in the United States, the South has often been considered by southern historians the most "American" region in the nation. C. Vann Woodward, one of the most respected members of that guild, wrote suggestively that the South's faults "are increasingly the faults of other parts of the country, standard American faults."[13] Historian Howard Zinn admirably summed up this perspective, viewing the South as a mirror of America: "For the South,... far from being utterly different, is really the *essence* of the nation. It is not a mutation born by some accident into the lovely American family; it has simply taken the national genes and done the most with them....Those very qualities long attributed to the South as special possessions are, in truth, *American* qualities, and the nation reacts emotionally to the South because it subconsciously recognizes itself there" (Zinn's italics).[14]

Many southern scholars have discussed "the Americanization of Dixie." John Egerton perhaps rightly observed, however, that the Americanizing process has also worked in the opposite direction and yielded a southernization of America.[15] If so, the South of the civil rights era remains a fairly accurate mirror on contemporary America. For if one excises its blatant sectionalism and its overt racism and thereby focuses on it essential images of America, the reactionary civil

---

[12] Grantham, *Democratic South*, 8.

[13] C. Vann Woodward, "The Search for Southern Identity," in *The Burden of Southern History*, 5.

[14] Howard Zinn, *The Southern Mystique* (New York: Simon & Schuster, 1972) 218.

[15] Egerton, *The Americanization of Dixie*.

religion of the civil rights era looks remarkably like the civil religion currently preached in contemporary American culture. Comparing the ideal national images of Reagan America to those of say, Jesse Jackson and his followers, one suspects that the civil religious conflict of the mid-twentieth-century South has become a wider, more contemporary, *American* conflict.

Such was the conclusion of this book in its original publication. The intervening fifteen years has afforded time to observe both black and white Baptists and the larger political and social discourse in America during the Reagan-Bush and Clinton eras. Thus it is now possible to do more than merely suspect "a wider, more contemporary *American* conflict." One might specifically argue that, with a certain broadening of the issues over which Americans and southerners have continued to fight, what began in the 1950s as civil religious conflict over race has become the "culture wars" of recent years. In 1992 students of American religion and politics, as well as ordinary American voters, discussed not only George Herbert Walker Bush and Dan Quayle, but also the two southerners—Southern Baptists, no less—who headed the Democratic party's presidential ticket. Then they heard defeated presidential candidate Patrick Buchanan tell the Republican National Convention that the nation was not just embroiled in a political campaign, but was involved in what he called "a religious and cultural war... for the soul of America." After that, journalists hungry for a story have made the phrase a standard part of contemporary political discussion.

Now, with the Clinton era officially over and a "compassionate conservative" Republican presiding over not only the nation, but over one of the most stridently partisan eras in American political history, it seems clear that the "culture war" is far from over. Recent skirmishes have centered on a Southern Baptist president of the United States who was vigorously opposed by his own denomination. This is in large measure because Bill Clinton and Al Gore represented the progressive wing of the Southern Baptist Convention, the segment that since 1979 has been out of power in the denomination's power

structure. In that year, the fundamentalist wing launched a jug-
gernaut intent on capturing control of the Convention, and by the
mid-1980s had removed progressives (or "moderates" as they called
themselves) from virtually every position of influence. Not coin-
cidentally, 1979 also marked the beginning of the Reverend Jerry
Falwell's Moral Majority and the rise of the Religious Right. Falwell,
Pat Robertson's Christian Coalition, and every Southern Baptist
Convention president since 1979 have all been central figures in the
culture war. As it happens, all of them, as well as the U.S. president
who embodied their opposition, have southern accents. Hence, the
connections between the religious traditions of the American South
and the culture war that preceded and outlived the Clinton administration are worth investigating.

By now, thanks largely to Pat Buchanan's 1992 speech, the term
"culture war" is common parlance among journalists and other
political junkies. More than likely, Buchanan got the phrase from the
title of a 1990 book by University of Virginia sociologist James
Davison Hunter. Hunter argues that our nation is indeed experiencing "Culture Wars," which divide citizens into two competing
ways of defining America. What he means is that Americans are
divided between two "visions of what kind of nation America ought
to be."[16] Religion and its role in American life are at the heart of this
debate. Religion enables individuals to answer questions of
identity—Who am I? What am I doing here? How do I fit in the larger
scheme of things? Religion also helps nations answer similar questions
of national identity—Who are we as a people? How does our nation
fit into the world? What is our purpose? Merely comparing, for
example, the religious visions of America set forth by the reverends
Jesse Jackson and Pat Robertson suggest at least competing images of
the ideal America. Buchanan's rhetoric suggested that Hunter is
correct and that competition has become conflict.

Interestingly, at the same time that Hunter and Buchanan were
telling us in different ways about our "culture wars," twin brothers
and political scientists Earl and Merle Black showed that winning the
"vital South is now indispensable to electing presidents. They argued
that as the largest and most cohesive region in the country, one which

---

[16] James Davison Hunter, *Culture Wars: The Struggle to Define America*, (New
York: Basic Books, 1990) 42-45, 50.

controls fifty-four percent of the electoral votes necessary to winning
the presidency, the South is "once again at the center of struggles to
define winners and losers in American politics.[17]

Voting for a president is often seen as qualitatively different from
voting for a local or state official. To vote for a president is to choose a
national official who, in the highest office in the land, in large measure represents the entire nation. A president serves the function of
pontifex maximus or "high priest," and as such symbolizes in his
(someday *her*) person the very meaning of the nation. Thus, to vote
for president is to vote for the candidate who best symbolizes what one
believes America ought to be. If this is true, and if the South now
largely determines who will be elected president, then it follows that
the South is also at the center of what Hunter calls "the struggle to
define America."

For the South to become dominant in national politics concurrently with a raging culture war strikes the historian of American
and southern religion as more than merely coincidental. These simu-
ltaneous realities raise the obvious question: How are America's
culture war and the South related to each other? All of the intricacies
of their relationship cannot be fully explored here, but the South has
clearly become the primary theater for the fighting of the culture war
that Hunter has described. Not that all southerners or only southerners
compete on one side of the culture war. African American and
conservative white southerners will usually differ markedly in their
ideal mythic images of America and many non-southerners share the
conservative views traditionally identified with the white South. And
though they are sometimes a very silent minority, there are white
southerners who willingly call themselves liberals. To some degree, the
battles do rage more fervently in southern venues, especially when
those white liberals manage to speak up. To say, however, that the
South is the primary theater of the culture war is to argue that the
conflict is in part an outgrowth of the South's cultural and religious
adjustment to once again being in a central place in American life.
During the post-World War II era, as the Bible Belt was transformed
into the Sunbelt, southerners have been forced to adjust to unprecedented levels of cultural and religious pluralism in their region and in

---

[17] Earl and Merle Black, *The Vital South: How Presidents Are Elected*
(Cambridge: Harvard University Press, 1992) 364-366.

modern America. The South's discontent with and reaction against
the secularizing tendencies of that pluralism is shared outside the
South by millions of citizens who alongside southerners have enlisted
to fight in the culture war. In light of what John Egerton has called
"the southernization of America," the culture war that has raged since
the 1980s can be considered the Americanization of Dixie's historic
concern to protect America from the dangers of unbridled pluralism.

A Historic Southern Concern

Since the beginnings of the American experiment, there have been two
different models for how society and religion ought to relate to each
other. One has been called the "custodial model," in which civil
authorities serve as the custodians of society's spiritual as well as
physical well-being. The Puritan leaders of the Massachusetts Bay
Colony were one example; evangelicalism's gradual cultural hegemony
over the South was another. Over against this model stood the
"pluralist" model of dissenters like Baptist Roger Williams, who
believed that religion was a matter of private concern, a matter of
individual conscience, and none of the government's business.[18] After
the First and Second Great Awakenings in the eighteenth century,
Evangelical Protestants (mainly Baptists, Methodists, and Presbyterians) gradually moved into numerical and cultural dominance
in the antebellum South. The poverty of the post-Civil War South led
later floods of immigrants to America largely to bypass the South,
making it possible for the region's Protestant homogeneity to persist
well into the twentieth century. As late as 1966, nine of ten southerners identified themselves as Protestants, and seventy-seven percent
did so in 1988.[19]

This longstanding religious consensus created a friendly relationship between church and state in the South. In spite of commitment to legal separation, the Evangelical South has been a chief

---

[18] These models of relations between church and state are suggested by Grant
Wacker in his helpful essay, "Uneasy in Zion: Postmodern Society," in George
Marsden, ed., *Evangelicalism and Modern America* (Grand Rapids: William B.
Eerdmans Publishing Company, 1984) 28.

[19] John Shelton Reed, *The Enduring South* (Chapel Hill: University of North
Carolina Press, 1983) 57; George Gallup, Jr and Jim Castelli, *The People's Religion*
(New York : Macmillan, 1989) 86.

representative of the custodial model. As custodians of antebellum southern church and culture, ministers and theologians produced biblical defenses of slavery that eventually melded into religious justifications of the Confederacy. These southern divines, however, did more than merely defend their society against northern abolitionism. As Eugene D. Genovese has argued, they also saw their society as the bulwark against an attendant apostasy and secularism. Orthodox ministers feared a Yankee victory would lead to theological liberalism and apostasy.[20] During the Civil War, a Greensboro minister representatively declared, "A pure Christianity is wrapped up in this revolution, and Providence is using the South for the grand work of its preservation and extension."[21] Just before the war, South Carolina's *Southern Presbyterian* noted "a religious character to the present struggle. Anti-Slavery is essentially infidel. It wars upon the Bible, on the Church of Christ, on the truth of God, on the souls of men."[22]

In the South's defense of both theological and racial orthodoxy, both before and after the Civil War, the region saw itself as called by God to spread what a Southern Baptist Home Mission Board official in the early 1900s called "the Anglo-Saxon evangelical faith."[23] As the twentieth century wore on, as they rose to numerical and cultural dominance among the South's evangelicals, Southern Baptists became the bellwether of the region's religious culture. Political scientist Oran P. Smith rightly argues that "deep within Southern Baptist religion

---

[20] On anti-abolitionism as a defense of Christian orthodoxy, see Eugene D. Genovese, *A Consuming Fire: The Fall of the Confederacy in the Mind of the White Christian South* (Athens: University of Georgia Press, 1998) 87; See also his foreword to James O. Farmer Jr., *The Metaphysical Confederacy: James Henley Thornwell and the Synthesis of Southern Values* (Macon: Mercer University Press, 1999) xi.

[21] J. Henry Smith, *A Sermon Delivered at Greensboro, N.C.,* 11, quoted in Drew Gilpin Faust, *The Creation of Confederate Nationalism* (Baton Rouge: Louisiana State University Press, 1988) 28.

[22] *Southern Presbyterian,* December 15, 1860, quoted in Mitchell Snay, *Gospel of Disunion: Religion and Separation in the Antebellum South* (Chapel Hill: University of North Carolina Press, 1993) 59. See especially 59-67, for Snay's cogent analysis of the interrelationships between the biblical defense of slavery, the critique of abolitionism, and the defense of religious orthodoxy.

[23] Quoted in Nancy Tatom Ammerman, *Baptist Battles: Social Change and Religious Conflict in the Southern Baptist Convention* (New Brunswick: Rutgers University Press, 1990) 39.

and politics lies the idea that the South is separate from the rest of the nation: a little more righteous, a little more virtuous; believers in the absolutes of scripture surrounded by relativists; a Christian nation-state snuffed out by barbarians." Smith also rightly affirms that this element remains a part of SBC mentality today.[24]

Much of Southern Baptists' hubris about their "divine mission" became a settled mentality because their denomination grew faster than the South's general population in the post-World War II era. The Southern Baptist Convention increased its membership from some five million in 1940 to almost ten million in 1960. Smith thus argues that such growth persuaded Southern Baptists that God's blessing was upon them and gave the denomination an overweening confidence in itself.[25] This denominational self-image as the bulwark against apostasy is reflected in the oft-repeated warning among SBC preachers that unless Southern Baptists hew to the line of biblical inerrancy and theological orthodoxy, they will "go the way of the mainline denominations." This review of its religious history reveals a South, and a Southern Baptist Convention, where calls for a "Christian America" were welcome and where religious and cultural dissent were not. In the South moral custodians were largely free to envision a happily homogeneous, WASPish Southland and nation.

Southern Discontent

Throughout the early part of the twentieth century the intended and accidental insularity of southern society protected the South from incursions of pluralism strong enough to threaten the cultural and religious status quo. The Jim Crow era created an uneasy truce with black southerners until after World War II, when slight changes in the stance of the federal government toward African Americans cracked the door open for an eventual transformation. Franklin Roosevelt's New Deal and his wife Eleanor's high-profile activism for civil rights brought about a major political realignment as African Americans began their movement toward the Democratic party. A war against Nazi racial ideology made the "American dilemma" even more ob-

---

[24] Oran Smith, *The Rise of Baptist Republicanism* (New York: New York University Press, 1997) 22.

[25] Smith, *Baptist Republicanism,* 38, 39.

vious to blacks and liberal whites. Harry Truman's desegregation of the armed forces and postwar civil rights policies, coupled with Branch Rickey and Jackie Robinson's noble efforts to integrate the national pastime, emboldened African Americans, putting the forces of change at the ready. All that was necessary to put these forces in motion was a catalyst. Thurgood Marshall and the NAACP's suits against public school segregation eventually lit the fuse, and the United States Supreme Court's 1954 *Brown v. Topeka Board of Education* ruling detonated a torrent of racial transformation in the South and the nation.

The enormous changes that swept over America and the South after 1940 created alarm among many devout southerners and set the stage for cultural conflict. In this period, the South became more urban, with the percentage of southerners living in cities increasing from thirty-seven percent to sixty-seven percent between 1940 and 1980. During the same period, urbanization of the non-South increased by only eleven percent—from sixty-six to seventy-seven percent.[26] The Sunbelt phenomenon also brought an influx of non-southerners into the South. Twenty percent of residents of the South in 1980 were born outside the region, up from only eight percent in 1950.[27] Higher education increased in the South as it did nationwide after 1950. In 1950 only 6.2 percent of Americans over twenty-five years of age had attended four years of college; in 1991 the proportion was 21.4 percent, with the percentage among southerners only slightly lower. All these social factors weakened the South's cultural and religious homogeneity. The percentage of Protestants fell from ninety to seventy-seven percent between 1966 and 1988, while nationwide the percentage of Protestants fell only two points, from 60 percent to 58 percent, during the same period.[28]

Linking these regional changes with the perception of moral crisis in America in the same period helps one see why many Americans and

---

[26] Carl Abbott, "Urban Growth," in Charles Reagan Wilson and William E. Ferris, eds., *Encyclopedia of Southern Culture* (Chapel Hill: University of North Carolina Press, 1989) 1444-1445.

[27] Earl and Merle Black, *Politics and Society in the South* (Cambridge: Harvard University Press, 1988) 16.

[28] Figures come from United States Census, 1990; Reed, 57-58; Gallup and Castelli, 86.

especially southerners felt that everything nailed down was coming up. The civil rights movement, the protests over the Vietnam War, the removal of school prayer, *Roe v. Wade*, Watergate, the secularizing tendencies of television, the growing violence in American life, and efforts toward gay rights all created among conservative Americans a discontent with pluralism. Having rejoined the national mainstream after World War II, the South found its religious adjustment to modern America very uncomfortable. With its custodial tradition still healthy, the region responded with the resurgence of the Religious Right in the 1980s. This might be considered a variation of a theme that may be visible elsewhere: "If Mama ain't happy, ain't nobody happy." If the Southland ain't happy, the nation ain't happy. While the Religious Right included many from across America, its leading voices speak with southern accents—think of Jerry Falwell, Jim Bakker, Oral Roberts, James Robison, Jimmy Swaggart, as well as Southern Baptist leaders Adrian Rogers, Paul Pressler, and Charles Stanley.

Perhaps the best evidence of the modern South's discontent with pluralism is the fundamentalist takeover of the region's dominant denomination, the Southern Baptist Convention. At the same time, as Jerome Himmelstein has suggested, the SBC's rightward shift is also "the most striking evidence of the strength of the New Religious Right."[29] Oran Smith's research explains Southern Baptists in terms of a Weberian theory of a "politics of lifestyle concern." He notes that cultural and religious conservatives often rally to defend against a perceived threat to their preferred way of life. As a percentage of southern population, Southern Baptists rose to twenty-five percent in 1930, peaked at thirty-six percent in 1960, then fell back to thirty-one percent by 1990. Until the 1960s, their membership rose to the point of dominating the South. Then after a thirty-year decline, Southern Baptists experienced a "fading majority" and began to fear losing their "cultural monopoly" in the South. Changes in the region and nation had threatened their accustomed place as religious and moral custodians, and they intended to fight back.[30]

---

[29] Jerome, Himmelstein, *The Right: The Transformation of American Conservatism,* quoted in Smith, *Baptist Republicanism,* 28.

[30] Smith, *Baptist Republicanism,* 71-72, 77.

While the Southern Baptist moderates and fundamentalists differed most sharply on whether there are errors in the Bible, evidence of the culture war among them was clear in their debate on various national issues. The 1982 Convention, dominated by the fundamentalist party, passed a resolution favoring a school prayer amendment. Prior to this, the SBC's tradition of church-state separation had led eight previous Convention resolutions to support the Supreme Court's 1963 ruling outlawing school prayer. Later W. A. Criswell, then pastor of the First Baptist Church, Dallas, Texas, forgot his Baptist history and claimed on television that the idea of church-state separation was "a figment of some infidel's imagination." Research by sociologist Nancy Ammerman in a survey of 800 Southern Baptist leaders discovered other indicators of discontent. Their views of the civil rights movement, the vanguard of pluralism's march into the South, reflect the divisions of the culture war. Of self-identified moderates, ninety percent agreed that the civil rights movement had moved America in the right direction, while only forty-five percent of self-identified fundamentalists agreed with the statement. Similarly, only fifteen percent of moderates favored the Moral Majority as compared to eighty-nine percent of fundamentalists surveyed. More directly, by probing their views of modernity and their relative acceptance of pluralism, Ammerman discovered that among Southern Baptists who disapproved of pluralism, fundamentalists outnumbered moderates almost ten to one.[31]

It is also instructive to note the timing of the SBC's lurch to the right. To a great extent it was a reaction against the developments in the nation and the denomination during the 1960s. Besides the threat to its "cultural monopoly," the SBC also saw an unprecedented political activity, as the denomination's progressive elite responded sympathetically to the civil rights movement and the issue of race in America and the South.

James Dunn, longtime director of the Washington lobby group, the Baptist Joint Committee on Public Affairs, saw 1968 as a watershed year for theological and racial liberals in the SBC. After conspicuous silence on racial matters, denominational agencies heads and a few liberal pastors were mortified by the upheaval in the nation

---

[31] Ammerman, 99-103; 151.

during the tumultuous year of 1968. The Tet Offensive and the increased antiwar protests it spawned, the assassination of Martin Luther King Jr and the racial riots in generated, and the assassination of Robert Kennedy, which took place during the annual meeting of the SBC, all led to the adoption of *A Statement Concerning the Crisis in Our Nation*. The *Statement* was Southern Baptists' most progressive statement of commitment to address the problem of race in America. According to Dunn, the Convention's adoption of the *Statement*, though not without considerable opposition from conservatives, marked a "programmatic commitment to an ecumenical political engagement that was not provincial."[32]

Oran Smith insightfully identified this document as a political awakening among Southern Baptist progressives. He argued:

> Convention moderates had moved from an irresolute statement in favor of *Brown v. Board of Education* in 1954 to a lengthy, up-front mea culpa in 1968 from none other than the executive committee of the Convention. This bold stance represented the first attempt at a political push in the SBC, an aggressive campaign by the middle and left that touched a match to conservative dynamite. Within a few short years, the conservative faction formed and the engine for takeover, the Baptist Faith and Message Fellowship, was being organized.[33]

Hence, to an important degree, concern about race and the changes brought about by the civil rights movement was a catalyst that set in motion the Southern Baptist fundamentalist takeover move-

---

[32] Dunn interview, quoted in Smith, *Baptist Republicanism*, 47. For a fuller discussion of the *Statement* as a response to the King assassination and the race issue, see Andrew M. Manis, "Silence or Shockwaves: Southern Baptist Responses to the Assassination of Martin Luther King Jr.," *Baptist History and Heritage* 15 (October, 1980) 19-27, 35.

[33] Oran Smith, *The Rise of Baptist Republicanism*, 47-48. The Baptist Faith and Message Fellowship was not only the precursor of what became the takeover movement, but it also included many fundamentalist Southern Baptists who had vigorously condemned King, the civil rights movement, and the 1968 *Statement*. For an important discussion of this organization, see David T. Morgan, *The New Crusade, The New Holy Land: Conflict in the Southern Baptist Convention, 1969-1991* (Tuscaloosa: University of Alabama Press, 1996) 24-28.

ment, its involvement with the Religious Right, its support of Ronald Reagan and the Republican party, and its enlistment in the culture war. Granted, it did not take long for their concerns to broaden to moral concerns and hot-button issues other than race. But back of the SBC's and the Religious Right's culture war against abortion, gay rights, feminism, the peace movement, and other expressions of the counterculture was a fearfulness about pluralism.

Southern accents have sounded the note of uneasiness with the increased pluralism and secularizing tendencies of modern America. As Rabbi Joshua Haberman has noted in another context that the Bible Belt seeks to be America's safety belt—protecting the nation from pluralism's many "dangers, toils and snares."[34] In the southern leaders of the Religious Right and in the fundamentalist-controlled Southern Baptist Convention, one finds combatants on one side of a conflict of civil faiths.

Over against them are those Americans and southerners more at home in modern America and more accepting of its pluralism. Just as during the 1950s their images of America conflicted with those of conservative Southern Baptists, so in the last half of the twentieth century have African Americans continued to stand for pluralism in America's civil religious battles. Ever since Roosevelt's New Deal, and particularly since the Kennedy and Johnson administrations, African Americans have been the Democratic party's most faithful constituency. Led by the black Baptist denominations, they strongly supported Jimmy Carter, as indicated by the participation of Martin Luther King Sr. in Carter's nominating convention and inauguration. In 1984 and 1988 one of their own ministers, the Reverend Jesse Jackson, largely funded his presidential primary campaigns from the offering plates of black Baptist churches.

Between July 1997 and September 1999, the National Baptist Convention, the largest of the black Baptist denominations, was forced by high level scandal to divert its attention from purely political concerns. Convention president Henry Lyons was discovered in an illicit affair with a Convention publicist and used church funds to purchase a lavish $700,000 waterfront home for himself and his girlfriend. All came to light when Mrs. Lyons discovered the

---

[34] Joshua O. Haberman, "The Bible Belt Is America's Safety Belt," *Policy Review* (Fall 1987): 40-44.

arrangement and torched the home. Lyons, pastor of the Bethel Metropolitan Baptist Church in St. Petersburg, Florida, used a secret bank account to swindle a number of companies out of some four million dollars. He was eventually convicted of five federal counts of tax evasion and bank fraud, along with Florida state convictions for racketeering and grand theft. He was sentenced to four years in prison. Following this prosecution, which Lyons had earlier claimed to be a plot of the white media to undermine his leadership, the Convention's attention was further distracted by a electoral battle royal to choose a presidential successor.[35] Finally, in September 1999, the Reverend William Shaw, a respected straight arrow, was elected in a close contest over the Reverend W. Franklyn Richardson and a number of other candidates. Nevertheless, amid this denominational turmoil, National Baptists and other African Americans aligned themselves with the group Hunter calls the Progressives, and became the most dependable and enthusiastic supporters of Bill Clinton, the lightning rod of the most recent phase of the culture war.

The South, Bill Clinton, and the Culture War

Throughout his two terms in office, the polarizing persona of America's forty-second president was the flashpoint of the culture wars. The South thus remained the primary theater of the conflict, as its response to Bill Clinton's presidency was mixed, though slanted toward his opponents. In 1992 Clinton won five southern states to George Bush's seven. Among white born-again Christians, Clinton garnered only two percent of the vote, compared to sixty-one percent for Bush and fifteen percent for Ross Perot. In ninety-six heavily Southern Baptist counties, Bush won forty-six percent to Clinton's forty and Ross Perot's fourteen percent.[36] In 1996 Clinton again won only five southern states (Kentucky, Tennessee, Arkansas, Louisiana, and Florida). Interestingly, as noted by Oran Smith, the southern states with the strongest anti-Clinton vote (Alabama, Georgia,

---

[35] *St. Petersburg Times*, March 17, 1999; *Newswire*, March 31, 1999; Bryan Robinson, "Lyons' Sentencing Provides Closure," Court TV, June 18, 1999. (This article was accessed on the Internet at www.courttv.com/trials/lyons/061899_ctv. html.)

[36] Voting percentages taken from *Baptists Today*, December 1992, 1.

Mississippi, South Carolina) are also the states with the highest Baptist population. This lends credence to Smith's contention that "the Republican party and the Southern Baptist Convention are not only in firm alliance, they are sometimes indistinguishable from each other."[37]

Since the 1992 election, readers' letters to southern newspapers have taken on the fearful sound of a moral apocalypse. Even the Baptist convention in Clinton's home state of Arkansas passed a resolution critical of his positions on certain moral issues, amending their statement to include a clause that in effect called on their un-favorite son to get right with God. All of this prompted Clinton to confide to a friend, "Pagans were kinder to me during the election than the Christians were."[38] As the Clinton era wore on, white flags of surrender and/or reconciliation were nowhere to be found, particularly within the former president's own denomination.

Particularly galling to fundamentalist Southern Baptists was the fact that Clinton was their denomination's wayward, not to say Prodigal, son. His coreligionists believed that as a Southern Baptist he should have known better. But then, he was more or less allied with the moderate faction of the Southern Baptist Convention, which was central to conservatives' problem with Clinton. His southern accent, his singing in the Immanuel Baptist Church choir, his carrying his Bible to church, and his familiarity with the language of Zion, all seemed to Southern Baptists (though not to black Baptists who always cheered him) a cloak of hypocrisy designed to hide his reputation as a pot-smoking, draft-dodging, womanizer with a penchant for weasel words. The Clintonian phase of the culture war began in earnest on his second day in office, when he introduced his intention to change the federal government's policy on gays in the military. The South's traditional support for the military combined with the fundamentalist South's homophobia to turn the new president into the

---

[37] Smith, *Baptist Republicanism*, 2, 192. The combined vote in these four heavily Southern Baptist states for Robert Dole and Ross Perot was as follows: Alabama, 56 percent; Mississippi, 55 percent; South Carolina, 55 percent; Georgia, 53 percent. See Almanac—United States—United States Government—Elections at www.infoplease.com.

[38] Author's conversation with Carolyn Y. Staley, Little Rock, Arkansas, December 30, 1992.

personification of everything conservatives believed was wrong with America.

Meeting in their annual convention meetings, Southern Baptists regularly leveled stinging criticism against Clinton. One Southern Baptist minister, Wiley Drake of Buena Park, California became something of a legend, chastising Clinton in at least one proposed resolution for every year he spent in the White House.[39] But if the effort to allow gays in the military sounded reveille, the Monica Lewinsky scandal signaled an all-out war. After revelations about the president's affair with Lewinsky, Convention president Paige Patterson called upon Clinton to resign "before he is instrumental in corrupting all our young people," Like former Republican Secretary of Education William Bennett, who asked, "Where is the outrage?" Patterson criticized Americans' willingness to give Clinton high approval ratings because of a strong economy. He viewed such approval as "a certain enthrallment with materialism, which is exactly what caused the demise of Rome, to say nothing of twenty-one other great civilizations. And it will kill us too."[40] The following year Convention messengers passed a resolution rebuking Clinton for proclaiming June 1999 as "Gay and Lesbian Pride Month." Calling the proclamation "an offense to...[the] sensibilities and an affront to...[the] religious heritage and convictions" of millions of Americans, the Convention also called on Clinton to rescind his appointment of James Hormel, a homosexual, as U.S. ambassador to Luxembourg.[41]

Hence, eight years of a white southerner and moderate Southern Baptist in the White House, especially the almost two years during which the nation was embroiled in the Lewinsky scandal and the impeachment process, saw perhaps the most vigorous prosecution of the culture war since its inception. Now, in a new millennium, the bitter defeat of Clinton's would-be successor with similar southern and Baptist credentials and the inauguration of a "compassionate conservative" southerner with four years to define America signals a healthy future for the culture wars—healthy for the war effort, if not necessarily for the nation.

---

[39] Chicago Tribune, June 16, 2000.

[40] Associated Press release, Sept. 7, 1998.

[41] "Resolutions Wrap-Up, June 17, 1999, www.sbcannualmeeting.org/sbc99/news63.htm.

Culture War, Civil War

Perhaps the most hotly contested battlefield in the southern theater is the lingering controversy over the Confederate flag. The issue relates directly to the most wrenching culture war of nineteenth century America, the Civil War, and touches upon symbolic meanings of both America and the Confederate South. Because it does, the battle elevates the emotional temperature wherever and whenever it is joined. The matter also generates powerful feelings because it divides southerners racially—those who cling to the flag are almost exclusively white, while virtually all African Americans oppose its use, many actively. Another important reason why this issue stirs up powerful emotions on both sides is precisely because it has to do with a flag. Flags are among the most sacred objects of any civil religion. For those who fly them, flags embody the mythic meanings and the sacredness of the nation they love, as well as the values for which it stands. To destroy a flag is not mere vandalism; it is a violation. It is a profanation of that which citizens believe to be sacred about their nation. For this reason more than any other, Americans refer to flag-burning as "desecration."

During the last decade of the twentieth century, the flag issue has arisen several times in a variety of southern venues. Early in the Clinton administration, controversies over the flag developed in Georgia, Mississippi, and Virginia in 1993. In Mississippi, the debate raged over use of the Confederate flag at University of Mississippi football games, when the 700 black undergraduates refused to sit in the student section because white students were there waving the controversial emblem. Related to this, three black members of the Ole Miss band put down their instruments, stood, and folded their arms to protest the playing of "Dixie."[42]

That same year, the city of Danville, Virginia, became embroiled in the debate, when the board of trustees of the city's Museum of Fine Arts and History voted to stop flying the flag from atop its building, which in fact is the historic "Last Capital of the Confederacy." (During the last week of the Civil War, as the Yankees closed in on Richmond, the Confederate government was moved west to Danville.)

---

[42] Douglas Lederman, Old Times Not Forgotten," *Chronicle of Higher Education*, October 20, 1993, A51-52.

"We Southern Americans are a little pissed off," protested a member of the Sons of Confederate Veterans, apparently speaking for many who expressed themselves in a slightly more genteel manner. Over the next few days, the *Danville Register and Bee* was flooded with over 7,000 phone calls, ninety-five percent of which indicated opposition to removing the flag. The paper also ran page upon page of letters to the editor reflecting similar feelings. Linwood Wright, president of the museum's board of trustees, also received a flurry of calls, some of which he described as "venomous."[43]

Some of the arguments for flying the flag rehashed old historiographical debates by which many white southerners assuaged their guilt by denying that the flag or the Confederacy represent slavery. They largely argued that the flag represented the Confederacy as a period of American history that, though tragic, could not be changed and should not be whitewashed. Most correspondents denied that the flag represented slavery, but stood for rather states' rights and the valor with which their great-great grandfathers fought and died. No one questions the courage of Confederate soldiers as they fought for principles in which they believed. But clearly, they believed in slavery even if they were a part of the eighty percent of antebellum southern whites who did not own slaves. Moreover, in reality it is the Rebel flag-wavers who attempt to rewrite history, or at least gloss over the most offensive part of it. White southerners have had a long tradition of avoiding the fact that the Civil War was *primarily*, though not exclusively, about the problem of slavery in a land that claimed that "all men are created equal." Slavery was philosophically founded upon and dedicated to the proposition that certain people were *not* created equal and were thereby legally enslaveable. Apart from that assumption, slavery based on race or color could not have existed.

Those who argue that the Confederate flag does not imply slavery or racism would do well to note a March 1861 speech by Vice-President of the Confederacy Alexander Stephens, in which he asserted that, unlike the "Old" Union, the Confederacy did not stand for the equality of the races. Rather, he continued: "Our new Government is founded upon exactly the opposite ideas; its foundations are laid, its cornerstone rests, upon the great truth that the Negro is not equal to

---

[43] *Danville Register and Bee,* June 8, 1993; June 12, 1993.

the white man, that slavery—subordination to the superior race—is his natural and normal condition."[44] Many others during the War saw their cause as the effort to maintain slavery. A Georgia editor in 1862 made it rather plain: "[N]egro slavery is the South, and the South is negro slavery." The *Mobile Register* wrote that "slavery and the cause must rise or fall together, for they are identical."[45] One could cite many other examples. Regarding states' rights, the question thus becomes, What did the white South want their states to have the right to do? The answer is, To continue to enslave black Americans. States' rights was clearly a means to the end of preserving slavery and was therefore a subsidiary rather than the primary cause. Moreover, the most self-evident result of the War was the end of slavery. Thus the causal connection between the War and slavery ought to be obvious. If the Confederacy's noble cause was to preserve slavery, only with blindfolds of illogic can white southerners deny that its flag at least indirectly symbolizes slavery and the racism upon which it was based. *That* is part of the southern heritage, and arguing that the flag does not symbolize that is precisely to gloss over and rewrite southern history. Historical analysis like this is reminiscent of the Simon and Garfunkel lyric, "A man hears what he wants to hear and disregards the rest."

But other arguments set forth in the Danville debate reflect connections with the current culture war, as many of its hot-button issues showed up in the tangential arguments of flag defenders. Political correctness, often the scourge of many of today's cultural conservatives, was seen as inspiring the decision to remove the flag. One Danvillian wrote, "Flying the flag...may not be politically correct, but it is historically correct." Another writer attributed the black response to the flag to being too easily offended. "It is precisely this type of thinking," he wrote, "which has driven God and prayer from our classrooms." Similarly, still another reader took aim at Danville city council member Joyce Glaise, who had applauded the Museum's decision. Comparing Glaise to America's most hated atheist, Madeline Murray O'Hair, the letter complained: "We're already had one woman single-handedly try to bring down the morals of our

---

[44] Quoted in Emory M. Thomas, *The Confederate Nation: 1861-1865* (New York: Harper and Row, Publishers, 1979) 10.

[45] See Faust, *Creation of Confederate Nationalism*, 59-60.

nation by having prayer removed from our schools. Now you want to remove another vital part of our heritage. *No way!*" Many writers called on the city to wave the Confederate flag as proudly as they would the American flag. Finally, reflecting the nostalgia for the good old days, one writer commented, "I think most of the people who live here liked our town the way it used to be."[46] Whether these citizens preferred Danville "the way it used to be" before the Civil War, or simply before the civil rights movement, is unclear, but there is little doubt that their arguments for the Confederate flag match up with many of the concerns of conservative culture warriors.

During the 2000 elections, the flag was raised as a campaign issue in both South Carolina and the presidential primaries. In May the South Carolina legislature approved a bill moving the flag from atop the statehouse to a Civil War monument on the capitol grounds. The measure was passed as a response to a five-month tourism boycott of South Carolina by the NAACP, and action that cost the state more than $20 million in revenue from conventions and conferences. The decision also led to protests among flag supporters.[47] As the NAACP boycott got under way, so did the presidential primary season. Covering the early primaries, reporters' questions forced candidates to take sides on the issue. Arizona Senator John McCain acknowledged its divisiveness, but said, "I believe it's a symbol of heritage." Eventual victor George W. Bush treaded lightly, saying it was a matter for the people of South Carolina to decide. Democrat candidate Al Gore supported the removal of the flag from the state capitol and criticized Bush for ducking the issue.[48]

In Georgia the flag became a *cause celebre* twice in recent years. In 1992 popular governor Zell Miller ran afoul of the electorate, and almost cost himself a second term, because of his plan to change the state flag, which incorporated the Confederate emblem. That version of the Georgia flag had been adopted only in 1956, Miller pointed out, as a protest against integration. He called it "the fighting flag of those who wanted to preserve a segregated South." By the time he gave his State of the State speech in 1993, Miller knew he did not have the votes

---

[46] *Danville Register and Bee*, June 5, 1993; June 9, 1993; *Danville Register and Bee*, June 10, 1993.

[47] CNN web reports, May 10 and July 1, 2000.

[48] CNN web report, January 16, 2000.

to change the flag. Yet he addressed the issue directly, and in terms reminiscent of both the Civil War and the contemporary culture wars. He identified the Confederate flag with "the dark side of the Confederacy—the desire to deprive some Americans of the equal rights that are the birthright of all Americans, and yes, the determination to destroy the United States if necessary to achieve that goal....Yet we maintain as a symbol of our state a flag that challenges the very existence of the United States of America."[49] The governor lost that fight by a large margin. But he correctly predicted that the issue would not die and that the Rebel-dominated flag of Georgia would not last too far into the future. In 2001, reacting to threats of a similar NAACP boycott against Georgia, and as these very words were being written, the Georgia State Senate followed the state House of Representatives and voted 34 to 22 to change the flag.

The controversy is more than just a "flag flap," as some derisively call it. The competition is between symbols of a *United* States, inclusive of all, and a *Divided* States, North and South, white and black. Those who defend the Confederate flag as "heritage not hate," forget that the flag symbolizes a society based on slavery as a way of preserving white supremacy. Those who defend the Confederate flag, as well as those who reject it, do so with the moral fervor of a culture war over how inclusive America will be in the twenty-first century. Perhaps the clearest and most vivid connection of this controversy to America's culture conflict is to be found in the state of Virginia, where every second Monday in January marks not simply the Martin Luther King Holiday, but a holiday commemorating an unlikely trinity of heroes—Robert E. Lee, Stonewall Jackson, and Martin Luther King. On the very same day, Virginians ironically reflect upon two competing understandings, two different visions of America— one homogeneous and exclusive; the other heterogeneous and inclusive. To whatever degree southerners may find honor and virtue in these sacred civil religious traditions, at the very least they celebrate two contrasting images of what America ought to be. The further irony is that both visions spring from the soil of the South. Thus, the South remains the once and future arbiter of which America provides the answer to Rodney King's famous question, "Can we all get along?"

---

[49] Miller quoted in Richard Hyatt, *Zell: The Governor Who Gave Georgia HOPE* (Macon: Mercer University Press, 1997) 325-326, 335-336.

Perhaps it is a new millennium after all, and the news from Atlanta may signal a kinder, gentler turn in America's culture war.

But don't bet on it. Odds are that race will continue to shape conflicting images of America into the twenty-first century for some time to come.

6

CIVIL RELIGIONS AND THE PROBLEM
OF RACE IN THE NEW MILLENNIUM

According to a popular story, a little boy was selling puppies by the road one day when an elderly gentleman came by and asked what kind of puppies the boy had for sale. "Democratic puppies," came the answer. The next week the gentleman returned and once again asked what sort of puppies the boy was tending. This time the answer came, "Republican puppies." The man then said, "Son, just last week you said they were Democratic puppies; how come now they are Republicans?" To which the boy replied, "Because *now* their eyes are open." For quite a long while now, it seems, South Carolina's Senator Strom Thurmond, the South's original Dixiecrat, has been telling that story to explain his conversion to the Republican party.

If, like Rip Van Winkle, we had closed our eyes after the high water marks of the civil rights movement, the Civil Rights Act of 1964 and the Voting Rights Act of 1965, only to have our eyes re-opened in this new millennium, we would now see very clearly two unmistakable realities about American politics and culture. One thing our newly opened eyes would see is a major transformation in which the white South has gone the way of Strom Thurmond and those puppies. At least in presidential elections, and increasingly at the local and state levels, the "Solid South" is still solid, but now solid with "Yellow Dog Republicans" instead of Democrats. To anyone who pays attention to American politics, this is so obvious as to barely need any corroborating evidence. Since 1964 Republican candidates have won the majority of southern (at least southern white) votes, except in 1976 when Republicans were still reeling from Watergate and southerner Jimmy Carter was the Democratic nominee.

The other reality we would see if we re-opened our eyes in the new millennium is that the solidly Republican white South, along with the rest of the nation, is embroiled in the "culture wars." The fires of battle, however, have raged for a good deal longer than the past eight years. University of Virginia sociologist James Davison Hunter actually he took the term from Otto von Bismarck's anti-Semitic and Catholic policy of *Kulturkampf* or "culture struggle" in nineteenth century Germany. In his 1990 book, *Culture Wars: The Struggle to Define America,* Hunter attempted to explain our contemporary battles over the family, art, education, law, and politics. He argued that the culture wars have produced a shrill partisanship and ideological incivility the likes of which have not been seen in America since the Civil War. On his way out of the Oval Office, without using the term "culture wars," Bill Clinton nonetheless summed up his opposition as a "basic attempt to delegitimize and de-Americanize your opponent."[1] Others would add the tactic of "demonizing" their political opposition. And in the wake of the disputed presidential election of 2000, skirmishes of the culture war broke out in Florida and Washington, DC as groups of Democrats and Republicans protested the final results with angry mutual accusations of trying to steal the presidency and complaints about the Supreme Court's "president-select."

Hunter viewed the factions' respective moral and religious commitments as the source of the culture wars. The combatants are true believers in "opposing bases of moral authority." The culture war is a struggle between "competing moral visions." Hunter argues that for most of American history cultural hostilities have occurred "within the boundaries of a larger biblical culture." Since the rise of modernity, however, and especially since the mid-twentieth century, Americans have been divided between those whose moral compasses lead them toward what Hunter calls the "impulse toward orthodoxy" and those with the "impulse toward progressivism." *Orthodoxy* is the belief in an external, definable, and transcendent moral authority, such as the Bible or the Judeo-Christian tradition. On the other hand,

---

[1]Bill Clinton, "The Exit Interview," *Esquire*, December 2000. See www.esquire.com.

Progressivism is the modern—some would say postmodern—tendency toward rational or subjective moral authority.[2]

While the nation ignores these competing moral understandings at its peril, it would seem that also at work here is what I have called a conflict of civil religions. What I interpret as a conflict of civil faiths, Hunter has described as a culture war. But his subtitle—"the struggle to define America"—suggests we may have been hunting the same game. Defining the nation in religio-patriotic terms is precisely what civil religions do. Listening to opposing culture warriors invoke the Bill of Rights, the "founding fathers," and "what America is really all about," Hunter acknowledges that "the contemporary culture war is ultimately a struggle over national identity—over the meaning of America, who we have been in the past, who we are now, and perhaps most important, who we, as a nation, will aspire to become in the new millennium."[3] Sociologist Robert Wuthnow has similarly described it as a divide between a liberal civil religion that exalts universality and a conservative civil religion that values American exceptionalism.[4]

There are, of course, some major differences between Hunter's analysis and my own. One obvious difference is my emphasis on the role of the American South as the venue for the civil religious conflict. In fact, if we remove its blatant sectionalism and overtly racist language, both of which now violate current canons of civility, the South of the civil rights era remains an accurate mirror on contemporary America. This suggests that a southernization of America has taken place and that the best evidence for it is the culture wars main combatants. One might add that the South is also *at the center* of the culture war.[5]

Another difference between my formulation and Hunter's is that, to be sure, his description of the conflict is thicker than mine. He examines a wider range of "hot button" social issues, while I have looked primarily at race. Of course, what I called a conflict of civil

---

[2] James Davison Hunter, *Culture Wars: The Struggle to Define America* (New York: Basic Books, 1990) 42-45.

[3] Ibid., 50.

[4] Robert Wuthnow, *The Restructuring of American Religion: Society and Faith Since World War II* (Princeton: Princeton University Press, 1988) 241-67.

[5] Earl and Merle Black, *The Vital South: How Presidents Are Elected* (Cambridge: Harvard University Press, 1990) 364-366.

religions has broadened from merely different understandings about the role of racial and cultural difference in America to a wider culture war fought on many fronts other than race. This, however, goes to my main argument. Hunter has significantly minimized race as a component of the culture war. Indeed, in a book of over 400 pages, Hunter discusses African Americans or race in only fifteen non-consecutive pages. If, as David W. Wills has suggested, race is one of the central themes of American religious history, and if, as many others have suggested, racism is America's "original sin," then one might hope to see more attention to those crucial issues in a book as important as Hunter's.[6] For that reason, the civil rights struggle of the mid-twentieth century is the best place to look for conflicting civil religious meanings of America.

Hunter sees the Civil War era as the last time in the nation's history that the national identity and purpose was as much a source of contention.[7] One could just as easily argue that the civil rights movement, called the Second Reconstruction by many historians, was really the last time America debated "the true meaning of its creed." In fact, historians Maurice Isserman and Michael Kazin have interpreted the civil rights era similarly in their recent book, *America Divided: The Civil War of the 1960s*. They write:

> To its northern and southern supporters, the civil rights move-ment was a "second Civil War."…In the course of the 1960s, many Americans came to regard groups of fellow countrymen as enemies with whom they were engaged in a struggle for the nation's very soul.…For better than three decades, the United states has been in the midst of an ongoing "culture war," fought over issues of political philosophy, race relations, gender roles, and personal morality left unresolved since the end of the 1960s.[8]

---

[6] See David W. Wills, "The Central Themes of American Religious History: Pluralism, Puritanism, and the Encounter Between Blacks and Whites," in Timothy E. Fulop and Albert J. Raboteau, eds., *African American Religion: Essays and Interpretations in History and Culture* (New York: Routledge, 1997) 12-20; Jim Wallis, "America's Original Sin: The Legacy of White Racism," *America's Original Sin: A Study on White Racism* (Washington: Sojourners Resource Center, 1992).

[7] Hunter, 50.

[8] Maurice Isserman and Michael Kazin, *America Divided: The Civil War of the 1960s* (New York: Oxford University Press, 2000) 3-4.

Just as Abraham Lincoln redefined the meanings of the Declaration of Independence with the Emancipation Proclamation and his Gettysburg remarks about a "new birth of freedom," so Martin Luther King Jr. and other civil rights preachers articulated a more pluralistic, more inclusive sense of purpose for the American nation. Just as armies of both North and South believed God to be on their side in a war to preserve their respective versions of a pure nation, so 100 years later both the integrationists and the segregationists believed God willed their respective images of America to be actualized. The civil rights movement was, however, not just the last time Americans debated the nation's identity and purpose; it was the beginning of this present culture war.

Were he around today, Lincoln might edit his Gettysburg Address to say, "Now we are engaged in a great *culture* war." And if he were unwilling to argue that this culture war is in the long view of history an extension of the civil war that began at Fort Sumter, he might very well say it began with Rosa Parks in the front of a Montgomery, Alabama bus. Hunter's idea of "competing moral visions" is very important; so are other hot button social issues taken up by the culture warriors. But *the heart* of the current *Kulturkampf* is a conflict between a homogeneous civil religion of exclusion and a pluralistic civil religion. Moreover, this particular phase of civil religious conflict began in the civil rights era and continues into this new millennium.[9] Thus, the culture war in essence began with the white backlash of the late 1960s, in North as well as the South, and is ultimately a debate about whether America should be exclusive or inclusive. To put it more bluntly, the culture war is at heart a civil religious battle over whether the sort of people who first dominated this country, namely white Anglo-Saxon (but *now* not necessarily Protestant) people, will continue to dominate it, or whether others will get an equal place at the table. To make these points, one must see

---

[9] To split historical hairs, one could argue that the conflict actually began when the Second Continental Congress' deleted Jefferson's antislavery clause from the original draft of the Declaration. One might also date its beginning with the Constitutional compromises on slavery, adding that the essential question of racial and cultural inclusion was left unresolved by the Civil War and Reconstruction and once again taken up in earnest in the mid-twentieth century. To simplify the argument, however, I maintain that the fervor and shrillness necessary to a culture war only really began with the civil rights movement.

the connections between white backlash against the civil rights movement and the array of social issues that now make up the culture war.

Theoretically, civil religion is supposed to unite citizens by focusing their allegiance on the religious meaning of their nation. Quite often, however, civil religions and their symbols can divide as well as unify. The best contemporary example of that is the Confederate battle flag, which means one thing to certain Americans and something else entirely to other groups of Americans. I have already alluded to the conflicting sentiments during the Civil War that both South and North fought in apocalyptic terms to preserve and purify their respective nations. As Lincoln said in his Second Inaugural, "Both read the same Bible and pray to the same God; and each invokes his aid against the other."

There was, of course, a similar conflict of civil religions dividing white and black southerners during the civil rights movement. Like most Christians throughout our history, both groups believed that America was in some way "God's Chosen People." In the civil rights movement they had directly conflicting mythic images of America. Both understood America as chosen and they both saw the nation as the not-quite-Christian beacon of freedom. They differed, however, on what kept America from being fully Christian. For whites it was the external threat of Communism (and to a slightly lesser extent, the power of Catholicism), while for blacks it was the internal threat of America's mishandling of its heritage of freedom. Basing their argument on the fact of America's pluralism, black Baptists saw integration as a symbol of hope that their images of the nation might be realized. On the other hand, the civil religion of Southern Baptist segregationists saw integration as a symbol of a endangered hope that America might continue to be a free, Anglo-Saxon nation.

Thus, during the civil rights era, two civil religions, two definitions of American reality, competed for the allegiance of southerners white and black. One version of the civil religion pulled them toward the racial status quo and the segregationist tradition; the other pulled them toward a messianic America in which "all men are created equal." To put it differently, during the civil rights era southerners and other Americans were caught between a civil religion of exclusion and a civil religion of inclusion. Those Americans operating with a civil religion of exclusion came to be a part of what is known as the "white backlash."

The White Backlash and the Culture War

Armed with this civil religion of inclusion the civil rights movement eventually won its primary victories on the streets of Alabama, first in Birmingham and then in Selma. Then came the commitment of the federal government to its goals in the Civil Rights Act of 1964 (resulting from the Birmingham protests), the Voting Rights Act of 1965, (resulting from the Selma to Montgomery March), and the Great Society programs (resulting from the assassination of President Kennedy and election of Lyndon Baines Johnson). But the victory would be short-lived, and political genius that he was, Johnson had an inkling of what was to come. On the very night that he signed the Civil Rights Act of 1964, LBJ explained to his press secretary Bill Moyers his reason for feeling downcast rather than elated, "Because, Bill, I think we just delivered the South to the Republican party for a long time to come."[10]

Johnson seems to have been right on the money both as to the white South's defection and its duration. Now we stand almost thirty years since Johnson's death and a return of a Prodigal white South to the Democratic party is nowhere in sight. Johnson's political instincts rightly told him that casting his party's lot with the agenda of black America would alienate his fellow white southerners. Indeed, many southerners viewed Johnson, a Texan, as a traitor to the South because of his racial liberalism, and though he won a landslide victory over Barry Goldwater in 1964, he lost the Deep South. One of my own loneliest days in elementary school in Birmingham, Alabama, was the day after election day, when I was impolitic enough to gloat among my classmates that my mother's candidate had won the presidency. Not long after that, I noticed the appearance of a particular license plate with a cartoon picture of a Democratic donkey with a

---

[10] Bill Moyers, "What a Real President Was Like," *Washington Post*, November 13, 1988.

Johnsonesque face, passing gas, and a caption that read, "LBJ Has Spoken."[11]

More significantly, since then the Democrats have lost not only most of the white South, but they have consistently lost the majority of white male votes in the entire nation. As former columnist Tom Wicker notes, "The Democratic party after 1964, lost a critical and growing share of the white vote, owing to the party's supposed devotion to black interests." Indeed, the last Democratic presidential candidate to win a majority of the nation's white males was Johnson in 1964.[12] The disaffection of whites from the Democratic agenda of the Great Society, increasingly perceived as the black agenda, was remarkably rapid. Non-southern white hostility to black advances can be seen in opinion polling data. When Johnson took office in 1963 a Harris poll found that only 31 percent of Americans polled believed that the federal government was pushing integration "too fast." Only five years later the figure had increased to 51 percent. A 1966 Gallup poll indicated the percentage was an even higher 72 percent.[13]

Thus a national reversal began within three years of the high water marks of the civil rights movement. In addition to the Democrats' "capture" by the civil rights agenda and its commitment to the spending programs of the Great Society, middle class white voters, especially in the South, were angered by the Watts riots of 1965, Martin Luther King's denunciation of the Vietnam War in 1967, and the civil disturbances after King's assassination in 1968. This helps explain their disaffection with black interests and their move away from the Democratic party.[14]

Two questions thus arise. First, to whom did middle and working class white voters angry at civil rights agitators and the counterculture

---

[11] On Johnson as traitor to the South, see Charles and Barbara Whalen, *The Longest Debate* (New York: New American Library, 1986).

[12] Wicker, 38.

[13] Louis Harris and William Brink, *Black and White: a Study of U. S. Racial Attitudes Today* (New York: Simon and Schuster, 1964) 100-117; George H. Gallup, *The Gallup Poll: 1935- 1971* (3 vols.; New York: Random House, 1972, III, 1933, 19041-43, 2011, 2021, 2128. See also Wicker, 8.

[14] Oran Smith, *The Rise of Baptist Republicanism* (New York: New York University Press, 1997) 89; Earl and Merle Black, *Politics and Society in the South* (Cambridge: Harvard University Press, 1987) 218-219; *Vital South*, 292-276; Wicker, 6, 13, 38.

go in the 1968 presidential election? Second, how then was this white backlash against the gains of the civil rights movement connected to the broader array of social issues that make up the culture war of recent days? The answer to both questions is the same: George Wallace. In two very important books, historian Dan T. Carter presents a solid case for the "fighting judge" and later governor of Alabama as the antecedent of what Carter calls "the politics of rage."

Through the 1980s and 1990s, the issues Wallace articulated and the enemies he excoriated "moved from the fringes of our society to center stage." Wallace did not create the conservative groundswell of the culture war, but, Carter argues, "he anticipated most of its themes.[15] By his 1968 third party run for the presidency, Wallace broadened his criticism beyond the traditional southern racial politics of his "schoolhouse door" phase to a wider range of social battles that were later joined by the Moral Majority and the Christian Coalition. Yet beneath it all lingered the slightly domesticated racism that had earlier demanded "Segregation today, segregation tomorrow, segregation forever." Carter points out that Wallace knew that a substantial percentage of the American electorate despised the civil rights agitators and antiwar demonstrators as symptoms of a fundamental decline in the traditional cultural compass of God, family and country, a decline reflected in rising crime rates, the legalization of abortion, the rise of out-of-wedlock pregnancies, the increase in divorce rates, and the proliferation of 'obscene' literature and films. And moving always beneath the surface was the fear that blacks were moving beyond their safely encapsulated ghettoes into 'our' streets, 'our' schools, 'our' neighborhoods.[16]

Thus fears of black criminality and associations with the disorder of the 1960s counterculture were not only central to Wallace's message, but in Carter's view were "the warp and woof" of the new social agenda of the conservative counterrevolution.[17]

The Wallace message and his enlarged following outside the South suggested, of course, the prevalence of racism outside the South, and in

---

[15] Dan T. Carter, *The Politics of Rage,* 472, 474.

[16] Dan T. Carter, *From George Wallace to Newt Gingrich: Race in the Conservative Counterrevolution, 1963-1994* (Baton Rouge: Louisiana State University Press, 1996) 14-15. Hereinafter cited as *FGWTNG.*

[17] Carter, *From George Wallace to Newt Gingrich,* 42.

the process came to the attention of Richard Nixon. As early as 1966, Nixon had decided to run for the presidency, and during a fund raising trip to South Carolina he told Harry Dent, aide to Strom Thurmond and chief architect of Nixon's Southern Strategy, that getting the Wallace vote in the South was the key to victory. In the 1968 campaign, Nixon taped a "law and order" political advertisement in which he echoed Wallace's themes. John Erlichman later told of his boss's effusive praise of the commercial, exulting, "It's all about law and order and the damn Negro-Puerto Rican groups out there."[18] After the 1968 election, which Nixon barely won and during which Nixon was the second choice of more than 70 percent of Wallace voters, Nixon vowed to stick with his southern strategy and do his best to keep the Wallace vote in his 1972 re-election bid. He certainly reflected the spirit, even if he avoided the exact phraseology of the famous Wallace line, spoken after a race-baiting opponent defeated him in the 1958 governor's race, that he intended never to be "out-niggered again." Soon, Nixon's domestic policies reflected Wallace's call for law and order and criticism of busing to achieve racial balance in the schools. Carter summed it up nicely: "When George Wallace had played his fiddle, the President of the United States had danced Jim Crow."[19]

Since then, at least in the voices that occupied the Oval Office, the Republican party has largely been George Wallace without the southern accent. As the dean of southern historians, C. Vann Woodward put it, "[S]outhern white Democrats have been Republicanized and northern white Republicans have been southernized."[20] Ronald Reagan echoed Wallace themes with a friendlier face. As a rising Republican spokesman for General Electric, and later as Governor of California, he opposed the Civil Rights Act of 1964. After his presidential nomination in 1980, he began his general election campaign announcing his commitment to states' rights in Neshoba County, Mississippi, where three civil rights workers were murdered in 1964. As president, he opposed renewing the Voting Rights Act of 1965. His justice department tried to allow Bob Jones University to

---

[18] Carter, FGWTNG, 30-31, citing John Erlichman, *Witness to Power: the Nixon Years* (New York: Simon and Schuster, 1982) 223.

[19] Carter, FGWTNG, 18, citing Gallup poll data; *Politics of Rage*, 471.

[20] From a publisher's blurb for Carter, FGWTNG.

discriminate against black and still receive a tax exemption. He opposed the Martin Luther King Holiday. When he retired as the most popular president of the second half of the twentieth century, blacks considered him a racist by a 3 to 1 margin.[21]

Then there was George Bush's 1988 "Willie Horton" ads that attacked Governor Michael Dukakis's prison furlough program. Or Senator Jesse Helms's ad against black opponent Harvey Gantt in which a white worker crumpled a job rejection letter with the voice-over: "You were qualified for that job, but it had to go to a minority because of quotas." Or Newt Gingrich's tirades against the counter-culture and the Great Society—both associated with African Americans by conservative middle class whites. Or his penchant for demonizing Democrats as more than just misguided, telling a reporter, "These people are sick." Or his suggested word list for defining Democrats: traitors, corrupt, bizarre, cheat, steal, devour, self-serving, and criminal rights.[22] Or Patrick Buchanan, Nixon's former speech writer who greatly admired Wallace and like him denounced the "whole rotten infrastructure of reverse discrimination" and "professional civil rights agitators."[23] As recently as his 2000 presidential campaign, Buchanan promised that his new Reform Party would "defend America's history, heritage and heroes against the Visigoths and Vandals of multiculturalism." His radio ads emphasized the culture war, claiming "It's time to take our country back from those who are tearing it down." He added: "In the culture war Al Gore is the enemy, and George W. Bush won't fight."[24]

To be sure, Buchanan's candidacy did not win the Republican nomination. Since Nixon and Wallace, however, the southern strategy has always been to put a friendlier face on the white backlash—to make it a "compassionate conservatism," if you will. True, Buchanan's Reform Party garnered only one percent of the 2000 popular vote, but many within the Republican party maintain a strong interest in pieces of Buchanan's message. More important, they are

---

[21] Wicker, 13-15; Carter, FGWTNG, 68.

[22] Wicker, 27-28; Carter, FGWTNG, 119; *Wall Street Journal*, May 10, 1988.

[23] Carter, FGWTNG, 93.

[24] Pat Buchanan August 13, 2000, Reform Party Convention, Long Beach; Bob Kemper, "Buchanan Maps Last-Minute Ad Blitz," *Chicago Tribune*, October 31, 2000. Both sources accessed on the Buchanan campaign's web site.

pragmatic enough not to waste their votes on a third party. Yet Buchanan, along with Reagan, the Bushes, Helms, and Gingrich, remain popular with the Religious Right who have been the shock troops of the culture war ever since Jerry Falwell invented the Moral Majority in 1979. And the 2000 election brought Falwell out of out of political semi-retirement to rally the Southern Baptist faithful to help defeat Al Gore.[25]

Having thus reacted against the pluralistic images of America and the racial gains of the civil rights era, the wider American nation has increasingly mythologized the nation in ways similar to the homogeneous civil religionists of the white South. And like southernness, the issue of race remains at the heart of the culture war. Michael Lind has correctly perceived that since Nixon and Reagan the Republican party has moved from relatively progressive racial policy to using race as a wedge. He adds: "The politics of 'culture war'…is, like so much else in the GOP, a transplant from the poisoned soil of the Bourbon South."[26]

Concluding Thoughts

The culture warriors of the Religious Right naturally deny that their agenda has primarily to do with race. As almost everybody says these days, racism is more subtle and more civil. Even some black liberal Evangelicals such as Stephen Carter note that for many America has become a culture "that many Americans see as threatening, not to themselves, but to their children—and in particular, to the ability of families to raise their children with religious values they consider vital."[27] Yet, even if race is temporarily factored out of the analysis, Americans are still dealing with the difficulties of living with pluralism in its free marketplace where all religions and cultures are created equal and with no religion or culture having a leg up on the others.

Perhaps the key reason why some white Christians believe themselves to be discriminated against in a multicultural society today is the many yesterdays when white Christianity dominated

---

[25] "Falwell Urges Baptists to Help Defeat Al Gore," press release, Associated Baptist Press, June 13, 2000.

[26] Michael Lind, "The Southern Coup," New Republic, 19 June 1995, 26, 29.

[27] Stephen L. Carter, God's Name, 44.

America's cultural landscape. Perhaps some white Christians today feel powerless in American culture mainly because they (or at least their spiritual progenitors) have been virtually *all*-powerful in the past, but no longer enjoy their earlier cultural dominance. Governmental and cultural neutrality *feels* like hostility because historically Evangelicals, particularly in the South, have enjoyed cultural favor. In their history they have grown accustomed to playing with an advantage and now that the playing field in America is level, it feels unfair. If one has been treated like a monarch for all of one's experience, being treated as an equal will seem like punishment. Since the ratification of the Constitution, Christianity has never reaped the benefits of a legally established religion, but it has enjoyed the advantage of cultural power. As a race, whites have obvious had a legal upper hand. Unfortunately, early on in American history whites Christians had become addicted to their power to dominate American life.

But by the mid-twentieth century, which also happened to be the beginning of the civil rights era, pluralism could no longer be denied. The civil rights movement cracked the door open and the counter-culture burst through. As George Marsden has noted, the South, historically less comfortable with racial or cultural pluralism, became the center of gravity for the Religious Right and the culture war. Faced with increasing pluralism and moral inclusivism, which they identified with the Democratic party, Republicans built a coalition around "militant, Christian, anti-secularist, and (formerly) anti-Communist heritage." Marsden could have added, "anti-Great Society, anti-black" to his list. He did add, however, that "as the end of the twentieth century approaches, this view of what it means to be an American conflicts sharply with a more inclusivist moral vision."[28]

As is well-known, during the 1960s Jerry Falwell spoke out against the civil rights movement. In the years immediately following those pronouncements, America saw an increasing racial equality and cultural diversity. Then later, after his emergence as leader of the Moral Majority and after the election of Ronald Reagan, Falwell celebrated that "America is back again." As theologian Walter Capps has noted, the America Falwell hoped for and the one whose return he

---

[28]George Marsden, "Religion, Politics, and the Search for an American Consensus," in Noll, *Religion and American Politics*, 388-389.

celebrated was the America that existed before the civil rights movement and the counterculture destabilized the status quo. Capps added that the Religious Right has given no evidence of honoring the sort of diversity introduced by the civil rights movement. Rather, Capps argues, its historical interpretations of America and its theology "reinforce the desire for a monochromatic society, even if these are not its declared objectives."[29]

Thus, the culture war, begun in the civil rights era as civil faiths in conflict over racial and cultural inclusiveness, continues in the twenty-first century. In the new millennium's first presidential election—a quadrennial exercise that always invites Americans to redefine their nation—a conservative thinktank called the Claremont Institute denounced Al Gore and Joe Lieberman as representatives of "the new civil religion of multiculturalism." Claremont spokesperson Ken Masugi chastised Gore's book *Earth in the Balance* for accepting in philosophical insights of Marxist Maurice Merleau-Ponty and Martin Heidegger, whom he exaggeratedly called a "Nazi theologian." With analysis reeking with McCarthyite guilt by association, Masugi warns that if we embrace the civil theology of multicultural openness, "dare we wonder what might come through that open door?"[30]

The open door of inclusiveness has always troubled a good many Americans. It was so in 1619, when those first twenty "negars" arrived on a Dutch man-o-war. It was so in Reconstruction days when the Fifteenth Amendment opened the door to the voting booth for their descendants. It was so in 1954 when the Warren court opened the door to equal education in America's public schools. And if it takes fighting a culture war for another millennium to keep that door open, God forbid that America let anyone close it.

---

[29] Walter H. Capps, *The New Religious Right: Piety, Patriotism, and Politics* (Columbia: University of South Carolina Press, 1990) 202, 210.

[30] Ken Masugi, "The New Civil Religion of Multiculturalism," Accessed on the Internet at www.claremont.org/publications/masugi000818.cfm.

BIBLIOGRAPHY

Because of the diversity of sources, the bibliography has been divided into several sections outlined as follows: Under the *Primary Sources* heading, subsections indicated references to books, articles, Convention annuals, and manuscript sources-in that order. Under the *Secondary Sources* heading, the reader will find subsections listing books and articles.

PRIMARY SOURCES

Books

Ahman, Matthew, ed. Race: *Challenge to Religion.* Chicago: Henry Regnery Co., 1963.
Brady, Thomas Pickens. *Black Monday,* Winona, Miss.: Association of Citizens Councils, 1955.
Brown, Robert R. *Bigger Than Little Rock.* Greenwich, Conn.: Seabury Press, 1958.
Campbell, Ernest Q., and Thomas F. Pettigrew. *Christians in Racial Crisis: A Study of Little Rock's Ministry.* Washington, D.C.: Public Affairs Press, 1959.
Carter, Hodding. *The South Strikes Back.* New York: Doubleday & Co., 1959.
Eckardt, Arthur Roy. *The Surge of Piety in America: An Appraisal.* New York: Association Press, 1958.
Frazier, E. Franklin. *The Negro in the United States.* Revised Edition. New York: Macmillan Co., 1957.
Herberg, Will. *Protestant-Catholic-Jew.* Garden City, N. Y.: Doubleday & Co., 1955.
Hill, Davis C. "Southern Baptist Thought and Action in Race Relations." Th.D. diss., Southern Baptist Theological Seminary, 1952.
Jackson, Joseph Harrison. *A Story of Christian Activism: The History of the National Baptist Convention, U.S.A.* Nashville: Townsend Press, 1980.
_____. *Unholy Shadows and Freedom's Holy Light.* Nashville: Townsend Press, 1967.
King, Martin Luther, Jr. Strength to Love. 2d ed. Philadelphia: Fortress Press, 1981.
_____. *Stride Toward Freedom: The Montgomery Story.* New York: Harper & Row, 1958.
_____. *Where Do We Go from Here: Chaos or Community?* New York: Harper & Row, 1967.
_____. *Why We Can't Wait.* New York: New American Library, 1964.
King, Martin Luther, Sr. *Daddy King: An Autobiography.* New York: Harper & Row, 1980.
Logan, Spencer, *A Negro's Faith in America.* New York: Macmillan Co., 1946.

Martin, John Bartlow. *The Deep South Says "Never."* New York: Ballantine Books, 1957.

Marty, Martin Emil. *The New Shape of American Religion.* New York: Harper & Brothers, 1958.

Maston, Thomas Buford. *Integration.* Nashville: Christian Life Commission of the Southern Baptist Convention, 1956.

Mays, Benjamin Elijah. *Born To Rebel.* New York: Charles Scribner's Sons, 1971.

_____. *Disturbed About Man.* Atlanta: John Knox Press, 1969.

Myrdal, Gunnar. *An American Dilemma: The Negro Problem and Modern Democracy.* 2 vols. New York: Harper and Brothers, 1944.

Robertson, A. T. *The New Citizenship: The Christian Facing a New World Order.* New York: Fleming H. Revell Co., 1919.

Stewart, Maxwell S. *The Negro in America.* New York: Public Affairs Committee, 1944.

Talmadge, Herman E. *You and Segregation.* Birmingham: Vulcan Press, 1955.

Articles

"Alabama Baptists Hit New Lay White Supremacy Group." *Baptist Record 80* (May 3, 1957): 1.

Amos, R. L. "How and When Will It End?" *American Baptist 79* (February 1, 1957): 2.

_____. "Inalienable Rights." *American Baptist 78* (December 7, 1956): 2.

_____. "Little Rock in a Big Role." *American Baptist 79* (October 25, 1957): 2.

_____. "Minutemen vs. Minutemen." *American Baptist 79.* (January 4, 1957): 2.

_____. "A Paradox of Paradoxes. *American Baptist 79* (August 30, 1957): 2.

_____. "We Would See Jesus." *American Baptist 79* (September 27, 1957): 2.

Austin, J. C. "To the Citizens of Our Great Democracy." *National Baptist Voice 24* (August 15, 1952): 1.

"Baptist world Alliance Hears Drs. Jackson and Ennals." *American Baptist 71* (July 22, 1955): 1 and 6.

Ballew, William H. "America and Civic Rights." *American Baptist 71* (November 18, 1949): 2.

_____. "America Needs a Revival." *American Baptist 71* (July 22, 1949): 2.

_____. "America's Challenge." *American Baptist 79* (April 19, 1957): 2.

_____. "America's Opportunity." *American Baptist 69* (July 11, 1947): 2.

_____. "Brotherhood Week Observed." *American Baptist 71* (February 11, 1949): 2.

_____. "Campaign Issues Evaded." *American Baptist 74* (October 17, 1952): 2.

_____. "Consider with Diligence." *American Baptist 76* (October 29, 1954): 2.

_____. "Count Your Blessings." *American Baptist 78* (November 16, 1956): 2.

_____. "A Cruel Opinion." *American Baptist 71* (March 4, 1949): 2.

_____. "A Day of Repentance, Fasting and Prayer." *American Baptist 78* (April 13, 1956): 4.

_____. "The Declaration of Independence Something to Live By." *American Baptist 69* (June 27, 1947): 2.

_____. "Have You a Constructive Offer?" *American Baptist 79* (January 18, 1957): 2.

_____. "Let's Not Defeat Ourselves." *American Baptist 76* (June 4, 1954): 2.

_____. "Let's Think and Talk Sense." *American Baptist 76* (May 28, 1954): 2.

_____. "Minority Progress." *American Baptist 76* (July 23, 1954): 2.

_____. "A Negro Youth Commended." *American Baptist 71* (July 29, 1949): 2.

_____. "Pressing Our Claims." *American Baptist 71* (Aug 12, 1949): 2.

_____. "Religion and Politics." *American Baptist 78* (March 16, 1956): 2.

_____. "Right Will Win." *American Baptist 78* (March 30, 1956): 2.

_____. "A Sane Approach." *American Baptist 76* (July 2, 1954): 2.

_____. "Self-Distruction" [sic]. *American Baptist 77* (December 9, 1955): 2.

_____. "Shadow Boxing." *American Baptist 69* (February 28, 1947): 2.

_____. "Signs of the Time." *American Baptist 69* (November 11, 1955): 2.

_____. "A Simple Plea." *American Baptist 77* (November 11, 1955): 2.

_____. "Social Progress." *American Baptist 69* (May 16, 1947): 2.

_____. "Southern Baptists Endorse Desegregation." *American Baptist 76* (June 11, 1954): 2.

_____. "Thanks." *American Baptist 78* (March 9, 1956): 2.

_____. "Thanksgiving Day." *American Baptist 77* (November 18, 1955): 2.

_____. "A Timely Suggestion." *American Baptist 74* (January 4, 1952), 2.

_____. "What God Hath Cleansed." *American Baptist 77* (June 24, 1955): 2.

_____. "Worth Commending." *American Baptist 77* (April 4, 1955): 2.

Barbour, J. Pius. "Among the Brethren." *National Baptist Voice 32* (January 15, 1948): 8.

_____. "A Bus Trip in Europe," part 5. *National Baptist Voice 32* (December 15, 1947): 5 and 13.

_____. "A Bus Trip in Europe," part 6. *National Baptist Voice,* 32 (January 15, 1948): 5 and 10.

_____. "The Catholic Threat." *National Baptist Voice 31* (August 15, 1947): 4.

_____. "The Catholics Are Coming." *National Baptist Voice 32* (May 1, 1949): 4.

_____. "Changing Presidents Makes No Difference." *National Baptist Voice 32* (October 15, 1948): 4.

_____. "The Defeat of Bilbo—. A Pyrrhic Victory." *National Baptist Voice 31* February 1, 1947): 4.

_____. "Editor Barbour Spends a Week in Alabama." *National Baptist Voice 31* (December 15, 1947): 3 and 14.

_____. "Editor Barbour Spends a Week in Kentucky." *National Baptist Voice 31* (October 15, 1946): 6 and 14.

_____. "Editor Barbour Spends a Week in Mississippi." *National Baptist Voice 31* (November 1, 1946): 3 and 14.

_____. "Editor Barbour Tours the Mississippi Delta." *National Baptist Voice 26* (July, 1954): 3.

_____. "Get Thee behind Me Satan–A Lenten Meditation." *National Baptist Voice 32* (March 1, 1948): 4.

_____. "Gradualism." *National Baptist Voice 34* (December 1, 1951): 4.

_____. "I Will Not Shout." *National Baptist Voice 26* (May 1954): 4.

_____. "A Mighty Blow to Segregation." *National Baptist Voice 32* (October 1, 1949): 4.

_____. "Paul Robeson, Walter White, and Ralph Bunche." *National Baptist Voice 32* (April 15, 1949): 4.

_____. "The Philosophic Basis of the Present Strife." *National Baptist Voice 31* (May 1,

1947): 1-2.

_____. "Race Prejudice Ruining America As a World Leader." *National Baptist Voice 32* (June 15, 1950): 4.

_____. "Randolph Lets the Cat Out of the Bag." *National Baptist Voice 32* (April 1, 1948): 4.

_____. "Report on National Baptist Convention." *National Baptist Voice 37* (October 1, 1947): 1-3, 5, 13.

_____. "What Is the Matter with the Negro Veteran?" *National Baptist Voice 31* (March 15, 1947): 4.

_____. "Wolves at Bay." *National Baptist Voice 31* (July 1, 1947): 4.

Booker, Merrel D. "I Served a White Church." *National Baptist Voice 31* (February 1, 1947): 6 and 14.

"Borders Re-elected President of Georgia Baptist Missionary and Educational Convention." *National Baptist Voice 32* (December 1, 1948): 3 and 10.

Brown, Earl. "American Negroes and the War." *Harper's Magazine*, April 1942, pp. 546-55.

Bryan, Gainer, E., Jr. "Georgia Baptists of White and Negro Conventions Join in Fellowship Meeting at Savannah." *Christian Index 126* (November 28, 1946): 5-6.

Buchanan, John H. "America at the Crossroads." *Alabama Baptist 117* (June 5, 1952): 4-5.

Butler, Henrietta P. "Race Relations Sunday." *American Baptist 69* (February 7, 1947): 2.

Carver, William Owen. "Some Aspects of Education in the Light of the War's Revelations." *Review and Expositor 17* (January 1920): 72-92.

Cayton, Horace R. "Fighting for White Folks?" *Nation*, September 26, 1942, pp. 267-70.

"Christian Nation." *Christian Index 135* (October 4, 1956): 7.

"Christian Spirit in Race Relations." *Christian Index 135* (April 12, 1956): 3.

"Christianity at the White House." *Alabama Baptist 120* (February 10, 1955): 4.

Correspondence. *Baptist Message 73* (March 15, 1956): 2.

"Criswell Clarifies Position on Recent Segregation Blast." *Baptist Message 73* (March 29, 1956): 1 and 4.

"Dallas Pastor Stirs Controversy with Statements on Integration." *Baptist Message 33* (March 1, 1956): 1.

"Dr. Nannie Burroughs Challenges Baptists in Her First Message as President of the Largest Organization of Negro Women." *National Baptist Voice 32* (October 1, 1949): 10 and 16.

"Eisenhower Message." *Christian Index 133* (January 14, 1954): 11.

Estell, Ernest C., Sr. "Great Interracial Meeting in Dr. Truett's Church, Dallas, Texas." *National Baptist Voice 32* (February 15, 1948): 1 and 13.

Fields, Wilmer C. "Mississippi Ranks Fourth in the Nation in Ratio of Church Members to Population." *Baptist Record 80* (November 4, 1956): 4.

_____. "The President and the Liquor Bottles." Baptist Record 80 (January 3, 1957): 3.

"Fifth Street Minister-Elect Announces Acceptance." *American Baptist 79* (June 7, 1957): 2.

Fisher, Miles Mark. "Keep Negro Churches Central." *National Baptist Voice 31* (January 15, 1947): 1-2.

Gallman, Lee. "We Can Avoid Bloodshed." *Baptist Standard 68* (September 22, 1956): 8.

Gardner, David M. "The Segregation Problem." *Baptist Standard 66* (October 14, 1954): 2.

_____. "Segregation's Problems." *Baptist Standard 66* (June 10, 1954): 2.

Gilbert, O. P. "Negroes North and south." *Christian Index 126* (October 3, 1946): 3.

"The Good and Bad Side on The Racial Front." *National Baptist Voice 32* (June 15, 1948): 1 and 13.

Goodrich, A. L. "Booming Baptists." *Baptist Record 38* (June 23, 1955): 3.

_____. "Crisis in Mississippi." *Baptist Record 37* (July 29, 1954): 3.

_____. "Independence Day." *Baptist Record 37* (July 1, 1954): 3.

_____. "The SBC Convention." *Baptist Record 37* (June 10, 1954): 3.

Green, Fletcher M. "Resurgent Southern Sectionalism." *North Carolina Historical Review 33* (April 1956): 222-40.

"Grenada First Dissents." *Baptist Record 37* (June 17, 1954): 4.

Grigg, W. R. "Separate But Equal." *Baptist Standard 68* (January 14, 1956): 6.

_____. "What's Wrong?" *Baptist Standard 68* (January 7, 1956): 9.

Grooms, H. H. "Christian Citizenship." *Alabama Baptist 119* (December 9, 1954): 4.

Gwaltney, Leslie Lee. "Focal Points." *Alabama Baptist 113* (February 12, 1948): 3.

_____. "Focal Points." *Alabama Baptist 115* (January 26, 1950): 3.

_____. "Thoughts on the Race Question." *Alabama Baptist 109* (August 10, 1944): 1.

_____. "The White and Colored Races." *Alabama Baptist 112* (January 23, 1947): 3.

Hamilton, Gerald. "It Seems to Me..." *National Baptist Voice 31* (July 15, 1947): 5.

"Here and There at the Convention." *National Baptist Voice 32* (October 1, 1949): 15.

Horace, James L. "Out of the Depths Back into the Kingdom Program." *National Baptist Voice 31* (August 15, 1947): 2 and 13.

"Humes Tiumphs in Mighty Struggle." *National Baptist Voice 26* (July 1954): 3.

Humes, Harrison H. "The Voice Pulpit: Victims of Cruel Influence." *National Baptist Voice 25* (March 1953): 11.

_____. "The Voices of a new Day." *National Baptist Voice 32* (August 1, 1949): 7.

Hurt, John Jeter. "Christian Morality." *Christian Index 135* (February 9, 1956): 6.

_____. "Convention Enlarges Mission Progress." *Christian Index 135* (November 22, 1956): 3.

_____. "It Can happen Here." *Christian Index 136* (October 3, 1957): 6.

_____. "Time for Calm." *Christian Index 133* (March 18, 1954): 6.

Hyman, Herbert H., and Paul B. Sheatsley. "Attitudes toward Desegregation." *Scientific American*, December 195,6, pp. 35-39.

"The Inevitable Result of White Primary Laws." *American Baptist 69* (March 7, 1947): 2.

Jackson, Joseph Harrison. "The Importance of America's Defense." *National Baptist Voice 26* (May, 1954): 5.

_____. "In Answer to the Southern Manifesto." *American Baptist 78* (March 30, 1956) 1.

James, E. S. "Christianity at the White House." *Baptist Standard 67* (January 28, 1955): 2.

_____. "First-Class Citizens." *Baptist Standard 68* (August 11, 1956): 2.

_____. "National Independence." *Baptist Standard 69* (June 29, 1957): 2.

"Jews, Negroes, and Russians Three Scapegoats." *National Baptist Voice 32* (March 15, 1948): 1.

Johnson, Charles S. "the Negro and the Present Crisis." *Journal of Negro Education 10*

(July 1941) 585-95.

Johnson, Guion Griffis. "The Impact of War upon the Negro." *Journal of Negro Education* 10 (July 1941): 596-611.

Johnson, Mordecai W. "The Voice Pulpit: America's Great Hour." *National Baptist Voice* 26 (May 1954): 11-12.

Jones, S. H. "Our American Heritage." *Baptist Courier 87* (June 30, 1955): 2-3.

_____. "Segregation and the Schools." *Baptist Courier 86* (June 3, 1954): 2.

_____. "The Segregation Issue." *Baptist Courier 87* (June 16, 1955): 2.

"Joyless Christianity." *American Baptist 78* (May 25, 1956): 2.

Kerry, Coleman W. "Mississippi Baptists Hold Great Meeting." *National Baptist Voice 32* (August 15, 1948): 3.

King, C. N. "Wake Up, America!" *American Baptist 79* (November 15, 1957): 2.

King, Martin Luther, Jr. "The American Dream." *Negro History Bulletin 31* (May 1968): 10-12.

_____. "The Current Crisis in Race Relations." *New South 13* (March 1958): 8-10.

_____. "Out of Segregation's Long Night: An Interpretation of a Racial Crisis." *Churchman 172* (February 1958): 7-9.

_____. "A View of the Dawn." *Interracial Review 30* (May 1957): 82-85.

"Klansmen Visit Baptist Church." *Baptist Record 80* (November 1, 1956): 1.

Langley, Ralph. "Poll on De-Segregation Nets Revealing Answers." *Baptist Standard 68* (March 10, 1956): 9.

Letters to the Editor. *Baptist Message 73* (March 29, 1956): 3.

Letters to the Editor. *Baptist Standard 68* (January 28, 1956): 3.

Lyon, Henry. "President's Address." *Alabama Baptist 120* (December 1, 1955): 4.

Macon, Leon. "American Legion Supports Religion." *Alabama Baptist 117* (January 31, 1952): 3.

_____. "America's Greatness." *Alabama Baptist 116* (April 26, 1951): 3.

_____. "A Christian Amendment." *Alabama Baptist 118* (August 13, 1953): 3.

_____. "The Christian Citizen." *Alabama Baptist 116* (August 30, 1951): 3.

_____. "The Christian Life Commission to Report on Race Relations." *Alabama Baptist 121* (April 26, 1956): 2.

_____. "Christianity Basic to Democracy." *Alabama Baptist 119* (June 17, 1954): 3.

_____. "Communism a Religion." *Alabama Baptist 120* (November 3, 1955): 3.

_____. "Communists Sense Our Weakness." *Alabama Baptist 119* (July 22, 1954): 3.

_____. "The Convention and Integration." *Alabama Baptist 122* (November 28, 1957): 3.

_____. "Convention Issues." *Alabama Baptist 119* (June 17, 1954): 3.

_____. "Dangerous Plans." *Alabama Baptist 119* (October 14, 1954): 3.

_____. "Freedom of Choice Amendment Needs Examination." *Alabama Baptist 121* (August 23, 1956): 3.

_____. "Georgia Baptists Take Stand on Private School Amendment." *Alabama Baptist 119* (November 4, 1954): 3.

_____. "Humanists on the March." *Alabama Baptist 117* (October 16, 1952): 3.

_____. "Integration." *Alabama Baptist 121* (May 3, 1956): 3.

_____. "Moral Conditions in Government." *Alabama Baptist 116* (October 18, 1951): 3.

_____. "New Developments." *Alabama Baptist 117* (March 27, 1952): 3.

_____. "New Developments." *Alabama Baptist 117* (June 12, 1952): 3.

_____. "New Developments." *Alabama Baptist 117* (September 11, 1952): 3.

_____. "New Developments." *Alabama Baptist 117* (November 6, 1952): 3.

_____. "New Developments." *Alabama Baptist 117* (November 13, 1952): 3.

_____. "New Developments." *Alabama Baptist 117* (December 18, 1952): 3.

_____. "New Developments." *Alabama Baptist 118* (February 19, 1953): 3.

_____. "New Developments." Alabama Baptist 118 (July 9, 1953): 3.

_____. "Our Freedoms." *Alabama Baptist 122* (July 4, 1957): 3.

_____. "Our Freedoms." *Alabama Baptist 117* (October 23, 1952): 3.

_____. "Our Moral Situation." *Alabama Baptist 121* (March 8, 1956): 3.

_____. "Our President Speaks." *Alabama Baptist 118* (January 8, 1953): 2.

_____. "The President's Plans." *Alabama Baptist 119* (August 12, 1954): 3.

_____. "Race Prejudice." *Alabama Baptist 118* (June 25, 1953): 2.

_____. "Religion in the Armed Forces." *Alabama Baptist 116* (February 14, 1952): 3.

_____. "Russia and Segregation." *Alabama Baptist 122* (October 10, 1957): 3.

_____. "The Segregation Problems." *Alabama Baptist 121* (March 8, 1956): 3.

_____. "The Supreme Court Decision." *Alabama Baptist 119* (May 27, 1954): 3.

_____. "The Social Gospel." *Alabama Baptist 120* (March 3, 1955): 3.

_____. "Thanksgiving Day." *Alabama Baptist 118* (November 26, 1953): 3.

_____. "Thought Control." *Alabama Baptist 117* (July 24, 1952): 3.

_____. "Time for Meditation." *Alabama Baptist 122* (October 3, 1957): 3.

_____. "Using Churches For Schools." *Alabama Baptist 123* (February 20, 1958): 3.

_____. "Where is Patriotism?" *Alabama Baptist 116* (August 9, 1951): 3.

Masters, Victor I. "Baptists and the Christianizing of America in the New Order." *Review and Expositor 17* (July 1920): 280-98.

Merriam, Charles E. "The Meaning of Democracy." *Journal of Negro Education 10* (July 1941): 309-19.

"Messengers Ban Specifics in Racial Issue." *Christian Index 135* (November 22, 1956): 4-5.

Moyers, Bill, "What a Real President Was Like," *Washington Post,* November 13, 1988.

"Nation's Leaders Caution about Religious 'Boom.'" *Baptist Record 80* (November 1, 1956): 1.

"Negroes in the Nation's Capital." *National Baptist Voice 32* (March 1, 1948): 1 and 13.

"One Hundred Thousand Colored Americans Will Go on a Thanksgiving Pilgrimage to the Lincoln Memorial, Washington, D.C." *National Baptist Voice 26* (June 1954): 12.

Our Readers Write. *Baptist Record 37* (June 24, 1954): 4-5.

Our Readers Write. *Baptist Record 37* (July 8, 1954): 4.

Our Readers Write. *Baptist Record 37* (September 2, 1954): 4.

"Pastor Fired Again." *Baptist Standard 67* (January 1, 1955): 6-7.

Pittman, W. I. "Brother Baraca." *Alabama Baptist 117* (July 4, 1952): 4-5.

"Preachers Pray on White House Steps." *National Baptist Voice 32* (January 15, 1948): 1.

"President Hails Prayer Meetings As Helping U.S. Prestige." *Baptist Message 73* (February 16, 1956): 1.

"President Opens Legion's Back to God Movement." *Baptist Message 72* (March 3, 1955) 1 and 4.

"President Sounds Religious Theme." *Christian Index 133* (January 14, 1954): 4.

Preston, T. J. "Baptists and Segregation." *Christian Index 134* (January 6, 1955): 8.

Ray, Sandy F. "Sandy F. Ray, Chairman of the Social Service Commission, National Baptist Convention, Pleads for Democracy at Home." *National Baptist Voice 31* (July 15, 1947): 6 and 14.

_____. "Sandy Ray, Baptists' Social Mongul Speaks." *National Baptist Voice 32* (January 15, 1948): 8.

_____. "Sixth Annual Report of the Social Service Commission of the National Baptist Convention, U.S.A., Inc." *National Baptist Voice 24* (November 1, 1952): 12.

"Report of the Social Service Commission of the South Carolina Convention." *Baptist Courier 86* (December 16, 1954): 6-7.

"Report on the National Baptist Convention, 1947." *National Baptist Voice 31* (October 1, 1947): 1-3, 5, 13.

Robinson, U. J. "Selma University's Place in Colored State Baptist Convention." *Alabama Baptist 120* (December 1, 1955): 5.

Routh, Porter, "An Alarming Trend." *Alabama Baptist 119* (January 7, 1954): 1.

"School Position Consistent." *Alabama Baptist 122* (November 28, 1957): 4.

"Segregation Reconsidered: The 'Separate But Equal' Failure." *National Baptist Voice 32* (April 15, 1948): 2.

"Shall the Roman Catholic Princess Control America?" *National Baptist Voice 32* (August 1, 1949): 3.

Singleton, O. "When Will Dear America Look at Her Own Unclean Hands?" *American Baptist 71* (February 18, 1949): 2.

"So They Say." *Baptist Message 72* (June 30, 1955): 1.

"Social Service." *Christian Index 135* (November 15, 1956): 3.

"A Sound and Sensible Approach." *American Baptist 76* (February 5, 1954): 2.

"Southern Baptist Leaders Call for Calm Appraisal of Court Ruling." *Baptist Record 37* (May 27, 1954): 1.

Strozier, A. L. "The Battle of the Giants." *Alabama Baptist 120* (July 14, 1955): 8 and 16.

Sullivan, H. T. "The Christian Concept of Race Relations." *Baptist Message 74* (October 10, 1957): 1 and 4.

Tinnin, Finley. "A Clear Mandate of the People." *Baptist Message 73* (November 15, 1956): 2.

_____. "Communists in the Segregation Fight." *Baptist Message 74* (June 6, 1957): 2.

_____. "Dr. Criswell's Remarks." *Baptist Message 73* (March 15, 1956): 2.

_____. "Hopes 1956 SBC Sidesteps Segregation." *Baptist Message 73* (May 3, 1956): 2.

_____. "Non-Segregation." *Baptist Message 71* (June 3, 1954): 2.

_____. "A Sane View on Segregation." *Baptist Message 73* (September 27, 1956): 2.

_____. "A Timely Protest." *Baptist Message 74* (August 8, 1957): 2.

Vander Zanden, James W. "The Ideology of White Supremacy." *Journal of the History of Ideas 20* (June-September 1959): 385-402.

"The Vatican Political Offensive: How American Freedom is Being Endangered by the World-Wide Militant Catholic Action." *National Baptist Voice 32* (November 15, 1947): 1-3.

Wilkinson, Horace C. "This Matter of Segregation." *Alabama Baptist 113* (February 5,

1948): 8.
Williams, J. Howard. "America's Unique Contribution to the World in Philosophy of
    Religious Liberty." *Alabama Baptist 122* (May 2, 1957): 16.

Convention Annuals

Annual of the Alabama Baptist State Convention. Birmingham, 1954-57.
Annual of the Louisiana Baptist Convention. Shreveport, 1954-57.
Annual of the National Baptist Convention, U.S.A., Incorporated. Nashville: Sunday School
    of Publishing Board, 1954-57.
Annual of the Southern Baptist Convention. Nashville, 1947-57.
Annual of the State Convention of the Baptist Denomination in South Carolina. Greenville,
    1954-57.
Minutes of the Baptist Convention of the State of Georgia. Atlanta, 1954-57.
Minutes of the Woman's Auxiliary to the National Baptist Convention, U.S.A., Incorporated.
    Nashville: Sunday School Publishing Board, 1954.
Minutes of the National Baptist Sunday School and Baptist Training Union Congress.
    Nashville: Sunday School Publishing Board, 1956.

Manuscript Sources

Abernathy, Ralph David. "Accepting the Challenge of This Age." January 28, 1964, pp. 1-
    6. Manuscript on file in the Southern Christian Leadership Conference (SCLC)
    Collection at the Martin Luther King, Jr., Center for Nonviolent Social Change,
    Atlanta, Georgia.
_____. "The Role of the Church and the Minister in Helping End Segregation." Speech to
    the Greater Atlanta Council on Human Relations, July 22, 1963. Manuscript on file
    in the SCLC Collection at the Martin Luther King, Jr., Center for Nonviolent Social
    Change, Atlanta, Georgia.
_____. Statement by the Chairman of the Executive Board of the Montgomery
    Improvement Association, October 16, 1958. Manuscript on file in the SCLC
    Collection at the Martin Luther King, Jr., Center for Nonviolent Social Change,
    Atlanta, Georgia.
_____. "Trying to Get Home Without Jesus." Sermon, October 8, 1961. Manuscript on
    file in the SCLC Collection at the Martin Luther King, Jr., Center for Nonviolent
    Social Change, Atlanta, Georgia.
Cowling, Dale. "A Christian Looks at Integration in Little Rock." Sermon preached at
    Second Baptist Church, Little Rock, Arkansas, September 1, 1957. On file at Boyce
    Centennial Library of The Southern Baptist Theological Seminary, Louisville,
    Kentucky.

SECONDARY SOURCES

Books

Ahlstrom, Sydney E. *A Religious History of the American People.* New Haven: Yale University Press, 1972.

Albanese, Catherine L. *America: Religions and Religion.* Belmont, Calif.: Wadsworth Publishing Co., 1981.

Alvis, Joel L. Jr. *Religion and Race: Southern Presbyterians, 1946-1983.* Tuscaloosa: University of Alabama Press, 1994.

Ammerman, Nancy Tatom. *Baptist Battles: Social Change and Religious Conflict in the Southern Baptist Convention.* New Brunswick: Rutgers University Press, 1990.

Ansbro, John J. *Martin Luther King, Jr.: The Making of a Mind.* Maryknoll, N.Y.: Orbis Books, 1983.

Ayers, H. Brandt, and Thomas H. Naylor, eds. *You Can't Eat Magnolias.* New York: McGraw-Hill, 1972.

Bailey, Kenneth K. *Southern White Protestantism in the Twentieth Century.* New York: Harper & Row, 1964. Reprint. Gloucester, Mass.: Peter Smith, 1968.

Barnet, Richard J. *Intervention and Revolution: America's Confrontation with Insurgent Movements around the World.* New York: Meridian Books, 1968.

Bartley, Numan V. *The Rise of Massive Resistance: Race and Politics in the South During the 1950s.* Baton Rouge: Louisiana State University Press, 1969.

Bellah, Robert N. *Beyond Belief: Essays on Religion in a Post-Traditional World.* New York: Harper & Row, 1970.

_____. "Civil Religion in America," *Daedalus* 96 (Winter 1967): 1-21.

_____. *The Broken Covenant: American Civil Religion in Time of Trial.* New York: Seabury Press, 1975.

_____. *Tokugawa Religion: The Values of Pre-Industrial Japan.* Glencoe, Ill.: Free Press, 1957.

_____, and Phillip E. Hammond. *Varieties of Civil Religion.* New York: Harper and Row, 1980.

Berger, Peter L. *The Sacred Canopy: Elements of a Sociological Theory of Religion.* Garden City, N.Y.: Doubleday & Co., 1969.

_____. *The Heretical Imperative: Contemporary Possibilities of Religious Affirmation.* Garden City, N.Y.: Doubleday & Co., 1979.

_____, and Thomas Luckmann. *The Social Construction of Reality: A Treatise in the Sociology of Knowledge.* Garden City, N.Y.: Doubleday & Co., 1966.

Billington, Monroe Lee. *The American South: A Brief History.* New York: Charles Scribner's Sons, 1971.

_____, ed. *The South: A Central Theme?* Huntington, N. Y.: Robert E. Krieger Publishing Co., 1976.

Black, Earl and Merle. *The Vital South: How Presidents Are Elected.* Cambridge: Harvard University Press, 1992.

Boddie, Charles E. *God's "Bad Boys."* Valley Forge, Pa.: Judson Press, 1972.

Brauer, Jerald Carl, ed. *Religion and the American Revolution.* Philadelphia: Fortress Press,

1976.

Burkett, Randall K. *Garveyism as a Religious Movement: The Institutionalization of a Black Civil Religion.* Metuchen, N.J.: Scarecrow Press, 1978.

Capps, Walter H.. *The New Religious Right: Piety, Patriotism, and Politics.* Columbia: University of South Carolina Press, 1990.

Carter, Dan T. *From George Wallace to Newt Gingrich: Race in the Conservative Counterrevolution, 1963-1994.* Baton Rouge: Louisiana State University Press, 1996.

_____. *The Politics of Rage: George Wallace, The Origins of the New Conservatism, and the Transformation of American Politics.* Baton Rouge: Louisiana State University Press, 2000.

Carter, Stephen L. *God's Name in Vain: The Rights and Wrongs of Religion in Politics.* New York: Basic Books, 2000.

Cherry, Conrad, ed. *God's new Israel: Religious Interpretations of American Destiny.* Englewood Cliffs, N.J.: Prentice-Hall, 1971.

Chidester, David. *Patterns of Power: Religion and Politics in American Culture.* Englewood Cliffs, NJ: Prentice-Hall.

Cone, James H. *The Spirituals and the Blues.* New York: Seabury Press, 1972.

Curti, Merle Eugene. *The Roots of American Loyalty.* New York: Columbia University Press, 1946.

Cutler, Donald R., ed. *The Religious Situation: 1968.* Boston: Beacon Press, 1968.

Douglas, Mary, and Steven M. Tipton, eds. *Religion and America: Spirituality in a Secular Age.* Boston: Beacon Press, 1982.

Egerton, John. *The Americanization of Dixie: The Southernization of America.* New York: Harper's Magazine Press, 1974.

Eighmy, John Lee. *Churches in Cultural Captivity.* Knoxville: University of Tennessee Press, 1972.

Eliade, Mircea. *Myth and Reality.* New York: Harper & Row, 1963.

Farmer, James O. Jr. *The Metaphysical Confederacy: James Henley Thornwell and the Synthesis of Southern Values.* Macon: Mercer University Press, 1999.

Faust, Drew Gilpin. *The Creation of Confederate Nationalism.* Baton Rouge: Louisiana State University Press, 1988.

Fenn, Richard K. *Toward a Theory of Secularization.* Storrs: University of Connecticut Press, 1978.

Ferguson, Robert Benjamin. "The Southern Baptist Response to International Affairs and Threats to Peace, 1931-1941." Ph.D. diss., Carnegie-Mellon University, 1981.

Fisher, Miles Mark. *Negro Slave Songs in the United States.* New York: Citadel Press, 1953.

Franklin, John Hope. *From Slavery to Freedom: A History of Negro Americans.* 3d ed. New York: Alfred A. Knopf. 1967.

_____, ed. *Three Negro Classics.* New York: Avon Books, 1965.

Gallup, George Jr and Jim Castelli. *The People's Religion.* New York : Macmillan, 1989.

Garrow, David J. *Bearing the Cross: Martin Luther King, Jr., and the Southern Christian Leadership Conference.* New York: William Morrow, 1987.

Gaston, Paul M. *The New South Creed: A Study in Southern Mythmaking.* Baton Rouge: Louisiana State University Press, 1970.

Geertz, Clifford. *The Interpretation of Cultures.* New York: Basic Books, 1973.

Genovese, Eugene D. *A Consuming Fire: The Fall of the Confederacy in the Mind of the White Christian South*. Athens: University of Georgia Press, 1998.

Grantham, Dewey W., Jr. *The Democratic South*. Athens: University of Georgia Press, 1963.

Harris, Louis and William Brink. *Black and White: A Study of U. S. Racial Attitudes Today*. New York: Simon and Schuster, 1964.

Hartsell, Robert L. "A Critical Analysis of Selected Southern Baptist Convention Presidential Addresses, 1950-1970." Ph.D. diss., Louisiana State University, 1971.

Hero, Alfred O., Jr. *The Southerner and World Affairs*. Baton Rouge: Louisiana State University Press, 1965.

Herskovits, Melville J., and Frances S. Herskovits. *Dahomean Narrative: A Cross-Cultural Approach*. Evanston, Ill.: Northwestern University Press, 1958.

Hill, Samuel S., Jr. *On Jordan's Stormy Banks: Religion in the South: A Southern Exposure Profile*. Macon, Ga.: Mercer University Press, 1983.

_____. Religion and the Solid South. Nashville: Abingdon Press, 1972.

_____. *Southern Churches in Crisis*. New York: Holt, Rinehart and Winston, 1966.

_____, ed. *Religion in the Southern States: A Historical Study*. Macon, Ga.: Mercer University Press, 1983.

Holland, DeWitte. *Sermons in American History: Selected Issues in the American Pulpit, 1630-1967*. Nashville: Abingdon Press, 1971.

Holt, Thomas C. *The Problem of Race in the Twenty-first Century*. Cambridge: Harvard University Press, 2001.

Hudson, Winthrop Still. *Religion in America*. 3d ed. New York: Charles Scribner's Sons, 1981.

_____, ed. *Nationalism and Religion in America*. New York: Harper & Row, 1970.

Hunter, James Davison. *American Evangelicalism: Conservative Religion and the Quandary of Modernity*. New Brunswick, N.J.: Rutgers University Press, 1983.

Kelsey, George D. *Racism and the Christian Understanding of Man*. New York: Charles Scribner's Sons, 1965.

_____. *Social Ethics among Southern Baptists, 1917-1969*. Madison, N.J.: Scarecrow Press, 1973.

Lincoln, Charles Eric. *The Black Church Since Frazier*. New York: Schocken Books, 1974. Published in a single volume with a reprint of Franklin Frazier, The Negro Church in America.

Loefflath-Ehly, Victor Paul. "Religion As the Principal Component of World-Maintenance in the American South from the 1830s to 1900 with Special Emphasis on the Clergy and Their Sermons: A Case Study in the Dialectic of Religion and Culture." Ph.D. diss., Florida State University, 1978.

Lovelady, Milton Charles. "The American Press and McCarthyism, 1950-1954." Master's thesis, University of Louisville, 1975.

Manis, Andrew M. *A Fire You Can't Put Out: The Civil Rights Life of Birmingham's Reverend Fred Shuttlesworth*. Tuscaloosa: University of Alabama Press, 1999.

Marsden, George, ed. *Evangelicalism and Modern America*. Grand Rapids: William B. Eerdmans Publishing Company, 1984.

Marty, Martin E. *A Nation of Behavers*. Chicago: University of Chicago Press, 1976.

_____. The New Shape of American Religion. New York: Harper & Brothers, 1959.

Mays, Benjamin Elijah. *The Negro's God*. New York: Atheneum Press, 1968.

McGuire, Meredith B. *Religion: The Social Context*. Belmont, Calif.: Wadsworth Publishing Co., 1981.

Mead, Sidney Earl. *The Nation with the Soul of a Church*. New York: Harper & Row, 1975.

Morris, Aldon D. *The Origins of the Civil Rights Movement: Black Communities Organizing for Change*. New York: Free Press, 1984.

Murray, Henry A. *Myth and Mythmaking*. Boston: Beacon Press, 1960.

Muse, Benjamin. *Ten Years of Prelude: The Story of Integration Since the Supreme Court's Decision*. New York: Viking Press, 1964.

Newman, Dorothy K., ed. *Protest, Politics, and Prosperity: Black Americans and White Institutions, 1940-1975*. New York: Pantheon Books, 1978.

Newman, William K. *The Social Meanings of Religion*. Chicago: Rand McNally College Publishing Co., 1974.

Noll, Mark A., et al., eds. *Eerdman's Handbook to Christianity in America*. Grand Rapids, Mich.: William B. Eerdmans Publishing Co., 1983.

Oates, Stephen B. *Let the Trumpet Sound: The Life of Martin Luther King, Jr*. New York: Harper & Row, 1982.

Paris, Peter J. *The Social Teaching of the Black Churches*. Philadelphia: Fortress Press, 1985.

Peterson, Thomas Virgil. *Ham and Japheth: The Mythic World of Whites in the Antebellum South*. Metuchen, N.J.: Scarecrow Press, 1978.

Reed, John Shelton. *The Enduring South: Subcultural Persistence in Mass Society*. Chapel Hill: University of North Carolina Press, 1972.

_____. *One South: An Ethnic Approach to Regional Culture*. Baton Rouge, Louisiana State University Press, 1982.

_____ and Dale Volberg, eds. *1001 Things Everyone Should Know About the South*. New York: Doubleday, 1996.

Reimers, David M. *White Protestantism and the Negro*. New York: Oxford University Press, 1965.

Richey, Russell, E., and Donald G. Jones, eds. *American Civil Religion*. New York: Harper and Row, 1974.

Roland, Charles P. *The Improbable Era: The South Since World War II*. Rev. ed. Lexington: University of Kentucky Press, 1976.

Rousseau, Jean-Jacques. "The Social Contract," in *Rousseau: Political Writings*, translated and edited by Frederick Watkins (New York: Nelson and Sons), 1953.

Sebeok, Thomas A.., ed. *Myth: A Symposium*. Bloomington: Indiana University Press, 1958.

Sellers, Charles Grier, Jr. *The Southerner as American*. Chapel Hill: University of North Carolina Press, 1960.

Sellers, James. *The South and Christian Ethics*. New York: Association Press, 1962.

Sherman, Billy Don. "Ideology of American Segregationism." ThD. Diss., Southwestern Baptist Theological Seminary, 1967.

Sherrill, Robert. *Gothic Politics in the Deep South*. New York: Grossman Publishers, 1968.

Simkins, Francis Butler, and Charles P. Roland. *A History of the South*. 4th ed. New York: Alfred A. Knopf, 1972.

Smith, Elwyn A., ed. *The Religion of the Republic.* Philadelphia: Fortress Press, 1971.

Smith, Kenneth L., and Ira G. Zepp, Jr. *The Search for the Beloved Community: The Thinking of Martin Luther King, Jr.* Valley Forge, Pa.: Judson Press, 1974.

Smith, Oran P. *The Rise of Baptist Republicanism.* New York: New York University Press, 1997.

Snay, Mitchell. *Gospel of Disunion: Religion and Separation in the Antebellum South.* Chapel Hill: University of North Carolina Press, 1993.

Sweet, Leonard I. *Black Images of America, 1784-1870.* New York: W. W. Norton Co., 1976.

Thompson, James J., Jr. *Tried As by Fire: Southern Baptists and the Religious Controversies of the 1920s.* Macon, Ga.: Mercer University Press, 1982.

Tindall, George Brown. *The Disruption of the Solid South.* Athens, Ga.: University of Georgia Press, 1972.

_____. *The Emergence of the New South*, 1913-1945. Baton Rouge: Louisiana State University Press, 1967.

_____. *The Pursuit of Southern History.* Baton Rouge: Louisiana State University Press, 1964.

Toulouse, Mark G. *The Transformation of John Foster Dulles: From Prophet of Realism to Priest of Nationalism.* Macon, Ga.: Mercer University Press, 1985.

Towns, James E., ed. *The Social Conscience of W. A. Criswell.* Dallas: Crescendo Publications, 1977.

Vandiver, Frank E. *The Idea of the South: Pursuit of a Central Theme.* Chicago: University of Chicago Press, 1964.

Washington, James Melvin. *Frustrated Fellowship: The Black Baptist Quest for Social Power.* Macon, Ga.: Mercer University Press, 1986.

Washington, James Melvin, ed. *A Testament of Hope: The Essential Writings of Martin Luther King, Jr.* New York: Harper & Row, 1986.

Whalen, Charles and Barbara. *The Longest Debate.* New York: New American Library, 1986.

Wheeler, Edward Lorenzo. "Uplifting the Race: The Black Minister in the New South, 1865-1902." Ph.D. diss., Emory University, 1982.

Wicker, Tom. *Tragic Failure: Racial Integration in America.* New York: William Morrow and Company, 1996.

Williamson, Joel. *The Crucible of Race: Black/White Relations in the American South Since Emancipation.* New York: Oxford University Press, 1984.

Wilmore, Gayraud S. *Black Religion and Black Radicalism.* Rev. ed. Maryknoll, N.Y.: Orbis Books, 1983.

Wilson, Charles Reagan. *Baptized in Blood: The Religion of the Lost Cause, 1865-1920.* Athens: University of Georgia Press, 1980.

Wilson, Charles Reagan and William E. Ferris, eds. *Encyclopedia of Southern Culture.* Chapel Hill: University of North Carolina Press, 1989.

Wilson, John F. *Public Religion in American Culture.* Philadelphia: Temple University Press, 1979.

Woodward, C. Vann. *The Burden of Southern History.* Rev. ed. Baton Rouge: Louisiana State University Press, 1977.

_____. *The Strange Career of Jim Crow.* Rev. ed. New York: Oxford University Press, 1966.

Yance, Norman Alexander. *Religion Southern Style: Southern Baptists and Society in Historical Perspective.* Danville, Va.: Association of Baptist Professors of Religion, 1978.

Zinn, Howard. *The Southern Mystique.* New York: Simon & Schuster, 1972.

Articles

Ahlstrom, Sydney E. "Religion, Revolution and the Rise of Modern Nationalism: Reflections on the American Experience." *Church History 44* (December 1975): 492-504.

Bellah, Robert N. "Civil Religion: The Sacred and the Political in American Life." *Psychology Today,* January 1976, pp. 58-65.

_____. "Commentary and Proposed Agenda: The Normative Framework for Pluralism in America." *Soundings 61* (Fall 1978): 355-71.

_____. "Rejoinder to [Joan] Lockwood: 'Bellah and his Critics." *Anglican Theological Review 57* (October 1975): 416-23.

_____. "Response to Panel on Civil Religion." *Sociological Analysis 37* (Summer 1976): 153-59.

Blackwelder, Julia Kirk. "Southern White Fundamentalists and the Civil Rights Movement." *Phylon 40* (December 1979): 334-41.

Buck, Paul Herman. *The Road to Reunion, 1895-1900.* Boston: Little, Brown & Co., 1937.

Capeci, Dominic J., Jr. "From Harlem to Montgomery: The Bus Boycotts and the Leadership of Adam Clayton Powell, Jr., and Martin Luther King, Jr." *Historian 42* (August 1979): 721-37.

Christenson, John A., and Ronald C. Wimberley. "Who is Civil Religious?" *Sociological Analysis 39* (Spring 1978): 77-83.

Cleveland, Len G. "Georgia Baptists and the 1954 Supreme Court Desegregation Decision." *Georgia Historical Quarterly 59* (Supp., 1975), 107-17.

Coleman, John A. "Civil Religion." *Sociological Analysis 31* (Summer 1970): 67-77.

Dunn, James M. "Reflections." *Report from the Capital 39* (April 1984): 15.

Elder, John Dixon. "Martin Luther King and American Civil Religion." *Harvard Divinity School Bulletin 1* (Spring 1968): 17.

Garrow, David J. "The Intellectual Development of Martin Luther King, Jr.: Influences and Commentaries." *Union Seminary Quarterly Review 40,* no. 4 (1986): 5-20.

Gaston, Paul M. *The New South Creed: A Study in Southern Mythmaking.* Baton Rouge: Louisiana State University Press, 1970.

Gehrig, Gail. "The Civil Religion Debate: A Source for Theory Construction." *Journal for the Scientific Study of Religion 20* (March 1981): 51-63.

Gravely, Willaim B. "The Dialectic of Double-Consciousness in Black American Freedom Celebrations, 1808-1863." *Journal of Negro History 67* (1982): 302-17.

Hammond, Phillip E. "The Sociology of American Civil Religion: A Bibliographical Essay." *Sociological Analysis 37* (Spring 1976): 169-82.

Harding, Vincent. "The Black Wedge in America: Struggle, Crisis, and Hope, 1955-1975." *Black Scholar 6* (December 1975): 28-46.

Hemmingway, Theodore. "Prelude to Change: Black Carolinians in the War Years, 1914-1920." *Journal of Negro History 65* (Summer 1980): 212-27.

Hesseltine, William B. "Sectionalism and Regionalism in American History." *Journal of Southern History 26* (February 1960): 25-34.

Hill, Samuel S., Jr. "The South's Culture-Protestantism." *Christian Century 79* (July-December 1962): 1094-96.

_____. "Southern Protestantism and Racial Integration." *Religion in Life 33* (summer 1964): 421-29.

_____. "The Strange Career of Religious Pluralism in the South." *Bulletin of the Center for the Study of Southern Culture and Religion 4* (July 1980): 17-25.

Jones, Faustine C. "Ironies of School Desegregation." *Journal of Negro Education 47* (Winter 1978): 2-27.

Kathan, Boardman, and Nancy Fuchs-Kreimer. "Bibliography on Civil Religion." *Religious Education 70* (September-October 1975): 541-50.

Lind, Michael. "The Southern Coup," *New Republic,* 19 June 1995, 26, 29.

Lovelady, Milton Charles. "The Baptist Press and McCarthyism, 1950-1954." *Quarterly Review 37* (April 1977): 56-65.

Manis, Andrew M. "Silence or Shockwaves: Southern Baptist Responses to the Assassination of Martin Luther King, Jr." *Baptist History and Heritage 15* (October 1980): 19-27, 35.

_____. " 'City Mothers': Dorothy Tilly, Georgia Methodist Women, and Black Civil Rights," in Glenn Feldman and Kari Frederickson, eds., *Race, Rights, and Reaction in the American South, 1940-1956.* Fayetteville: University of Arkansas Press, forthcoming 2003.

Marsden, George. "Religion, Politics, and the Search for an American Consensus," in Mark Noll, *Religion and American Politics: From the Colonial Period to the 1980s.* New York: Oxford University Press, 1989.

Masugi, Ken. "The New Civil Religion of Multiculturalism." Accessed on the Internet at www.claremont.org/publications/masugi000818.cfm.

McBeth, Leon. "Southern Baptists and Race Since 1947." *Baptist History and Heritage 7* (July 1972): 155-69.

Niebuhr, Reinhold. "The Effect of the Supreme Court Decision." *Christianity and Crisis 14* (June 14, 1954): 76-77.

Owsley, Frank L. Review of Road to Reunion, 1865-1900, by Paul H. Buck. *Yale Review* (new series) 27 (September 1937): 171-73.

Phillips, Ulrich B. "The Central Theme of Southern History," *American Historical Review 34* (October 1928): 30-43.

Potter, David M. "The Enigma of the South." *Yale review 51* (Autumn 1961), 143-51.

_____. "The Historian's Use of Nationalism and Vice-Versa." *American Historical Review 67* (July 1962), 924-50.

Price, Joseph L. "Attitudes of Kentucky Baptists toward World War II." *Foundations 21* (April-June 1978): 123-38.

Roland, Charles P. "The Ever-Vanishing South." *Journal of Southern History 48* (February 1981): 3-20.

Smylie, James H. "On Jesus, Pharoahs, and the Chosen People." *Interpretation 24* (January

1970): 74-91.

Thornton, J. Mills, III. "Challenge and Response on the Montgomery Bus Boycott, 1955-1956." *Alabama Review 33* (Supp., 1980), 163-235.

Tomberlin, Joseph A. "Florida and the School Desegregation Issue, 1954-1959." *Journal of Negro Education 43* (Fall 1974): 457-67.

Wallis, Jim. "America's Original Sin: The Legacy of White Racism," in *America's Original Sin: A Study on White Racism* (Washington: Sojourners Resource Center, 1992).

West, Cornel. "Black Politics Will Never Be the Same," *Christianity and Crisis 44* (August 13, 1984): 302-5.

Wills, David W. "The Central Themes of American Religious History: Pluralism, Puritanism, and the Encounter Between Blacks and Whites," in Timothy E. Fulop and Albert J. Raboteau, eds., *African American Religion: Essays and Interpretations in History and Culture.* New York: Routledge, 1997, 12-20.

INDEX

black spirituals, 157
Bob Jones University, 188
Borders, William Holmes, 35
Brady, Thomas P., 98, 99, 118, 121, 122, 123, 135
Brookhaven, MS, 98
Brown v. Board of Education, 5, 10, 11, 29, 40, 56, 86, 87, 88, 89-102, 108, 115, 124, 126, 134, 136, 151, 165, 168
Buchanan, John H., 67, 95, 133
Buchanan, Patrick, 159, 160, 189
Burroughs, Nannie Helen, 112
Bush, George, 159, 170, 188
Bush, George W., 176, 189
Byrd, Harry F., 116

Campbell, Ernest Q., 107, 117, 132
Capps, Walter, 191
Carmichael, Stokeley (Kwame Ture), 10
Carter, Dan T., 186-88
Carter, Jimmy, 169, 179
Carter, Hodding, 37
Carter, Stephen, 190
Carver, Carter, 45
Carver, W. O., 66, 74
Catholicism, 62, 69, 70, 71, 72, 73, 74, 78, 79, 85, 86, 184
Central High School (Little Rock, AR), 103, 104, 106
"central theme of southern history", xi
Chavez, Cesar, 153
"Christian America," 164
Christian Coalition, 160 187
Christian Index, 58, 97
Christian Life Commission
    of the Alabama Baptist
    Convention, 119, 133; of the
    Southern Baptist Convention, 40,
    96, 102, 108; of the South Carolina
    Baptist Convention, 146; of the
    Louisiana Baptist Convention, 146
Christianity, ix, xii, 26, 29, 49, 65, 66, 68, 76, 109, 110, 120, 163, 190
Christianity and Crisis, 58
chosenness (America as chosen land), 2, 18, 23, 65, 66, 132, 139, 150, 156, 157, 184
church (African American), 25, 30
church (white), 38

(White) Citizens Council, 8, 9, 10, 37, 38, 101, 102, 103, 105, 123, 135
"city on a hill," x, xi,
city councils, 142, 145, 146, 150, 155
civil disobedience, 33
civil religion, xiii, xvii; ; archaic versions of, 17, 18, 154; conflicting versions of, 3,7, 8, 10, 11, 14, 22, 93, 108, 125, 126, 152, 180, 192; debate, 1, 14, 18; definitions of, ix-x, 14-25; idolatrous versions of 17, 18, 22; "inclusive" perspective on, 4-5; "interactive" perspective on, 3, 5, 7, 87; modern versions of, 17, 154; mytho-cultural model of, 19-22; priestly expressions of, 15n4, 18, 153, 155; prophetic expressions of, 4, 8, 15n4, 16, 18, 109, 110, 153; ritual dimension of, 21; southern civil religion, 23; versions, 149; working definition of, 21; world civil religion, 18
civil rights, 4, 6, 10, 11, 30, 31, 32, 39, 54, 61, 111, 135, 190, 191, 192
Civil Rights Act (1957), 104
Civil Rights Act (1964), 179, 185, 188
civil rights movement, x, xi, xii, xiii, xvii, 5, 6, 11, 25, 34, 87, 109, 111, 122, 139, 145, 152, 166, 184, 186, 191
Civil War, x, 2, 3, 23, 37, 43, 44, 115, 116, 118, 162, 173, 176, 179, 182, 184
Claremont Institute, 192
Clinton, Bill, 11, 159, 160, 170, 171, 172, 173, 179
code, religion as, 15
Cold War, 5, 6, 57, 60, 62, 63, 69, 72, 118, 123
Colquitt County (Georgia) Baptist Association, 108
Committee on Civil Rights, 6, 61
Communism, 17, 29, 62, 64, 65, 67, 68, 69, 71, 72, 73, 74,76, 78, 80, 86, 97, 99, 105, 107, 111, 117, 118, 121, 122, 123, 184
Communist Party, 75
Compassionate conservatism, 159, 172
Cone, James H., 26, 29
Confederacy, 163, 174, 177
"confusionism," 33